gestalt is

— a collection of articles about gestalt therapy and living by:

Frederick S. Perls

Wilson Van Dusen

Stephen A. Tobin

Barry Stevens

John O. Stevens

Robert K. Hall

John B. Enright

Stella Resnick

Paul Goodman

Cooper C. Clements

Marc Joslyn

edited by *John O. Stevens*

Copyright© 1975
Real People Press
Box F
Moab, Utah 84532

Standard Book Number   *911226-14-1 clothbound $7.00*
                             911226-15-X paperbound $3.50

Cover Photography by Ernest Braun

Library of Congress Cataloging in Publication Data:

Main entry under title:

Gestalt is.

    1. Gestalt therapy--Addresses, essays, lectures.
I. Perls, Frederick S.   II. Stevens, John O.
RC489.G4G47   616.8'914   74-25590
ISBN 0-911226-14-1
ISBN 0-911226-15-X pbk.

Other useful books from Real People Press:

GESTALT THERAPY VERBATIM, By *Frederick S. Perls.* 280 pp. 1969 Cloth $5.00
Paper $3.50

IN AND OUT THE GARBAGE PAIL, by *Frederick S. Perls.* Illustrated. 280 pp.
1969 Cloth $7.00 Paper $4.00

DON'T PUSH THE RIVER, by *Barry Stevens.* 280 pp. 1970 Cloth $7.00 Paper $3.50

NOTES TO MYSELF, by *Hugh Prather.* 150 pp. 1970 Cloth $4.00 Paper $2.00

EMBRACE TIGER, RETURN TO MOUNTAIN: the essence of T'ai Chi, by *Al
Chung-liang Huang.* Illustrated. 185 pp. 1973 Cloth $7.00 Paper $3.50

PERSON TO PERSON, by *Carl Rogers and Barry Stevens.* 276 pp. 1967 Cloth $4.50
Paper $3.00

AWARENESS, by *John O. Stevens.* 275 pp. 1971. Cloth $7.00 Paper $3.50

The name *Real People Press* indicates our purpose: to publish ideas and ways that a
person can use independently to become more *real*—to further his own growth as a human
being and to develop his relationships and communication with others.

1   2   3   4   5   6   7   8   9   10   printing   79   78   77   76   75

Contents

Introduction

John O. Stevens and Barry Stevens

This book is a collection of writings on gestalt therapy. It contains all of Fritz Perls' previously published uncollected papers, some of which have been very difficult to obtain. One paper which appeared under Fritz' name, "The Anthropology of Neurosis," has been omitted. Laura Perls says that it was actually written by Paul Goodman, who asked Fritz to put his name on it because Goodman already had two other articles in the same issue of *Complex* (#2 Summer 1950).

The Perls papers were originally published in the 50's and 60's, and Van Dusen's articles originally appeared in the 60's. These papers show important aspects of the development of gestalt during that period. All of the other articles were either published within the past five years, or were written for this book. These show some of the developments that are now taking place in the theory and practice of gestalt.

These articles have been chosen simply on the basis of our preference. To us, they are the clearest, most interesting, original and vital of current writing on gestalt.

The title of this book reflects our view that gestalt simply is—no capital G, no glorification. Gestalt is a word for an orientation, a description of the process involved in individual human awareness and functioning. Most studies of people measure only a few events or variables and use large numbers of people for statistical validity, ignoring large areas of experience. Gestalt dares to focus on the moment-to-moment functioning of an individual in all its detail and complexity. The writing here attempts to outline some of the regularities underlying this complexity. Like a road map, these writings can serve as a guide through unfamiliar territory by describing *some* of its features. But the road map is not the country that you travel through. The reality *is:* the description is only as good as our observation. Your life is, and at best these writings may serve as guides to unaware aspects of your life.

Perhaps the most remarkable, and yet obvious, message from gestalt is this: If you see the events of your life clearly, then your living goes well, without confusion and unnecessary misery. Sometimes life is difficult and painful, and sometimes life is joyful and full. With awareness you can minimize the pain and maximize the joys and satisfactions.

Gestalt is really more of a personal practice, a way of living, than it is a professional "therapy" or a "cure." It is something that you do *with* others, not *to* them. Walter Kempler says it well:

"Gestalt therapy, although formally presented as a specific type of psychotherapy, is based on principles considered to be a sound way of life. In other words, it is first a philosophy, a way of being, and superimposed on that are ways of applying that knowledge so that others may benefit from it. Gestalt therapy is the service organization of the gestalt philosophy. Hopefully, the gestalt therapist is identified more by who he is than by what he is or does. The presumption then is that the fundamental premises underlying the psychotherapeutic model are as appropriate at home as they are at the office, as applicable to a healthy child as to a disturbed child, as relevant at a party as at a seminar: as a teacher or a student, as a supervisor or a senator." *

Gestalt philosophy serves as an orientation to living, a reminder that awareness is always useful, and provides a number of specific strategies and techniques that we can use to move toward greater awareness.

*Walter Kempler "Gestalt Therapy" in *Current Psychotherapies*, edited by Raymond Corsini © 1973 F. E. Peacock, Itasca, Ill. p. 273.

All of us who are involved in gestalt have imperfect awareness. We are like the windows in old buildings with bubbles, wavy areas, dirty spots, bits of paint, and other obstructions and distortions. Each of us has areas of clarity and areas of obscurity. Each of us has areas of human experience in which we see clearly and walk easily, and others in which we are unclear and confused. Each of us can work as therapist more easily with certain people than with others.

In this book, each of us is writing about areas in which we are gaining clarity, moving out from the personal foundation of our own experiencing.

There is a "gestalt explosion" going on. There is widespread popular interest in gestalt, and there are gestalt therapists and gestalt institutes even in smaller cities. Gestalt ideas are being used or adapted for use in other than "therapy" settings: schools, organizations, churches, etc. There are already some 20 books about gestalt and another 15 or so are in process as this is written.

As with so many things, wide acceptance is even more dangerous than rejection. Much of the "adaptation" is emasculation. Many "gestalt" therapists are retread therapists who have picked up a few gestalt gimmicks so they can hop on the bandwagon. Other therapists are sincerely moving into gestalt and are presently in transition. Some of the institutes have been set up by people with very little experience and ability.

Even among those with many years of experience and training in gestalt there is a wide variety of orientation and practice. Some of this variety is the result of sincere and valid experimentation, development, and specialization. Some of this variety is the result of contamination by the symptoms, blind spots, conceptions, and misconceptions of the therapist. Beneath the "gestalt" label there is a very wide spectrum of experience and practice.

So, as in all things, you have to find your own way, trust your own experiencing. If you find some writing or some person who is useful to you and good to be with, rejoice.

Shura, Utah
June 1975

It is obvious that an eagle's potential will be actualized in roaming the sky, diving down on smaller animals for food, and in building nests.

It is obvious that an elephant's potential will be actualized in size, power and clumsiness.

No eagle will want to be an elephant, no elephant to be an eagle. They "accept" themselves; they accept them-"selves." No, they don't even accept themselves; for this would mean possible rejection. They take themselves for granted. No, they don't even take themselves for granted, for this would imply a possibility of otherness. They just are. They are what they are what they are.

How absurd it would be if they, like humans, had fantasies, dissatisfactions and self-deceptions! How absurd it would be if the elephant, tired of walking the earth, wanted to fly, eat rabbits and lay eggs. And the eagle wanted to have the strength and thick skin of the beast.

Leave this to the human—to try to be something he is not—to have ideals that cannot be reached, to be cursed with perfectionism so as to be safe from criticism, and to open the road to unending mental torture.

Friend, don't be a perfectionist. Perfectionism is a curse and a strain. For you tremble lest you miss the bulls-eye. You are perfect if you let be.

Friend, don't be afraid of mistakes. Mistakes are not sins. Mistakes are ways of doing something different, perhaps creatively new.

Friend, don't be sorry for your mistakes. Be glad for them. You had the courage to give something of yourself.

It takes years to be centered; it takes more years to understand and to be *now*.

—Fritz Perls
In and Out the Garbage Pail

Gestalt Therapy and Human Potentialities

Frederick S. Perls

Gestalt therapy is one of the rebellious, humanistic, existential forces in psychology which seeks to stem the avalanche of self-defeating, self-destructive forces among some members of our society. It is "existential" in a broad sense. All schools of existentialism emphasize direct experience, but most of them have some conceptual framework: Kierkegaard had his Protestant theology; Buber his Judaism; Sartre his communism; and Binswanger his psychoanalysis. Gestalt therapy is fully ontological in that it recognizes both conceptual activity and the biological formation of *Gestalten*. It is thus self-supporting and truly experiential.

Our aim as therapists is to increase human potential through the process of integration. We do this by supporting the individual's genuine interests, desires and needs.

Many of the individual's needs contend with those of society. Competitiveness, need for control, demands for perfection, and immaturity are characteristic of our current culture. Out of this background emerge both the curse and the cause of our neurotic social behavior. In such a context no psychotherapy can be successful; no unsatisfactory marriage can be improved. But, more importantly, the individual is unable to dissolve his own inner conflicts and to achieve integration.

Conflicts extend to the external as well. In demanding identification and submission to a self-image, society's neurotic expectations

Reprinted from *Explorations in Human Potentialities*, edited by Herbert A. Otto, Ch. 35. © 1966 Charles C. Thomas, Springfield, Ill.

1

further dissociate the individual from his own nature. The first and last problem for the individual is to integrate within and yet be accepted by society.

Society demands conformity through education; it emphasizes and rewards development of the individual's intellect. In my language I call the intellect a "built-in computer." Each culture and the individuals composing it have created certain concepts and images of ideal social behavior, or how the individual "should" function within its framework of reference. In order to be accepted by society, the individual responds with a sum of fixed responses. He arrives at these responses by "computing" what he considers to be the appropriate reaction. In order to comply with the "should" demands of society, the individual learns to disregard his own feelings, desires and emotions. He, too, then dissociates himself from being a part of nature.

Paradoxically, the more society demands that the individual live up to its concepts and ideas, the less efficiently can the individual function. This basic conflict between the demands of society and one's inner nature results in tremendous expenditures of energy. It is well known that the individual ordinarily uses only 10 to 25 percent of his potential. However, in times of emergency, it is possible for the conditioned responses to collapse. Integration becomes spontaneous. In such situations the individual is able to cope directly with obstacles and, at times, achieve heroic results. Gestalt therapy seeks to bring about integration without the urgency of emergency situations.

The more the character relies on ready-made concepts, fixed forms of behavior and "computing," the less able is he to use his senses and intuition. When the individual attempts to live according to preconceived ideas of what the world "should" be like, he brackets off his own feelings and needs. The result of this alienation from one's senses is the blocking off of his potential and the distortion of his perspective.

The critical point during any development, both collectively and individually, is the ability to differentiate between *self*-actualization and the actualization of a *concept*. Expectations are products of our fantasy. The greater the discrepency between what one can be

2

through one's inborn potential and the superimposed, idealistic concepts, the greater the strain and the likelihood of failure. I give a ridiculously exaggerated example. An elephant wants to be a rose bush; a rose bush wants to be an elephant. Until each resigns to being what they are, both will lead unhappy lives of inferiority. The self-actualizer expects the possible. The one who wants to actualize a concept attempts the impossible.

In responding to "should" demands, the individual plays a role not supported by genuine needs. He becomes both phony and phobic. He shies away from seeing his limitations and plays roles unsupported by his potential. By seeking cues for behavior from the outside, he "computes" and responds with reactions not basically his own. He constructs an imaginary ideal of how he "should" be and not how he actually is.

The concept of perfection is such an ideal. In responding, the individual develops a phony facade to impress others what a good boy he is. Demands for perfection limit the individual's ability to function within himself, in the therapeutic situation, in marriage as well as other social situations.

One can observe in marital difficulties that either one or both of the marriage partners are not in love with the spouse but with an image of perfection. Inevitably, the partner falls short of those expectations. The mutual frustration of not finding perfection results in tension and increased hostility which results in a permanent status quo, an impasse or, at best, a useless divorce. The same condition applies to the therapeutic situation. Either a status quo of many years or a change of therapists occurs, but *never* a cure.

By turning his perfectionistic demands toward himself, the neurotic tears himself to pieces in order to live up to his unrealistic ideal. Though perfection is generally labeled an "ideal," it is actually a cheap curse which punishes and tortures both the self and others for not living up to an impossible goal.

At least two more phenomena interfere with the development of man's genuine potential. One is the formation of character. The individual then can act only with a limited, fixed set of responses. The other is the phobic attitude which is far more widespread than psychiatry has been willing to recognize thus far.

3

Freud was the genius of half-truths. His investigations of repression, blocks and inhibitions reveal his own phobic attitude concerning phobias. Once an impulse becomes dangerous, we turn, according to Freud, actively against it and put a *cordon sanitaire* around it. Wilhelm Reich made this attitude still more explicit in his armor theory. But danger is not always aggressively neutralized. More often we avoid and flee from it. Thus, by avoiding the means and ways of avoidance, we miss half the tools for a cure.

The organism avoids actual pains. The neurotic avoids imaginary hurts such as unpleasant emotions. He also avoids taking reasonable risks. Both interfere with any chance of maturation.

Consequently, in gestalt therapy we draw the patient's attention to his avoidance of any unpleasantness. We work through the subtle machinations of phobic behavior in addition to working through the blocks, inhibitions and other protective attitudes.

To work through imaginary pains and unpleasant emotions we need a fine balance of frustration and support. Once the patient feels the essence of the "here and now" and "i and thou," he begins to understand his phobic behavior.

At first the patient will do anything to keep his attention from his actual experiences. He will take flight into memory and expectation (past and future); into the flight of ideas (free associations); intellectualizations or "making a case" of right and wrong. Finally, he encounters the holes in his personality with an awareness of nothing (no-thing-ness), emptiness, void and the impasse.

At last the patient comes to realize the hallucinatory character of his suffering. He discovers that "he does not have to" torture himself. He acquires a greater tolerance for frustration and imaginary pain. At this point he begins to mature.

I define maturity as the transition from environmental support to self-support. In gestalt therapy maturity is achieved by developing the individual's own potential through decreasing environmental support, increasing his frustration tolerance and by debunking his phony *playing* of infantile and adult roles.

Resistance is great because the patient has been conditioned to manipulate his environment for support. He does this by acting helpless and stupid; he wheedles, bribes and flatters. He *is not* infantile but *plays* an infantile and dependent role expecting to control the situation by submissive behavior. He also plays the roles of an infantile adult. It is difficult for him to realize the difference between mature behavior and "playing an adult." With maturation the patient is increasingly able to mobilize spontaneously his own resources in order to deal with the environment. He learns to stand on his own feet, thus becoming able to cope with his own problems as well as the exigencies of life.

Human potential is decreased both by inappropriate demands of society and by the inner conflict. Freud's parable of the two servants quarrelling, with the resultant inefficiency, is again, in my opinion, but a half-truth. Actually, it is the masters who quarrel. In this case the opposing masters are what Freud named *superego* and *id*. The *id* in Freud's concept is a conglomeration of instincts and repressed memories. In actuality we observe in each and every case that the *superego* is opposed by a personalized entity which might be called *infraego*. In my language I call the opposing masters topdog and underdog. The struggle between the two is both internal and external.

Topdog can be described as righteous, bullying, punishing, authoritarian and primitive. Topdog commands continually with such statements as, "You should," "You ought to" and "Why don't you?" Oddly enough, we all so strongly identify with our inner topdog that we no longer question its authority. We take its righteousness for granted.

Underdog develops great skill in evading topdog's commands. Only half-heartedly intending to comply with the demands, underdog answers: "Yes, but . . . ," "I try so hard but next time I'll do better," and "Manana." Underdog usually gets the better of the conflict.

In other words, top- and underdog are actually two clowns performing their weird and unnecessary plays on the stage of the tolerant and mute self. Integration, or cure, can be achieved only when the need for mutual control between top- and underdogs ceases. Only then will the two masters mutually listen. Once they come to their senses (in this case listening to each other) does the door to integration and unification open. The chance of making a whole person out of a split becomes a certainty. The impasse of the status quo or the eternal conflict of the nonending therapy can be overcome.

A gestaltist integration technique is dream work. We do not play psychoanalytical interpretation games. I have the suspicion that the dream is neither a fulfilled wish nor a prophecy of the future. To me it is an existential message. It tells the patient what his situation in life is and especially how to change the nightmare of his existence into becoming aware of and taking his historical place in life. In a successful cure the neurotic awakens from his trance of delusions. In Zen Buddhism the moment is called the great awakening *(satori)*. During gestalt therapy the patient experiences a number of lesser awakenings. In coming to his senses he frequently sees the world brightly and clearly.

In actual practice I let the patient act out all the details of his dream. As therapists we do not imagine we know more than the patient does himself. We assume each part of the dream is a projection. Each fragment of the dream, be it person, prop or mood, is a portion of the patient's *alienated* self. Parts of the self are made to encounter other parts. The primary encounter, of course, is between topdog and underdog.

To illustrate the method of integrating top- and underdogs by working through a dream, I relate a case of a patient who impressed everybody with his psychotic eccentricities. During one of my group sessions he related a dream in which he saw a young man enter a library, throw books about, shout and scream. When the librarian, an elderly spinster, rebuked him, he reacted with continued erratic behavior. In desperation the librarian summoned the police.

I directed my patient to act out and experience the encounter between the boy (underdog) and the librarian and police (topdogs). In the beginning the confrontation was belligerent and uselessly consuming of time and energy. After participating in the hostile encounter for two hours, the different parts of my patient were able to stop fighting and listen to each other. True listening *is* understanding. He

6

came to recognize that by playing "crazy" he could outwit his top-dog, because the irresponsible person is not punished. Following this successful integration the patient no longer needed to act crazy in order to be spontaneous. As a result he is now a freer and more amenable person.

When topdog feeds underdog expectations of success, results, improvements and changes, underdog generally responds with pseudo-compliance or sabotage. The result is inefficiency and spite. If the underdog sincerely tries to comply, he has the choice between an obsessional neurosis, flight into illness or "nervous breakdown." *The road to Hell is paved with good intentions.*

Externally, top- and underdogs struggle for control as well. Husband and wife, therapist and patient, employer and employees play out roles of mutual manipulation.

The basic philosophy of gestalt therapy is that of nature—differentiation and integration. Differentiation by itself leads to polarities. As dualities these polarities will easily fight and paralyze one another. By integrating opposite traits we make the person whole again. For instance, weakness and bullying integrate as silent firmness.

Such a person will have the perspective to see the total situation *(a gestalt)* without losing the details. With this improved orientation he is in a better position to cope with the situation by *mobilizing his own resources.* He no longer reacts with fixed responses (character) and preconceived ideas. He doesn't cry for environmental support, because he can do for himself. He no longer lives motivated by fears of impending catastrophes. He can now assess reality by *experimenting with possibilities.* He will *give up* control-madness and let the *situation* dictate his actions.

The ability to resign, to let go of obsolete responses, of exhausted relationships and of tasks beyond one's potential is an essential part of the wisdom of living.

Group vs. Individual Therapy

Frederick S. Perls

Marshall McLuhan has written a book in which he expands the notion: the medium is the message.

What is the message we receive from the medium of group therapy? Group therapy tells us, "I am more economical than individual therapy." Individual therapy counters, "Yes, but you are less efficient." "But," asks group therapy, "who says *you* are efficient?"

You will notice that on my private stage these two therapies immediately begin to fight, to get into a conflict.

For a while, I tried to solve this conflict in gestalt therapy by asking my patients to have both individual and group therapy. Lately, however, I have eliminated individual sessions altogether, except for emergency cases. As a matter of fact, I have come to consider that all individual therapy is obsolete and should be replaced by workshops in gestalt therapy. In my workshops, I now integrate individual and group work. This is effective with a group, however, only if the therapist's encounter with an *individual patient within the group* is effective.

To understand the effectiveness of gestalt therapy in workshops, we have, first, to consider another conflict: the dichotomy in present-day psychology between the *experiential* and the *behavioral* approaches. Then we can understand how gestalt therapy integrates both branches of psychology.

The behaviorist is usually thought of primarily as a conditioner. If

Reprinted from *Etc: A Review of General Semantics*, Vol. 34, No. 3, 1967, pp. 306–312, by permission of the International Society for General Semantics.

he were willing to disassociate himself from the activity of conditioning—from a compulsion to change behavior, essentially by the external means of drill and repetition—he could become an observer, a describer of ongoing processes. He would then learn that learning is discovering, that it is a matter of new experience. On the other hand, he has one advantage over the majority of clinical psychologists: he works in the here and now. He is reality-oriented, though in a rather mechanical way; and he is more observation-oriented than the clinician, who, for the most part, is guided by abstractions and computations. But the clinician has what the behaviorist omits—full concern with the phenomenon of awareness. Whether he calls it consciousness, sensitivity, or awareness does not matter at all.

Freud assumed that the mere transposition of unconscious *memories* into conscious ones would be sufficient for a cure. Existential psychiatry has a similar, though somewhat broader, outlook: to assimilate and to make available *all* those parts of the personality that have been alienated.

What can hinder the experientialist is this: though his focus is on experience, he turns easily away from the here and now of the behaviorist. Either he becomes concerned, like Freud, with the past and with causality, or he becomes concerned, like Adler, with intentions. The actual behavior of *both* the therapist and the patient is usually explained away as "transference" and "counter-transference."

Interest in observable behavior developed early in psychotherapy. The hypnotist wanted not only to relieve the patient of his symptoms, but also to change objectionable habits into desirable ones. The Freudian school saw behavior patterns parallel with the three recognized erogenous zones: oral, anal, and genital. Reich's interest in character formation was largely centered on a person's *motoric* behavior. He tried to take a short cut, and so, like most therapists, he neglected to observe the details of *voice* and *verbal* behavior.

The gestalt school has investigated much of our sensoric behavior. Since our contact with the world is based upon sensory awareness, especially seeing, hearing, and touching, these means of external-object-awareness play as great a part in gestalt therapy as does the internal proprioceptive system of self-awareness. Since all sensing takes place in the here and now, gestalt therapy is "present time" oriented, as is the behaviorist.

The sum of the types of overt motoric and verbal behavior—that which is easily observable and verifiable—we call character. We call the place where this behavior originates the mind. Even our secret verbal behavior is called thinking or intellect. But it is actually fantasy, or, as Freud has seen it, to play in life—the rehearsal stage on which we prepare for the roles we want.

The intellect—the whole of intelligence—we might liken to a computer. It is, however, a pallid substitute for the vivid immediacy of sensing and experiencing. The psychoanalyst and the so-called rational therapist, by playing interpretation and explanation games, only reinforce this deceptive dominance of the intellect and interfere with the emotional responses which are at the center of our personality. In the emotional desert of neurotic patients, we seldom find any feelings other than boredom, self-pity, and depression.

In short, the clinical psychotherapist lacks full involvement with actuality, with the here and now, whereas the behaviorist denies the importance of awareness. In gestalt therapy, we integrate the two sides of the coin by doing microscopic psychiatry, by investigating the awareness and avoidance of awareness of every detail of the patient's and the so-called therapist's behavior. This is the true integration of the two psychologies—not just eclectic, not a compromise. But it is most difficult to achieve this synthesis in the combination of group and individual therapy.

A neurotic may be defined as a person who is unable to assume the full identity and responsibility of mature behavior. He will do anything to keep himself in the state of immaturity, even to playing the role of an adult—that is, his infantile concept of what an adult is like. The neurotic cannot conceive of himself as a self-supportive person, able to mobilize his potential in order to cope with the world. He looks for environmental support through direction, help, explanations, and answers. He mobilizes not his own resources, but his *means of manipulating* the environment—helplessness, flattery, stupidity, and other more or less subtle controls—in order to get support.

The psychoanalyst can play right into the hands of the neurotic who resorts to such behavior by disregarding the essence of human relationships and by turning any relationship into an infantile one, such as father-figure, incest, super-ego dominance. The patient is not made responsible, but the unconscious, the Oedipus complex or what-you-will, receives the catharsis of cause and responsibility.

The basic behavior of a student of mine was wailing. His father was a professional wailer: a cantor. The student *was* aware that he was like his father in many respects and fought this attitude; but the insight was of no help to him, because it never clarified what the essence of his wailing was. The louder he wailed, the greater his disappointment that there was no result. He failed to realize that he *and* his father were barking up the wrong tree. There could be no answer, because nobody, no God, no magician, was there to help him. The father imitation is not the problem. The irrational behavior of both father and son is.

Freudianism barks up the wrong tree of cause and interpretations; psychology in general does it by mixing up mind and fantasy. Every patient barks up the wrong tree by expecting that he can achieve maturation through external sources—through being psychoanalysed, reconditioned, hypnotized, or marathonized, or by taking psychedelic drugs. Maturation cannot be achieved *for* him; he has to go through the painful process of growing up by himself. A therapist can do nothing but provide him with the opportunity—by being available both as a catalyst and as a screen upon which he can project his neurosis.

The basic theory of gestalt therapy is that maturation is a continuous growth process in which environmental support is transformed into self-support. In healthy development, the infant mobilizes and learns to use his own resources. A viable balance of support and frustration enables him to become independent, free to utilize his innate potential.

In contrast, a neurosis develops in an environment that does not facilitate this maturation process adequately. Development is, instead, perverted into a character formation, into a set of behavior patterns that are meant to control the environment by manipulation.

The child learns, often by copying some adult, to secure environmental support by playing helpless or stupid, by bullying, by flattering, by trying to be seductive, and so on and on. Thus any helpful and too supportive therapist or member of the group who is sucked in by a patient's manipulations will only spoil that person more—by depriving him of the opportunity to discover his own strength, potential, and resources. The therapist's real tool here is skillful frustration.

At the core of each neurosis lies what the Russians call the *sick point*. Realizing that they can do nothing to cure it, they are satisfied to reorganize it and to sublimate their energies around this sick point. In gestalt therapy, we call this sick point the *impasse*; and I have as yet seen no method other than gestalt therapy capable of getting through it. Furthermore, I doubt if it is possible to get through the impasse in individual therapy, and I know that the integration of individual and group therapy holds the possibility to do so.

When approaching the existential impasse (and this does not mean minor hang-ups), the patient gets into a whirl. He becomes panic-stricken, deaf and dumb—unwilling to leave the merry-go-round of compulsive repetition. He truly feels the despair which Kierkegaard recognized as "sickness unto death." The existential impasse is a situation in which no environmental support is forthcoming, and the patient is, or believes himself to be, incapable of coping with life on his own. So he will do anything to hold on to the status quo—rather than grow up and use his own powers. He will change marriage partners, but not his expectations; he will change therapists, but not his neurosis; he will change the content of his inner conflicts, but he will not give up his self-torture games; he will increase the subtlety of his manipulations and his control-madness to secure the environmental support without which he imagines he cannot survive.

Now, in the group situation something happens that is not possible in the private interview. To the whole group it is *obvious* that the person in distress *does not see* the obvious, does not see the way out of the impasse, does not see (for instance) that most of his misery is a purely imagined one. In the face of this collective conviction of the group, he cannot use his usual phobic way of disowning the therapist when he cannot manipulate him. Somehow, trust in the group seems to be greater than trust in the therapist—in spite of all so-called transference confidence.

Behind the impasse there lurks the threatening monster that keeps the patient nailed to the cross of his neurosis. This monster is the catastrophic expectation that, so he imagines, spells his doom and prevents him from taking reasonable risks and enduring the growing pains of maturation.

It is at this point that rational thinking has its place: in the assessment of the degree to which catastrophic expectation is mere imagination or exaggeration of real danger. In the safe emergency of the therapeutic situation, the neurotic discovers that the world does not fall to pieces if he gets angry, sexy, joyous, mournful. Nor is the group's support for his self-esteem and appreciation of his achievements toward authenticity and greater liveliness to be underestimated.

In my gestalt workshop anyone who feels the urge can work with me. I am available, but never pushing. A dyad is temporarily developed between myself and the patient; but the rest of the group is fully involved, though seldom as active participants. Mostly they act as an audience which is stimulated by the encounter to do quite a bit of silent self-therapy.

There are other advantages in working with a group. A great deal of individual development can be facilitated through doing collective experiments—talking jibberish together, or doing withdrawal experiments, or learning to understand the importance of atmosphere, or showing the person on the spot how he collectively bores, hypnotizes, or amuses the environment. In grief or similar emotionally charged situations, chain reactions often occur. The group soon learns to understand the contrast between helpfulness, however well-meaning, and true support. And at the same time, the group's observation of the manipulative games which the neurotic plays, the roles he acts out in order to keep himself in the infantile state, facilitates their own self-recognition.

In other words, in contrast to the usual type of group meetings, *I* carry the load of the session, by either doing individual therapy or conducting mass experiments. I often interfere if the group plays opinion and interpretation games or has similar purely verbal encounters without any experiential substance, but I keep out of it as soon as anything genuine happens.

It is always a deeply moving experience for the group and for me, the therapist, to see previously robotized corpses begin to return to life, gain substance, begin the dance of abandonment and self-fulfillment. *The paper people are turning into real people.*

Acting Out vs. Acting Through

Frederick S. Perls and Cooper C. Clements

Fritz: Before you ask questions I want to say something about "acting out" in general. This term, acting out, takes me back to the time when I was a psychoanalyst, and where acting out was a bad thing. Freud's rigid demand was, "You should not act out, but remember instead." In his preoccupation with the past, Freud said people should remember instead of acting out. But his idea, in my opinion, was that they should be aware and have enough distance from this way of living so that they could work on it. They should be, in Freudian terms, more conscious of what they were doing. In a way, Freud's idea was correct. He believed that people lived certain neurotic attitudes and by living them and acting them out, they escaped treatment. Now in gestalt therapy when we talk about "acting out" we do not mean living out but "Be an actor." We have a script in the form of a dream or a fantasy. We see that the dream or fantasy is a story, a drama, and we act it out again in therapy to make us more aware of what we are, of what is available.

Cooper: And this is acting out the role in the therapy situation.

Fritz: Exactly. So the trouble lies partly on a semantic level. The acting out idea of Freud should say, "Be aware that you act out a role." But instead a taboo was presented by Freud as, "You should not act out because it is a bad thing." Now in Freudian therapy you don't bring this into the therapy, and so maybe the prohibition makes sense.

Reprinted from *Voices, the Art and Science of Psychotherapy*, Vol. 4, No. 4, Winter 1968, pp. 66–73.

Cooper: In gestalt therapy you are aiming for conscious awareness of the acted out roles?

Fritz: Exactly. The difference between us and Freud is that he stressed remembering and we stress being aware. We stress the difference between *deliberate acting* and being unaware of living in a certain way. The latter is living a part of one's life script and doing it compulsively, without knowing that it is a pathological way of living. I want to emphasize that in Freudian terminology acting out is a dirty word. And many things are then covered as "acting out" and a taboo is put on things which might just as well be a genuine expression of the personality. Freud's idea was that everything is predetermined and whatever happens is just a repetition of something that happened before. In other words, this Freudian analysis does not leave room for creative living because if everything happened before, it's an automatic repetition. Again this might often be the case so far as the Freudian type of acting out is concerned.

Cooper: So we want to look ahead to what is authentic living, in addition to the process of getting out of the neurosis.

Fritz: My opinion is this: Any unfinished situation, any incomplete action, will come to the surface and will be or wants to be completed. Now much of what Freud called "the repetition compulsion" (compulsive repetitiveness) is the unfinished situation. Freud thought this is just maybe a habit formation, a petrified way of living. And I maintain it's just the other way around. These compulsive repetitions, the living out of something in a very similar way, are our attempts (futile attempts in most cases) to solve the situation. This is because very often something is left out in this acting out; there is something one is not yet aware of.

Cooper: This would bring in the avoiding part. There's always some avoiding.

Fritz: Yes, yes.

Cooper: It's a crucial element. And then you try to get at this, particularly in dream work and body language work?

Fritz: I don't try to get to this. The organism gets to this, and whether it gets to this in the form of acting out or dreaming out—perhaps poetrying out—it is just a matter of chance the way this person expresses himself. To talk in old-fashioned words, the extrovert would rather live it out and the introvert would make a poor piece of poetry out of it. But in both cases it points to some arresting in one's development by avoiding taking a certain step, taking a certain risk.

Cooper: So you would relate it to the general thing of a person trying to experience and express himself?

Fritz: Look, consider a cat which plays and climbs up a curtain and uses its claws. When the cat is young it cannot avoid using the claws. Claw-using is unfinished business for the young cat; so it does not "act out" at this moment clawing you. Now if a grown-up cat would always use the claws, would act out the claw bit, then something is missing in its development. The moment that it learns to walk without using the claw, then the differentiation has taken place.

Cooper: So you're looking at the development of the individual and his needs for completion, rather than focusing on a prohibition or taboo.

Fritz: Yes. Now let's take an example of a human being learning to do something, say typing. When I've learned to type well and formed the gestalt by practice, then I'm free to attend to the content and not the mechanics of typing. But if my typing is still faulty, like doing an *m* for an *n,* then a lot of effort must still be invested in the unfinished situation. The whole acting out bit of Freud is something similar. We are repeating a certain unfinished situation. For example, we always get disappointed in the same friend or we are always being sucked in by certain personalities. All this is because we avoid something in the relationship that would lead to a closure, to an understanding of that person, or to the ability to "let go" if this is not the right person. Sure psychoanalysts probably think in the same terms. They would say we have to cure, we have to work through that complex. But the complex is not worked through in the form of coming to closure but only in retracing the event to some so-called trauma, some happening in childhood. This is something quite different from completing the person.

Cooper: And picking up on what's happening here and now.

Fritz: And working on what's here and now and what's missing in that person.

19

Cooper: I wonder if you would like to relate acting out to the four layers of therapy and neurosis that you were talking about in the group this morning. You described the role-playing layer as first, then the implosive layer leading to the impasse, then the explosive layer, and finally authentic living. Would you see acting out as related to the third layer, the explosive one?

Fritz: Yes, that's very interesting. We are "acting out" in the first layer in playing out roles but this is definitely not in the Freudian sense of thinking that this is an unfinished situation that is bad. We are acting out the patient in the therapy situation so eventually an explosion can be achieved. The acting out in the Freudian sense, the incomplete situation without awareness, is the *blocking* of the explosion.

Cooper: I am thinking of the four areas of explosion you've mentioned in this third layer: explosions into sexual love, into anger, into joy, and into grief. The anger and the sexual love are the ones that get the most attention and that is where the therapists get most concerned with social consequences.

Fritz: I would say Freud is very much in favor of living out, acting out, the grief. He's done beautiful work on the mourning labor. I don't see much of him ever written about the acting out of joy. He, Wilhelm Reich, Adler, and many others have written a lot about anger and they are completely off the mark by having real semantic confusion. Sometimes they talk about aggression, then sadism or cruelty, then anger, then hostility.

Cooper: Hostility seems to be popular these days.

Fritz: Yes, and they never make clear what is going on. These are completely different forms of functioning. A salesman can be aggressive, having initiative, without being hostile.

Cooper: His assertion could also be quite appropriate.

Fritz: I want to give you my favorite example. If I swallow my food, forcing the food down on the basis of greediness, and I am not aggressive toward the food (do not try to destroy the food), then I might get stomach trouble and also develop a certain amount of "introjective tendency" instead of understanding assimilation.

Cooper: In gestalt the aggression is a necessary part of the assimilation process.

Fritz: In gestalt? In nature! The supermarket made us forget that we kill in order to survive. Every being kills in order to survive. Only the human being kills out of greed more than he needs. He kills out of habit formation.

Cooper: We've been talking mainly, I think, about acting out in terms of working through the process with the person in the therapy situation. Many times when the acting out taboo comes up, it's that the patient is doing something outside the therapy situation. He is acting out sexually or aggressively in ways that the therapist gets concerned about. The therapist feels the person may not be contributing to his development by this behavior.

Fritz: Okay, I'll give you an example of mine. When I was in analysis, I had no relationship to that guy. He hardly ever spoke in therapy. Five minutes before the therapy hour was finished, he scratched the floor as a signal that the hour was over. He believed in completely passive therapy. Now I noticed what he cherished. He called me an Omar Khayyam when listening to my adventures. So all I did during the time I was in analysis with him was go out for more and more adventures so as to be able to tell him something. I acted out, and the acting out was to please him. He never discussed this with me.

Cooper: So you were trying to have something to report.

Fritz: Sure, and this happens with other therapists. The whole thing is so silly, the acting out bit. Just as silly as psychoanalysis itself among gestalt therapists. The acting out, the compulsion! Come rain, come shine, the person goes every day to the same place for an hour whether he is depressed or happy, whether he wants to go or not, he goes. What rigid compulsion, rigid acting out that is! And then the hour must not be one minute less or one minute more than fifty, notwithstanding the fact that most of the people don't say a real thing except for the last two minutes. Suddenly then they have something urgent to say so as to torture the therapist, to prolong and put him into a quandry on how he can finish up and get his ten-minute rest. Have you not seen that?

Cooper: Yes, and I've done it myself.

Fritz: That's crap and being compulsive, the 50 minutes. Look at our workshop advantage. Sometimes we work 20 minutes with a person, sometimes an hour and a half. This whole individual therapy crap is completely obsolete. It's a fossilized survivor of the Freudian period when they thought psychoanalysis was a means to cure people.

Cooper: So you see this general term of acting out as a taboo that Freud got started.

Fritz: Not only that. I go a step further. Consider the deep phobia of Freud who was a very, very sick man; what was he acting out? He was acting out the business of not going out, *not* acting out. Such pain he had to cross the street, what pain to talk to any person. He was so embarrassed and so self-conscious. However, in a true deep meaning of Freud, I think he was saying be careful of acting out as a means of avoiding; bring your real problems to this place of therapy, this is better. Notwithstanding this, I'm very suspicious whether the taboo of acting out is not just as much a rationalization of Freud's phobia.

Cooper: How would you relate the acting out taboo to different cultural mores and settings? Like in one setting they may allow more sexual freedom and more aggressive expression.

Fritz: Freud never meant this by acting out. Freud meant by acting out that some type of pathological behavior is slipping out and is executed as a piece of living, instead of as a piece of discussion on the couch. What you are talking about is freedom of action, a full awareness that this is permissible and that is not permissible. This is fine to an extent but has nothing to do with the specific thing Freud meant by acting out. If you go that far, then the only way to live would be not to do a thing.

Cooper: So you want to look more in terms of the process going on in the person and how much awareness he has of what he's doing.

Fritz: Yes, as well as what awareness he has of what he's not doing.

Cooper: What he's avoiding.

Fritz: Yes.

Cooper: And that would be the basis for differentiating between role playing in these earlier layers of neurosis and authentic living?

Fritz: Yes, yes. It is to say that somebody cannot see himself as a grownup. He has to have parents; hanging on to a real mother, a dead mother, a psychoanalytical mother, anything not to let go.

Cooper: This is related to what you call the Dummy Complex in your book *Ego, Hunger, and Aggression,* isn't it?

Fritz: Yes. Hanging on to the idea that one is a child, and this is Freudian acting out—one repeats what has happened before, investigates what has happened before, and it is part of keeping the patient in an infantile state. Now acting out in a good sense means letting go, let the dead bury the dead, let the parents be the parents. The other man does so and so but I am a free agent, a free agent on my own. I don't relate to this guy out of a fixation; I relate to him because I want to and to the degree that I feel relatedness.

Cooper: A here and now experience with the person.

Fritz: Yes, yes.

Cooper: Could you relate acting out to the balance concept in gestalt, the figure-ground balance of the person you are working with?

Fritz: Yes, in this acting out material (the repetition of something), one of the polarities is always hidden. Let's take the basic acting out. What do we act out as our usual moral or self-improvement system? The topdog-underdog system. You know this game. We are aware of the inefficient underdog part in ourselves, but we are not aware of the character of the top part in ourselves. Our own righteous behavior, we take that for granted. And thus the balance between the submissive behavior and the bullying behavior, between the aggressive and the frightened, cannot be achieved. Let's go back to Freudian terms. He would say there is not a strong ego because the patient is all superego. What Freud misses is that there is an infra-ego balancing the superego. What do you call acting out there? If I torture myself, sure then I am acting out. But where is the exact point of where you put in that the acting out is bad? Just because you are naughty and don't bring your therapist these things? .

I feel this is good to take a new look at acting out and what some of the confusion has been. This is the bloody thing always when somebody creates a wrong notion. This wrong notion is then accepted as a reality where there should be nothing. And then the whole world has to start to refute and fight the nonsense. Look what it did to Wilhelm Reich to take the libido as something real instead of as just a conceptual whim of Freud. He went completely off his rocker. Are there some questions you'd like to ask?

Cooper: I know in groups I've been in with you, you usually say you take no responsibility for an individual's behavior outside the group situation. Would that be your view of the patient's behavior outside the therapy situation, that it's up to him?

Fritz: Exactly. I'm responsible only for myself. If you decide to go crazy, it's your business. If I am a responsible therapist I invest my skilled knowledge into working with you.

Cooper: If he wants to bring this into the therapy situation and work, then you're there to work with him?

Fritz: Yes. I don't have a compulsion to win or be the Almighty or the best therapist in the world. Anyone not willing to limit his responsibility to himself is beset with the need to be omnipotent. This is a distorted view of the self and of one's potential.

Cooper: He's expecting more of himself than he can really deliver.

Fritz: Sure.

Cooper: I wonder if we can relate acting out some more to the different layers: role-playing, implosive, explosive, authentic. The first or role-playing layer is obviously related; we see all kinds of behavior which could be labelled acting out.

Fritz: Sure.

Cooper: What about the second layer, the implosive one? What would you see happening there?

Fritz: What is happening is not acting out. There is fear of being, a basic contraction or freezing. This is the equivalent with what Freud sensed as the death instinct. But it is not an instinct for death; if anything, it is the opposite. As you see when it's worked out to the explosion, it's very much being alive! Look at my hand. If I keep an exact balance of extensor and contractor muscles, I can get an extremely rigid claw which can't move. A very rigid position. Yet there is a double amount of energy here, two parts of myself trying to take control and in exact balance. This is life still; it is catatonic.

Cooper: You don't have any figure-ground shifting.

Fritz: Exactly. This is the impasse—being stuck—neither acting out nor not acting out. The slightest acting out here, a slight trembling, is the beginning of dissolution of the implosive layer.

Cooper: How about the third layer, the explosive one? Here you mention explosions into sexual love, anger, joy, grief.

Fritz: These are explosions from the center of the personality which is the soul, also called the center of emotion. This brings the ability to feel and live again.

Cooper: It starts coming out in strong form at that point?

Fritz: Not necessarily strong. In some cases there are extreme explosions at this point. In other forms there is just a slight trembling. Explosions can be like those in your auto engine, not that noticeable. The thing is that the contractions are beginning to work again. The implosive layer is kind of like hibernating. A hibernating animal freezes up, contracts. It's not dead, it preserves life. And then it finally begins to vibrate again.

Cooper: Do people get to the explosive layer, then back up to the implosive layer before they get going with authentic living?

Fritz: Yes. Sometimes you find that only a certain segment is freed by explosion, and then the energy is freed in the total personality. The person becomes more alive. He then is able to cope with other of the feeling levels better. The one emotion easiest to reach is usually grief because it is, in most cases, socially acceptable. The explosion into love is often difficult. The hardest for the neurotic is the explosion into joy.

Cooper: Could you talk about the way you work with, say, anger and sexual love in therapy, the kinds of limits you put on?

Fritz: I don't put any limits on any explosion, including fucking! It doesn't really come to fucking, but there are no taboos in my kind of therapy. You can at least fuck in fantasy and aggress against a pillow.

Cooper: Here in the workshop one time you had people fighting with just their feet. Wasn't this a way to limit what they could do to each other?

Fritz: No, no, the leg thing came about because some of the people had no legs. Legs are very important for self-support. I suggested they move further apart as they began to use their legs so they would not accidentally hit the genitals or something. There are small precautions. But in the extreme, I've very nearly been killed quite a few times. But if you don't want to take the risk, don't be a therapist.

Cooper: In a group situation you have some support from the group to help control explosions.

Fritz: What do you mean "control explosions?" We don't want to control explosions!

Cooper: Okay. Prevent injury, shall I say?

Fritz: These injuries are not true explosions. True explosions I've seen are usually like those into joy where people dance around. Exceptions are real psychotic cases, a psychotic episode when somebody really wants to kill. Instead of exploding into impotence and realizing the impotence of impotence, they try to avoid impotence by killing. Killing is always a sign of impotence.

Cooper: So you just take your chances?

Fritz: EXACTLY!

Morality, Ego Boundary and Aggression

Frederick S. Perls

The idea of absolute morality, the conviction that good and bad do exist and that what is good or bad is fixed once and for all, is as old as human culture. In the Bible the snake tempts Adam with the promise that he can, by eating an apple, know good and bad. (Note that he acquires such knowledge by eating.) Even such a man of the Enlightenment as Sigmund Freud shows traces of such an idea when he says, "The Unconscious is not always bad; sometimes it is better than the conscious person." Psychoanalytical investigations show indeed that at least our consciences behave as if there were an absolute morality; conscience evaluates our deeds as good and bad. The absoluteness of morality has a tremendous advantage. It provides the believer with a sense of security. He knows how to act, he knows what is right and wrong. The law demands from a sane person that he should be able to distinguish right and wrong. He may not like it, but he can avoid doubt and stay out of "trouble."

The idea of the relativity of morality is not new either. The proofs of it are so overwhelming that we can hardly understand why mankind has been going along suffering the notions of sin and guilt, often driven to despair, suicide, saintliness, insanity, or voluntary incarceration. But we truly suspend between the two poles: the uncertainty of relative morals and the despair of absolute morality, between the Scylla of reason and the Charybdis of revelation.

Is there a way out for us? Can we find a unifying absoluteness

Reprinted from *Complex*, #9, 1955, pp. 42–52.

behind the relativity of morality, a point of view from which faith, conviction and rationality can be unified? I believe so; but I do not think it can be done without attaining a new attitude toward aggression. Morality and aggression, I intend to show, are essentially linked.

We may consider absolute and relative morality with respect to the total personality or the situation. In the story of Dr. Jekyll and Mr. Hyde, the total personality is good or bad. It is even represented by two people with two names. So in ordinary language we say, "He is a different person," "You are a bad boy," "She used to be such a nice person," "You are a liar." In each case we identify the total personality. Consider the devastating consequences of this kind of as-if-identification: label your child a liar a few times for having a vivid fantasy life, and he will feel under the obligation to live up to the epithet "liar"; he will actually become a chronic liar, if mother says so, because mother knows best. As to situations, think of the Victorian morality and compare then and now. The best theme for comparison is the attitude toward sex. The condemnation of sex at that time was so strong that "immoral" meant sexually immoral. Compare the Victorian ideal with our ideal. The Victorian ideal was to be beautiful, chaste, and thrifty; the present American ideal is to be glamorous, sexy, and efficient. Because of economic independence and the ever-deepening conflict between religion and science, the simplicity of faith and the greediness of progress, the social situation has altered.

From the psychiatrist's point of view, we can say that on the whole the battle against neurosis-producing sex-repression has been won, but a great many mopping-up operations still remain to be done. For instance, while the quantity of sex is abundant, the quality of the sexual act as the most intimate and intense expression of love leaves much to be desired. Instead of satisfaction and gratitude we find emptiness and disgust, frigidity and perversions as the companions of what is meant to be the ecstatic climax of human experience. The danger of today's outlook is this: while in Victorian times most of the evil was attributed to sex, we now attribute it too easily to the repression of sex.

Yet we may safely say that in the sexual sphere there is less misery. We can now press on to the next bogeyman of mankind, aggression, which is now regarded as being the "root of all evil." Aggression shares this place with money, but I am of the opinion that the curse of money cannot be solved until we come to a better understanding of aggression. For instance, let me merely mention that without solving the riddle of aggression we cannot understand greed.

There is an interesting mixture of relative and absolute morality within the individual. We use the expression "double standard"; this means that we have two yardsticks of moral measurement, one for ourselves and one for the others. "Quod licet Jovi, non licet Bovi"—what is permissible for Jupiter is forbidden to cows. In psychiatry we find an illness that has this double morality as its main symptom. I mean paranoia. The paranoiac is always a moralist, and very proud of it. He is unfairly treated, victimized, wronged, but he does not realize for a moment that *he* is doing all the victimizing and wronging. But we all have such double standards, though some of us are adept at covering up with good rationalizations.

For a physician and a psychologist the problem of morality boils down to one question: can we, dissatisfied with absolute and relative morality, find an unequivocal answer in the morality of the organism? Can we find, on the non-verbal level, experiences that can be labeled good and bad? If there are such experiences and they occur as a normal process, we can make them the basis of a useful morality—I might even go so far as to say that an objective outlook without evaluation is an impossibility.

My contention is that there is such a morality of the organism. Good and bad are responses of the organism. But the *label* "good" or "bad" is then unfortunately projected onto the stimulus; then, isolated, torn out of context, these labels are organized into codes of conduct, systems of morals, often legalized, and connected with religious cosmologies. Let us take this up piecemeal.

Good and bad are responses of the organism. We say, "You make me mad," "You make me feel happy," less frequently, "You make me feel good," "You make me feel bad." Among primitive people such phrases occur with extreme frequency. Again we use expressions like "I feel good" "I feel lousy," without considering the stimulus. But what is happening is that an ardent pupil makes his teacher feel good, an obedient child makes his parents feel good. The victorious boxer makes his fan feel good, as does the efficient lover his mistress. A book or a picture does the same when it meets your aesthetic needs. And *vice versa:* if people or objects fail to meet needs and produce satisfaction, we feel bad about them.

The next step is that instead of owning up to our experiences as ours we project them and throw the responsibility for our own responses onto the stimulus. (This might be because we are afraid of our excitement, feel that we are failing in excitement, want to shirk responsibility, etc., etc.) We say the pupil, the child, the boxer, the lover, the book, the picture "is" good or bad. At that moment, labeling the stimulus good or bad, we cut off good and bad from our own experience. They become abstractions, and the stimulus-objects are correspondingly pigeon-holed. This does not happen without consequences. Once we isolate thinking from feeling, judgment from intuition, morality from self-awareness, deliberateness from spontaneity, the verbal from the non-verbal, we lose the self, the essence of existence, and we become either frigid human robots or confused neurotics.

Nature has not provided us with the deep sense of feeling good or bad without deep meaning for survival; this emotional compass indicates a direction for us on even the most abstract and refined levels of existence. To speak in summary fashion: Feeling good for the organism means identification, be one with me; feeling bad means alienation, you go away. In the feeling of good and bad we see the discriminating function of the organism; this is a work of what we call, in gestalt therapy, the ego boundary.

Let us consider the nature of this ego boundary. I want to make two points. (1) The ego boundary is flexible. In the healthy person it is changeable as situations change; but in psychopathological states it is rather rigid. Such rigidity looks as if it would make for stability, but the stability is the stability of a "principled" person who disregards his emotions and the evidence for the sake of his preconceived ideas. One of the greatest dangers of absolute morality is that it makes for rigid ego boundaries. (2) The ego boundary can be thought of as a meeting of opposite sets of emotions, acceptances and rejections, identifications and alienations, positive and negative emotions.

Let us bear in mind that "I" is not a real existing object or a part of the organism. "I" is a symbol of a symbol. "I" indicates a state or a functioning. What underlies is more closely given in words like "intuition" or "mood." Like the indescribable something which we call the "mood" of a person, the "I" is experienceable but has no fixity.

When I say "I am here," I mean to say "Here is an organism in front of you with whose functions the speaker identifies himself." If this organism should say, for instance, "I didn't do it," there is an alienation, a "not I" involved.

Perhaps the basic function of the ego boundary is discrimination. And we can say that neurotic conflict is simply the conflict between two types of discrimination, an "introjected" or alien discrimination (somebody else's choosing that we have incorporated) and the discrimination of the organism. Karen Horney, for instance, spoke of the idealized image and Sullivan of the self-system as the introjected discrimination. Bergler, like many psychoanalysts before him, found the mainspring of conflict in conscience. Freud used the name super-ego.

Now peculiarly it has been overlooked that the conflict between these discriminations must involve aggression, for aggression is the essence of conflict. Without aggression, peace of mind would prevail. Thus, whatever the neurotic conflict may be about, we must first of all get hold of the aggression that causes and maintains the conflict.

Let us return to Dr. Jekyll and Mr. Hyde. In that story the conflict is apparently finished as far as the Doctor is concerned. He has disavowed all unwanted properties and has become an ideal. His discrimination has kept everything that was in his time considered to be good, and has projected everything bad onto Mr. Hyde. For instance, we can say that he has disowned his animal nature. His ego boundary runs between the two personalities. Everything inside the boundary is good, everything outside bad. We should actually call our hero Mr. X, for as you see by now, the Doctor and Mr. are two parts of a split person, and the split, the insulating layer, is the ego boundary. The idealist in this person, of course, would like to become a killer himself, namely to kill the animal nature in him, but this would mean suicide and the end of the story, for you cannot kill nature.

More generally, on the inside of each ego boundary we find the cohesive forces of integration which we call good, and on the other side the destructive forces of aggression that we call bad. On the inside is what we accept and what is familiar, outside is what we reject as strange. The laws of the ego boundary, identification and alienation, apply to all boundary phenomena. They apply to interpersonal relations, as "you are mine," "I don't know you any more," "This can't be my son." They apply intrapersonally as in Mr. X. We can fill whole books with examples of dissociations of parts of ourselves, due to repressions, projections, self-control, and other means of alienating the organismic discrimination. Identification and alienation occur in social organizations as well, a nation, a club, a racial group, a fraternity. The laws are especially pronounced where the "otherness" is stressed, as in nationalisms, cults, systems of exploitation or reform. The closer the inner ties of the members of a group, the more aggression and hostility gathers outside the boundaries. It is because the Montagues and Capulets are such cohesive clans that they are so hostile to each other. One's own god is always the good one, the strange god is rejected. One's own soldiers are brave heroes. The enemy is a raping villain.

Aggression and cohesion are mutually dependent. After the aggression of Pearl Harbor, the inner cohesion, the feeling of oneness within the United States, increased considerably, and the aggression hitherto invested in party and class strife went to the boundary as a powerful means of defense.

So we have quite naturally come to the theme of aggression. If one's discrimination calls whatever is outside the boundary bad, then a real danger arises. For the closer neighbors are in space or spirit, the greater is the danger of identification between them, which means a danger of losing one's own identity. So the need for destroying the threat arises. And, contrariwise, if a unit wants to expand, as in the growth of an individual personality or of a nation, or the need of a reform movement to make proselytes, the unit needs aggression to destroy the resistance encountered. So let us discuss a moment this word "destroy."

We often think of destroying as annihilation, but we cannot destroy a substance important to us in such a way that it is made *nihil,* nothing. To destroy means to de-structure, to break into pieces. Aggression has a two-fold purpose: first, to de-structure any threatening enemy to the point where he becomes impotent; and, second, in an expanding aggression, to de-structure the substance that is needed for growth and to render it assimilable. Even Hitler, when setting out to destroy Czechoslovakia, was careful not to destroy the armament factories that he wanted to incorporate into his greater Germany.

Thus aggression is essential for survival and growth. It is not an invention of the devil, but a means of nature. We can understand the wish of parents that aggression be merely a neurosis of naughty children, or of psychiatrists in mental hospitals that aggression can be discharged like a physical excretion, to get rid of something unpleasant. Actually nature is not so wasteful as to create such a powerful energy as aggression just to be "got rid of" or "abreacted." In cases of pathological aggression, we have simply instances of unorganized, useless aggression. As a tool of nature, aggression is valuable; as the tool of moralistic discrimination, it becomes an instrument for non-survival. For example, a case of nervous breakdown is due to too much self-control, and this means that the person is directing aggression against his own spontaneous impulses.

In order to live, an organism must grow, physically and mentally. To grow, we must incorporate external substance, and in order to make it assimilable, we have to de-structure it. Let us consider just the elementary tool of aggressive de-structuring, the teeth. To build up the highly differentiated proteins of human flesh, we have to de-structure the molecules in our food. This occurs in three stages, biting, chewing, digesting. For biting, we have incisors, the front teeth, in our culture somewhat replaced by the cutting knife. The first step is the cutting of large pieces into morsels. Secondly, we grind down the morsels to a pulp with the help of our molars, or culturally, with millstones. (A patient told me he couldn't see anything aggressive in chewing, though he could in biting; but how would he feel if he were lying between two millstones?) Lastly, there is the chemical de-structuring in our stomachs, by means of dissolving acids. (For example, in cases of resentment, which is an incomplete aggression, we often have the effect of stomach ulcers.)

Not only the teeth, of course, are tools of aggression, but the muscles of the jaw, the hands, the words. The aggression is given in the organic working-together of all the parts of the personality.

Now if we want to integrate the neurotic personality, we first de-structure the symptoms. In other words, we do not try to get rid of the headaches or obsessions by annihilating them, by cutting them out. This would cripple the patient if it were possible; we leave such attempts to lobotomists. But we aim to re-organize, to de-structure and re-structure the personality. Invariably when we do so, we find considerable aggression that has been bound up either in self-control, self-punishing, even self-destruction. We find aggression that has been projected and appears as chronic fear of an impending catastrophe. We find destructive aggression in irritability, withdrawing, withholding. In short, we find a lot of "surplus" aggression. But to hold that this aggression as such is responsible for the pathological distortions, like Hitlerism or sadism, is like holding the sexual drive responsible for the perversions. It is not aggression, any more than sex, that is responsible for the neuroses, but the unfortunate organization of aggression that occurs in our institutions and families, especially in the inability to cope with industrial progress and the inferno of urban living. We have neglected our organic discrimination and thus we have diminished the amount of satisfaction in our lives. Caught in rush and worry, we don't have the time to finish situations. Most of all, perhaps, instead of being attracted by what is interesting to them, people are driven by "duty," by the need to earn a living in occupations that are not appropriate to them, not true vocations, by greed for things instead of appetite for meaningful relations, by greed for entertainment instead of the effort for happiness.

In my opinion, all of this is importantly connected with the poor organization of our habits of eating; and in every therapy I devote considerable time to restructuring these habits. Disturbances of breathing produce symptoms of anxiety; disturbances of adequate and satisfactory intake of food produce, via the unemployed biological aggression, many neurotic troubles.

Let us collect our various threads.

The growth of the organism takes place by integrating our experiences, that is by assimilating to the organism the physical, emotional, and intellectual substances that the environment offers and that meet a need.

If no assimilation occurs, we are left with the introjects, the things swallowed whole, the foreign material that we have not made our own. Such is an introjected morality: it is the result of an incomplete aggression, an incomplete biting-off and chewing-up and digestion of the standards of parents, teachers, and society. Some of that food was perhaps not fit for the organism to begin with; it would never have been bitten off but was force-fed. This part must be vomited back. Other of it might have been potentially wholesome enough, but it was fed at the wrong time or in the wrong doses, so it was never digested. This part must be regurgitated, chewed through again, and digested.

Further, since the aggression was incomplete, since the organic de-structuring of the food was interrupted, there occurs a dissociation of part of the aggression into free-floating aggression; and the corresponding starvation recurs as greed. The essence of what is taken in by greed is that it does not satisfy; greed requires more and more to fill the bottomless pit—for the food does not nourish. On the plane of self-esteem, for example, if you are in need of praise, then no amount of praise you get will ever be enough, for the praise is not assimilated; it is deprecated (swallowed without savor) or becomes a source of boasting (vomiting it back). And the free-floating aggression, that should have been used for the assimilation, finds its way into tyranny, sadism, irritation, and so forth.

Encumbered by its introjection, the organism loses its proper discrimination; the stomach and mouth are sour or desensitized; there is no appetite. Then wrong choices are made, nourishment is looked for in the wrong direction, according to alien "needs." The result of this must be still further fixing of the habits of faulty and incomplete de-structuring, for without savor, appetite, and need, how can we expect a complete mobilization of the functions of aggression, whether toward food, sexual satisfaction, knowledge, or social relationships? Healthy aggression is nothing but applying oneself for the achievement of self-realization.

In therapy, on the contrary, step by step with re-structuring the habits of aggression we examine and reevaluate the acts of discrimination. For example, with an exercise in chewing might come first gagging and vomiting, but then new sensations of taste and a more vigorous appetite. And, *vice versa*, with a reevaluation of what objects are disgusting and what objects have been sought out, might come first pains or cramps in the jaws and other muscles of aggression, but then a new strength to reach out for and bite off what is organically needful.

When appetite and aggression follow from the needs of the organism and the objects are discriminated by the organism, there is the security that was rigidly given by absolute moral standards. At the same time there is the flexibility and relativity necessary and delightful in the changing circumstances of the world, for there is no anxiety about losing the self: it is the self that is choosing.

In practice, of course, the greatest obstacle to re-organizing aggression is the patient's fear to hurt, or by retaliation, his fear of being hurt. Mostly, however, this fear to hurt can be shown to be nothing but self-deception and hypocrisy, for though he inhibits his action or scotomizes his wishes from hurting directly, he always hurts indirectly instead. He does it by showing the cold shoulder, by being late, by disappointing, by being in a bad humor, by being clumsy and breaking something, etc., etc., ad infinitum. It is not the conflict and the aggression brought to a conclusion, often to a creative and surprisingly satisfactory conclusion, that causes the misery, but the avoidance of bringing the fight into the open and clearing the air. Let me mention an extreme case, one of my patients in South Africa. He had lost a button off his jacket. For three weeks he felt acute resentment against his wife because she did not mend the button. But he did not speak to her about it, nor invest the five minutes necessary to mend the button himself. Instead he made himself and his wife miserable with his sulking for three weeks.

What is our conclusion with regard to morality and aggression?

The organism cannot tolerate an unfinished situation. With every finished situation, we feel good; with every unfinished situation, we feel bad. To finish a situation, in order to achieve well-being and stability, we mobilize our forces to attack the problem. The more obstacles that stand in the way, the more energies we are required to bring into play. In hunger, there is oral aggression; wants and frustrations of other kinds involve other muscular aggressions. In language, when we feel good or are achieving the desired conclusion, our speech is soft and friendly; when we feel bad or are being frustrated, our voices grate and we curse. With regard to our fellows, when we feel good, we feel thankful, we have a sense of harmonious contact; when we feel bad, we attack in some way and try to change the environment. If we prevent ourselves from aggressing, we feel resentment or guilt instead.

So we must say: it is not aggression itself that is good or bad, but when we feel bad we feel aggressive.

The Theory of "The Removal of Inner Conflict"

Frederick S. Perls and Paul Goodman

Psychoanalysis has classically devoted itself to the uncovering of "inner conflicts" and their "removal." Certainly there is a world of truth in this concept, but even so we must inspect it much more closely than is usually the case. "Inner" presumably means either within the organism, inside the skin, or "within the psyche." For instance, a conflict between sexual tension and shrinking from pain, or between instinct and conscience. Opposed to these, and non-neurotic, would presumably be conflicts with the environment or with other persons. But put this way the distinction between "inner conflicts" and other conflicts is not valuable, for clearly there are non-"inner" conflicts that are profitably called neurotic. To the extent that a child has not yet grown free-standing from the child-parent field—is still suckling, learning to talk, economically dependent, etc.—it is pointless to speak of the neurotic disturbances (unawares starvation, unawares hostility, unawares deprivation of contact) as either within the skin or within an individual's "psyche." The disturbances are in the *field;* they spring from the "inner conflicts" of the parents, and they result in the introjected conflicts in the later free-standing offspring, but their essence is in the disturbed felt-relation, irreducible to the parts. So the lapse of community in political societies is reducible neither to the neuroses of individuals (for indeed they become "individuals" because of the lapse), nor to the bad institutions (which are maintained by the citizens); it is a

Reprinted from *Resistance,* Vol. 8, No. 4, March 1950, pp. 5–6.

disease of the field. The distinction of "intra-personal" and "inter-personal" is a poor one, for all individual personality and organized society develop from functions of coherence that are essential to both person and society, such as nourishment, love, learning, communication, sympathy, identification; and indeed the contrary functions of division are also essential to both: rejection, hate, alienation, etc. Contact-and-boundary is prior to intra and inter, or to inner and outer. And disturbances that could be called neurotic occur also in the organism-natural-environment field, for instance the magic rituals of primitives that develop, quite without personal neurosis, from starvation and thunder-fear: or our contemporary disease of "mastery" of nature rather than healthy symbiosis, for quite apart from personal and social neuroses (which are, to be sure, here working overtime), there is a dislocation in the interaction of sheer material quantities and dearths, caused by unawares abuses. The primitive says, "The earth is starving, therefore we are starving," and we say, "We are starving, therefore let us wrest something from the earth"; symbiotically both are dreams.

In short, let us speak of "unawares conflicts" rather than "inner conflicts." This change is a fundamental simplification; for previously it was necessary to say, "we uncover the inner conflicts and bring them to the surface, make them awares," but now we can say "we make the unawares conflicts awares."

The classical wording, however, contains a very important truth, stated characteristically upside-down: namely that the inner conflicts, those inside the skin, within the organism—the opposed tensions and checks and balances of the physiological system—are for the most part reliable and not neurotic, they can be trusted to be self-regulating; they have proved themselves for thousands of years and have not much changed; they are not the subject of psychotherapy; when they are unawares they can be left unawares. It is, on the contrary, the meddling-inward of outside-the-skin social forces that deliberately upsets the spontaneous inner-system and calls for psychotherapy. These forces are new-comers and often ill-considered. Psychotherapy is, importantly, a process of disengaging these properly outside-the-skin forces from meddling inside the skin and disturbing organism-self-regulation. And by the same token, it is a process of disengaging such more distant unreliable economic and political forces, as competition, money, prestige, power, from meddling inside the primary personal system of love, grief, anger, parenthood, dependence and independence.

We come then to the terms "conflict" and "removal of conflict." Obviously in the classical formula "conflict" does not mean simply the opposition of tensions and the system of checks and balances that we have spoken of. The word is used pejoratively: conflict means "bad conflict," hence conflicts must be removed. Again let us distinguish carefully. The badness of conflicts seems, in the theories, to mean one or all of the following things: (1) all conflicts are bad because they waste energy and cause suffering; (2) all conflicts excite aggression and destruction, which are bad; (3) some conflicts are bad because one or both of the contestants are anti-social and, rather than let the conflict rage, the offender should be eliminated or sublimated, e.g. pre-genital sexuality or various aggressions; (4) false, mistaken, conflicts are bad. Now from our point of view, only the last of these propositions is unequivocally sound: conflicts that are unreal, dummy, projected, displaced, etc. must be removed. But even in this case we must remember that behind every false conflict – that is, where the contestants are erroneously conceived or are masks – there is a true conflict, of opposing real forces. The errors are tendentious, the masks express the real. Therefore we can say that, fundamentally, no conflicts should be removed by psychotherapy; but the goal of psychotherapy is to make awares unawares conflicts and to remove false conflicts. And indeed this may be simplified by omitting the last part, for once a false conflict is in awareness it dissolves of itself; one cannot be aware of what is not the case.

Here, on points (2) and (3) let us say only the following: where the contestants are natural drives they cannot be reduced, although they may be postponed by organism-self-regulation or even deliberately suppressed. When all the contestants are in awareness, a man may make his own hard decisions, he is not a patient; most often indeed, in such a case, a difficult drive spontaneously finds its measure by organism-self-regulation, without the need of deliberate choice.

41

Let us, then, consider conflict itself, awares and attended by suffering. The notion that conflict, whether social, interpersonal, or intrapsychic, is wasteful of energy, is plausible but superficial. Its plausibility is that if the work to be done could be got at directly, then it is wasteful for the contestant that will do the work to have to fight off an opponent; and perhaps both opponents can be made to join in as partners. But this is superficial, for it assumes that one knows beforehand what the work is that is to be done, and where energy is to be expended. Then the opponent must be deceived or he is lying. But where a conflict is real, *what* to do is just what is being tested. Even more, the true work to be done is perhaps *first being found out in the conflict;* it was not hitherto known to anybody and certainly not to the contestants. Surely this is true of any creative collaboration among persons: the best efficiency is attained not by establishing an *a priori* harmony among their interests and by their compromising their individual interests to a pre-arranged goal; rather, so long as they are in contact and are earnestly aiming at the best creative achievement, the more sharply they differ and have it out, the more likely they are to produce an idea better than any of them knew individually. It is the competition in games that makes the players surpass themselves. (We do not mean, of course, that *habitual* competitiveness is not a neurotic symptom.) In personal creation, also, as in art or theory, it is the warring of disparate elements that suddenly leaps to a creative solution. A poet does not reject an image that stubbornly but "accidentally" appears and mars his plan; rather he respects the intruder and suddenly discovers what *his* plan is, he discovers and creates himself.

The question is whether the same must not be true of intrapsychic emotional conflict. In ordinary healthy situations there is no problem: by organism-self-regulation a flexible instinct-dominance establishes itself, e.g. a strong thirst puts other drives in abeyance until it is satisfied. And longer range orderings healthily occur the same way: biting-chewing-drinking establish themselves over suckling, and the genitals establish themselves as the final aim in sexuality; genital orgasm is the conclusion of a sexual excitement. In the development of these orders there were conflicting tensions, but the conflicts worked themselves out. Now suppose the situation is unhealthy: e.g. the genital primacy was not strongly established because of oral unfinished situations, genital fears, so-called "regressions," and so forth. And suppose now that all these contestant drives are brought into the open, into open contact and open conflict, with regard to object-choices, behavior, interest. Must not this conflict and its attendant suffering and hardships be the means of coming to a self-creative solution, presumably the normal primacy? The conflict is severe because there is much to be destroyed. Is the destructiveness to be inhibited? If this is the meaning of conflict, it is obviously unwise to allay it or to suppress some of the contestants, for the result must then be to prevent a thorough destruction and assimilation, and therefore to condemn the patient to a weak and never perfectly self-regulating solution.

From the physician's point of view, the danger in an emotional conflict is that its raging may destroy the patient, tear him to pieces. This is a true danger. But it must be met not by weakening the conflict but by strengthening the self and the self-awareness, so that as the conflict emerges and is attended to and sharpens, the self may sooner reach an attitude of creative indifference and identify with the coming solution.

Theory and Technique of Personality Integration

Frederick S. Perls

In the development of man from the lower animal to his present stage, there occurred at least three events of decisive interest especially for the psychotherapist. The first was the development of the cortex specific for the homo sapiens. For the first time an animal acquired faculties different from those which other animals developed in the struggle for survival. The human brain developed the faculty of delaying responses and thus modulating instinctive behavior, and made possible the consulting of previous experiences. This resulted in the development of tools and deliberate action; in other words, at that stage deliberateness supported the spontaneous instinctive behavior in the pursuit of gratification of man's organismic needs and his defenses.

The second stage began when man was required to use his deliberateness not for the support but for the harnessing of instinctive behavior. This occurred at a time when the survival of society assumed more importance than the survival of the individual. However, the instincts were merely harnessed and channelled; there was no tendency to eliminate them as something evil.

The third period began with Greek philosophy, when man became conscious of himself as an object and when he discovered the "mind." Beginning with the Christian notion of the "sin of thought," man then turned his will power against himself, forgetting more and more that the organismic needs are the very soil on which he thrives.

Reprinted from *American Journal of Psychotherapy*, Vol. 2, No. 4, October 1948, pp. 565–586.

Dichotomy was born, and it has reached in our time a stage where it defeats its own purpose. The individual in our time lives no more for the benefit of society of which he is a part but for the sake of the production of machines and money. Personal development is, like initiative and many other primary characteristics, projected. The fetish of our time is industrial development, a development in which the workman is more and more required to be an automaton. He produces machine-made parts which, and this is of decisive importance, must show no variation. In this process, the individual and society are rapidly losing their survival value.

The dichotomy of the human personality can be approached from three angles: From the point of view of the dualistic structure of *personality,* of the dualistic *behavior,* and of the dualistic *language.* Man could regain his survival value if these dualisms could be reintegrated, if he could create a unitary language and a sufficient number of unitary personalities. Individually, we are already capable of doing the latter, but we are far from producing unitary personalities on the conveyor belt. The essential requirement for reintegration would be the production of an adequate tool, and this instrument would have to be the unitary language.

Leonardo da Vinci, Goethe, Freud and Einstein started with the structure of events and kept up the primary contact with the non-verbal world, verbalizing only *a posteriori* what they had found. How different is the approach of most of us! We *begin* with words. We hear "complex," "repression," "libido," "obsession," "schizoid." Then we try to grasp the meanings of those words and go out on our search to find the confirming facts. We shout enthusiastically, "Freud is right! These things *do* exist." Or, if we do not like what we find, we become para-Freudians, accepting bits and pieces here and there and rejecting others. But if we have enough discrimination left and if we do not simply swallow the collected works—those millions of words—we can still hope for progress. However, we must not get stuck in the morass of our own theories. We must not be deceived by the double-tongued, glib, compartmental thinkers who tell us at one moment that the master himself regarded his ideas as mere theories, and at the next moment react with indignation when we have ideas of our own about "libido" and some other treasured labels of their jargon.

Because of the significance of the language problem, it is important that we try to understand it. What makes language so attractive and so concealing? Can one conceive a means-whereby we can penetrate the linguistic veil that hides reality? Shall we return to our belief in magic or shall we denounce the effectiveness of language altogether? Finally, is our language adequate to the task which we have undertaken; namely, the integration, or rather the reintegration, of human beings?

Our present-day language seems to be a totally inadequate instrument for our undertaking. If this is true, how handicapped we are! After all, language is our professional tool, and certainly, any craftsman is seriously handicapped by poor tools. While the surgeon is improving his technique, the physicist building better cyclotrons, the general practitioner using more efficient drugs, the farmer modernizing his implements, we still try to do the impossible: to integrate personalities with the help of a non-integrative language. A unitary language which would create, or result from, unitary personalities is a condition *sine qua non* for an integrated personal or social structure; but today the development of such a language is in its infancy. (Among others, Korzybski and L. L. White have concerned themselves with the creation of a unitary language.)

At present we are dissociated, dualistic personalities with a dualistic language, a dualistic mentality, a dualistic existence. The deep split in our personality, the conflict between deliberate and spontaneous behavior, is the outstanding characteristic of our time. Our civilization is characterized by technical integration and personality deterioration. The statistics of industrial production and of personality disorder show a parallel increase.

If the assumption is correct that the split personality is the normal, perhaps even unavoidable product of our time, doubt arises as to whether or not an integration is possible, or if so, whether or not it has market value or at least survival value. If an integrated personality, or as I prefer to call it, a unitary person should have a unitary language, how much of an understanding between him and those who use the present-day dualistic language could be achieved?

47

The examples of Heraclitus, Spinoza, Bach, and Goethe, who were such unitary personalities, are evidence that this is not merely a fantastic goal. On the other hand, Freud, like Beethoven, was a dualistic giant. He produced an apparently balanced scientific system of opposing energies even at the cost of having to introduce his mysterious death instinct, but he did not achieve that degree of unification of his own personality which would have seen dualities as different aspects of the same phenomenon and not as irreconcilable contradictions.

Let us look at some of the prevailing dualisms, for instance the conception of "body and mind." Philosophers tried to glue the two together in a psycho-physical parallelism. Illnesses are made out to have either psychological or organic causes. In the unitary concept of the organism-as-a-whole, the "body" becomes the visible aspect of the personality while the "mind" appears as a number of functions, especially as attention, which means as a subject/object relationship.

"God and World" is another dualistic concept in the conviction of most believers. The integration which Spinoza accomplished was *pre*-mature; it had no decisive *social* consequences. In contrast, present-day society accepts the integration of time and space, of mass and velocity, as a *timely* expression of our quantitative century, and Einstein's theory of relativity is—at least for the time being—a valid unitary interpretation.

Let us compare Freud's concept of "libido" with that of "attraction." "Libido" as opposed to "aggression" is dualistic; a unification cannot be brought about by integration, but only by behaving like a young dog that tries to bite its own tail. Thus it is not astonishing that we meet in the Freudian language monstrosities like "aggressive libido" and "latent negative transference."

"Attraction" belongs to the unitary approach. It is not irreconcilably opposed to "separation"; both expressions mean movement of a body in relation to a field. Thus Karen Horney's ideas about "moving-toward" and "moving-away" types have integrative value. Freud himself saw the antithetical meaning of many root words; e.g., the Latin "altus" which we translate with either "high" or "low." He saw the dialectical relationship of a number of processes like sadism and masochism, but in more decisive concepts he retained his dualistic outlook. After he had crystallized, and thereby solidified, his system, it was completed, and no further development can be expected from there.

Alfred Adler was the first to outgrow Freud's system. He saw how one-sidedly Freud had looked at the past and at causes, but he himself was equally prejudiced, over-emphasized the future and purposiveness. Wilhelm Reich refused to accept Freud's vague notions on the means-whereby a repression takes place. He found the answer in the muscular tensions co-existent with every neurosis and called the totality of these spasms the motor armor.

The general trend however, seems to go away from the biological foundations of our existence and instead stresses the characterological aspect and our situation within society (as if a character were put on like the mask in Greek tragedy, and as if we were not society ourselves). Security and adjustment seem to be more important than personality development.

The problem we have to face can now be formulated: How can we achieve the transition from the split into the unified personality, from the dualistic to a unitary language, from the antithetical to a truly comprehensive philosophy?

We should not underestimate either the importance or the difficulty of the task. A progressive dichotomy threatens the survival of mankind. Whether or not mankind is committing suicide or preparing for a more adequate form of existence, nobody can tell at this time. The latter would have to be a re-integrated existence, not an artificially glued-together edifice of incoherent approaches. It entails the acceptance of the organism-as-a-whole with the sincerity of William Alanson White or Kurt Goldstein and not with the lip-service which so many of the present-day movements pay to this concept. Their unitary outlook is blocked by blind spots. They have a piece of the cake and imagine that they have the whole. Their personality is crippled, and their organism-as-a-whole concept corresponds to the specific aspect of themselves which they permit to exist.

The concept of the organism-as-a-whole is the center of the *gestalt* psychological approach which is superseding the mechanistic association psychology. New York, which as no other place in the world has many different movements attempting to come to grips with psychotherapy, also attracted the three great *gestalt* psychologists, Koehler, Wertheimer and Kurt Goldstein. Goldstein broke with the rigid concept of the reflex arc. According to him, both kinds of nerves, the sensor *and* the motor, stretch from the organism to the environment. The concept that sensing is a passive, mechanistic phenomenon has to be replaced by the insight that we are active and selective in our sensing. I have called the sensory apparatus our means of orientation and the motor one that of manipulation. With this linguistic adjustment, the senses, far from being purely mechanical means for the transport of acoustic and other waves, become once more an aspect of personality itself. Thus the vista is open for an approach in which an individual may again come to his senses.

Now we meet on familiar ground. The senses are the means of awareness, consciousness, attention. Lack of awareness is characteristic for the neurotic. Insufficient awareness of past traumatic experiences has been considered by Freud as the cause of the neurosis. Frigidity and scotoma are two more examples of diminished awareness. I have studied extensively the corresponding phenomena of the alimentary tract.

Quite briefly, my theory is the following: Difficult situations create wishful and magic thinking, scientific manipulation, propaganda, and the philosophy of the free will; in short, deliberateness in place of spontaneity. Human behavior, as far as it was and is objectionable to a person or a group, has to be changed. But "goody-goody" behavior does not replace, but only supersedes the spontaneous attitude. Instincts as the source of unwanted behavior cannot be eliminated, only their expressions can be modified or annihilated. Generally, it is the expression and execution of the organismic needs, of the biological, original personality which is scotomized and paralyzed. Consequently, the modern individual has to be re-sensitized and re-mobilized in order to achieve integration.

If we set out with the idea of correlating the sensory-motor nervous system to orientation and manipulation, we arrive at an unbroken chain of interdependencies which begins with the rapid automatic reaction, the so-called reflex, and progresses to the delayed responses of medium and high order. A convenient example of the medium order response is rifle shooting. A perfect and continuous co-ordination of orientation and manipulation, a permanent adjustment to the changing situation, is required to hit a moving target. The property of the human brain to delay action is already pronounced in this example. Climbing up the ladder of abstractions, we come to the high-order activities of planning, blue-printing, theorizing, and finally, to philosophizing. Every theory, every philosophy is a map from which we take our orientation for our actions. An adequate map is one that represents reality as truthfully as possible at any particular time. However, if one opens an atlas one finds all kinds of maps; some give an orientation about the geography of a country, others tell about the political or ethnographic situation. In addition, one can get information about wind movements, data on economics, or whatever aspect of reality one is interested in.

In other words, reality *per se* does not exist for the human being. It is something different for each individual, for each group, for each culture. Reality is determined by the individual's specific interests and needs.

Everything is in flux. Only after we have been stunned by the infinite diversity of processes constituting the universe can we understand the importance of the organizing principle that creates order from chaos; namely, the figure-background formation. Whatever is the organism's foremost need makes reality appear as it does. It makes such objects stand out as figures which correspond to diverse needs. It evokes our interest, attention, cathexis or whatever you choose to call it.

Bring the Sunday's *Herald Tribune* into a large family and watch the diversity of interests. Father seeks orientation in the business section, while mother skims the paper for basement bargains. Alec looks for instances of hardships of the suppressed classes, while Jack gets enthusiastic about a football game. Aunt Jenny indulges in the obituary columns, and the twins fight over the funnies.

The most important fact about the figure-background formation is that if a need is genuinely satisfied, the situation changes. The reality becomes a different one from what it was as long as the situation was unfinished. A neurosis is always characterized by the great number of unfinished situations. The patient is either not aware of them or is incapable of coping with them, which means that he is limited in his orientation or his manipulation or in both.

The healthy organism rallies with all its potentialities to the gratification of the foreground needs. Immediately as one task is finished it recedes into the background and allows the one which in the meantime has become the most important to come to the foreground. This is the principle of organismic self-regulation. Wilhelm Reich has dealt with this principle in connection with the orgasm and has contrasted it with the principle of moralistic regulation. I would prefer to call it the principle of deliberate regulation.

The psychotherapist's philosophy determines his specific approach. The priest will purify the soul with methods that increase the awareness of the sinfulness of the forbidden deeds; the medicine man will attempt to change behavior by the use of bromides; the witch doctor will apply magic. The Freudian is concerned with the extraction of childhood traumata; the Adlerian with pumping confidence into his arrogant (inferiority-stricken) patient. If a school regards the inconsistencies of character as the root of all evil, it will endeavor to reconcile them; if the self-system is at fault, its stabilization will bring security into the interpersonal relations. If the perfect sexual orgasm produces the perfect personality, the therapeutic effort will be concentrated in that direction; and if incomplete awareness and immobility, as I suggest, are the scapegoats of the personality disorder, the method in question will be the re-sensitizing of the figure-background awareness and the re-mobilizing of all potentialities of the personality. This includes the harmonizing of both deliberate and spontaneous attitudes.

The ultimate goal of the treatment can be formulated thus: We have to achieve that amount of integration which facilitates its own development. This is in accordance with the fact that the dissociated person is inhibited or even degenerating in his development. To repeat once more, the criterion of a successful treatment is: *the achievement of that amount of integration which facilitates its own development.* A small hole cut into an accumulation of snow sometimes suffices to drain off the water. Once the draining has begun, the trickle broadens its bed by itself; it facilitates its own development. This facilitation of its own development should be given an important place in child education. The child requires, firstly, the gratification of its immediate needs and, secondly, the facilitation of its development.

But the child is, even with well-meaning parents, seldom given the facilitation of development of its inherent potentialities. It has to be shaped into something that finds the approval of parents and society. This entails two kinds of processes: the crippling of *some* attitudes and an artificial development of others. The spontaneous personality is being superseded by a deliberate one. On the behavior level we see the same dualism at work as we discussed previously in regard to the linguistic level. Spontaneity and deliberateness fight each other, producing conflicts, inconsistencies, distortions, discomfort in our civilization, while the integration of spontaneity and deliberateness could produce men capable of self-expression and self-realization.

Volition, conscience, living up to expectations, or whatever one chooses to call these deliberate attitudes, does not necessarily mean an inconsistency within the personality or a conflict with the environment, but it will lead to dichotomies if it is in conflict with the deeper layers of the personality, if it leads to the production and accumulation of unfinished situations within the personality. The unfinished situations cry for solutions, but if they are barred from awareness, neurotic symptoms and neurotic character formation will be the result.

Man is part of nature, he is a biological event; therefore, society is also part of nature. Speaking is a time-space event; so is thinking. Every abstract notion is as much a process as is the visualization of an object. Deliberate activity, self-control, conscience, are *social* and at the same time *biological* functions. Re-integration can be successful only if every human activity, deliberate as well as spontaneous, thoughts as well as instincts, are regarded and treated as biological processes.

Even at the risk of being redundant, this theme merits elaboration. A symptom is like a book, a precipitation of processes. The processes of observing, verbalizing, writing, selling, printing; the processes of making paper, ink, compositor's metal; the processes of distributing, advertising, and many more make up a book. Once it has become form it can partake in a variety of further processes. It can become a weapon to be thrown at one; an object to barter for a bit of food; something with which to show off, or something to hide from parents; something to be burned by the Nazis; it can even become something to be read. In the latter case, the receptive processes are considerable and vary from staring at it to introjection, and even to digestion and assimilation.

Likewise, a neurotic symptom is the precipitation of processes; a hysterical headache, for instance, may be the end-result of being touchy, wanting to cry, being heroic about it, then squeezing the eye muscles until they hurt. Such a symptom can be used to get sympathy, an aspirin, or a thorough neurological examination. It can also be analyzed and its contributing processes integrated.

Functional and evolutional experimentation are the characteristics of global organic life. The baby is experimenting with sounds; the kitten with the strength of the branches it wants to climb. The schoolboy experiments with the teacher—how to cheat him or how to be in his good books. Once he has developed attitudes which appear to function adequately, he proceeds to other experiments.

The neurotic is always characterized by inadequate functions, mostly in the direction of unnecessary activity. This is most obvious in the obsessional type, but all neurotic character features are of a compulsive, rigid nature in contrast to the healthy experimental elastic attitude. The malfunctions of the neurotic become manifest in his lack of genuine self-expression. He cannot reveal himself before himself, and still less before others. His interpersonal relations as well as his development will, consequently, more and more deteriorate.

What technique is at present available to integrate the personalities of our patients: that is, to restore the organismic balance and to open the way for productive self-realization?

Freud's experiments with hysteria made him finally reject the hypnotic technique and develop a procedure which is now rigidly followed by the classical school. His pioneering spirit is found in the unorthodox rather than in the orthodox movement. Nature is experimenting lavishly; many of the species and individuals it produces show no survival value. In the same way, many of our attempts to find a solution will be abortive; but a *movement* which is petrified is an absurdity, a contradiction in itself. As long as it does not cope with changing situations and does not assimilate whatever valuable knowledge is available outside the temple, it will cease to remain a factor in the development of mankind. The psychotherapist who is scotomized with regard to semantics and *gestalt* psychology, to mention only two tools developed since Freud, will soon be out of date.

At present, my technique is based on function and experiment. What I will do next year, I cannot tell. Our aim is integration, and the analytical procedure is only one of many instruments towards this goal. I try to find out as much as possible about the patient's personality disorder by observation and discussion. Some dissociation or other is bound to become manifest in the first interview. Some anxiety, some talking around the subject will provide the opportunity to show him the existence of unrealized conflicts.

These conflicts have one pattern only: the identification/alienation pattern. This means: the patient identifies himself with many of his ideas, emotions and actions, but he says violently "No!" to others. Integration requires identification with all vital functions. Every attempt at integrating is bound to bring to the foreground some kind of resistance, and it is this bit of resistance I am after and not the content of the "unconscious." Every bit of *re*-sistance that is changed into personality *as*-sistance is a double gain as it sets free the jailer and the jailed.

I am fully aware that the patient cannot be immediately successful in the tasks which I put before him. If he could, he would not need my assistance. In this connection let us investigate the basic Freudian experiment: the demand that the patient should say whatever is in his "mind." Actually no patient is free in his self-expression. In an attempt to comply, he often gets the feeling that resistances are something bad, something that he should not have. He develops a technique of apparent compliance but keeps his statements on a dead verbal level. He talks *around* his resistances instead of *about* them; the barriers—embarrassment, fear, and disgust—which produce the dissociation are not experienced. The analysis is often kept on a level of unreality, for everything is related to a transference, that means to something that actually does not matter. The contact with the analyst is a blank; in it, interpersonal relations cannot be examined and discussed. Free associations, originally meant to clarify the meaning of a symptom, degenerate into a flight of ideas.

I can see no other way out of this dilemma than to start with the obvious, with the situation in which the patient finds himself during the interview. I suggest, for example, the following experiment: Let him begin every sentence with the words "here and now" and observe how he reacts to it. He may be co-operative or he may be a "slick customer" and begin a few sentences with "here and now" and then slip into yesterday and tomorrow at the first suitable occasion. Or he may be one of the obsessional types who attempt to make fools of other people. He might ridicule the experiment by saying, "Here and now on Friday I visited my friend." Another might ask, "What has *this* to do with *my* problems?" You can already appreciate from these few examples that the attitude of the patient is, as everywhere, also coming out in the session. Thus, if his character changes in his relation to the analyst it might also change in his other relationships. Already the first reactions give the analyst and the patient an opportunity to discuss some basic attitudes, the tendency to escape from the present, that is, from contact with reality, or the tendency to fool oneself and others (this is mostly not conscious) or the knack for plausible rationalizations.

Sentences like "Here and now" or "Now I am aware of" are chosen not only to bring out the top layer of the patient's character formation and some of the more primitive resistances but also to clear the path to the recognition of all his functions, especially, his disfunctions, conflicts, attitudes of escape.

I have previously discussed the relativity of reality and its determination through the figure-background formation. When I use as synonyms, reality and actuality; when I stress the importance of "Here and now," I expect the Freudian to ask: "What about the past and the causes of the neuroses?" and the Adlerian to protest: "What about the future and the aims of our existence?" To these I must say: Unitary thinking does not recognize past, present, or future; it only recognizes processes to which we can artificially ascribe a beginning. If we like, we can call the beginning "cause" and the future event "purpose." Unitary thinking recognizes, however, *recordings* of previous events and forms as precipitations of previous functions. It recognizes as aspects of the so-called future: planning, hope, predictability and vectors—but it maintains that these processes take place here and now. Moreover, a single sentence, even a word, is a time-space event. When reading a complex sentence, one may, as might be said, return to the past in order to pick up the lost thread, or as I would formulate it, consult quickly one's acoustic recordings to produce a meaningful *gestalt.*

Existence is actuality. It is awareness. For Freud, the present included the past 48 or so hours. For me, the present includes a childhood experience if it is vividly remembered now; it includes a noise on the street, an itch on my cheek, the concepts of Freud and poems of Rilke, and millions of more experiences whenever and to whatever degree they spring into existence, into *my* existence in the moment.

The initial difficulties in putting across the concept of functional thinking are sometimes considerable. Perhaps one can generalize and say: The toughest resistance is provided by what to the patient appears as obvious. To him it is obvious that one does not insult the analyst. It is obvious that one produces memories and, if possible, childhood memories. It is obvious that resistances are something undesirable, that one should not have them. It is obvious that one's difficulties have causes; that talking will bring the solution; that the therapist is either God or a fool.

Peculiarly enough, all great progress was made by examining the obvious. After taking over unsuccessful cases from other therapists, I have frequently discovered that the obvious had been taken for granted, not only by the patient, but by the therapist as well.

Here are several examples.

A man had had sixteen months of analysis. He liked his analyst and the analysis, but he had the impression that he had not made much progress. The obvious consisted in his case in the fact that the analysis meant for him lying on a couch and telling to the analyst all the unpleasant experiences of the previous few days. This obvious attitude was his means of preserving the status quo; namely, to bring up whatever he could not stomach. Instead of tackling any of the unpleasant experiences and profiting from them, he just "swallowed" them and "vomited" them out in his analytical sessions. He was not aware that he gulped down all his physical and mental food, but he was very much aware of a troubled stomach. He was not aware that he did not assimilate his experiences, but he knew that he had difficulty in understanding the world.

A lady who had considerable experience with psychotherapists put herself on the couch, lay stiff as a corpse, talked like an automaton and produced associations entirely irrelevant to her present life. She was dismayed to realize that I was not interested in the material she produced but only in how she produced it. Her previous analyst had not even noticed the obvious; namely, that this playing the corpse, this desensitization and immobilization was the center of her armor, of her resistance. The personality behind this armor showed a degree of disintegration approaching the psychotic border. I do not hesitate to make the classical technique responsible for this state of affairs. After six months of treatment she showed good recovery and a noticeable degree of integration.

A girl's obvious behavior was characterized by her continuous complaining about this or that person. She was full of complaints about her previous analyst. On my asking her what *he* had had to say about these complaints, she answered that they were never discussed! And this happened with an analyst who believes in the transference mechanism! After having shown her that the complaining about someone to somebody else—for instance, about me to a friend— instead of to his face was her way of avoiding aggressive contact, we proceeded to experiment with her attacking me. In this process a good deal of the previously unrealized fear and embarrassment came into the foreground.

A sculptor had derived satisfactory benefit from treatment by a progressive analyst; finally, it was decided to change analysts because two important symptons stubbornly remained: his inability to work and his obsessional thought of killing his wife. After one of the first interviews I suggested that he should experiment with sculpturing the killing of his wife. The next day he returned enthusiastically, informing me that for the first time in years he had worked for three hours with interest and pleasure. His ability to express himself with pencil and clay, that is, on the nonverbal level, continued to be a great help in his treatment. The obvious that was overlooked in his case was that modeling, not language, was his means of expression.

In contrast to these cases there are those with whom I can achieve only little or no satisfactory integration. Apparently, they take their customary outlook so much for granted that no other orientation seems feasible to them. In these cases I either lack the ability to show them convincingly the need for change and re-orientation, or else myself am insufficiently integrated to be aware of the crucial resistance.

A psychologist was sent to me because she showed a number of characterological symptoms: among them was the desire to become a psychoanalyst. In spite of occasional emotional outbursts there was no possibility of breaking through an armor of confused verbosity, a state which Landauer so beautifully called *faselige Verbloedung*. She refused to accept her need for personal treatment. We finally parted after she had decided that she could not afford a therapeutic analysis although she was willing to invest money to obtain the "easy and glamorous" life of a psychoanalyst.

At present, there are two more cases with me which look very doubtful. One is a paranoid man; the other is a near-schizoid young woman. The first's slogan for life is: "Rather to be important than healthy." The other's: "Rather to be clever and crazy than healthy and stupid." In both of these cases I have not been able to obtain satisfactory co-operation. Whatever experiment I suggest to the former, he proves to me that he can do it and leaves it at that. He behaves like a soldier who goes to war, shows his officer that he is able to hit the target and then thinks that he can go home. For him the war is over. What characterizes both cases more than anything else is their crippled spontaneity. Scheming and deliberate acting, blue-printing and preparing for all eventualities, in short, the futuristic thinking has become the obvious approach to life; thus contact with actuality has lost all meaning. Both are most of the time *beside* themselves and not *within* themselves. They are not "all there," in the true sense of the phrase.

Once one has worked through the basic character resistance, the battle is won. Not that the patient can achieve awareness entirely on his own, but from that point on the increasing integration reverses the vicious circle of the neurosis. More and more, the "I" against "you" turns into a "we." Especially the second phase, the recognition of the motor tensions, of Reich's muscular armor, may evoke the patient's interest. Many a neurotic is given to hypochondriasis and other forms of introspection, and this phase of the treatment gives him plenty of opportunity for self-observation and, at the same time, a technique to cope with certain gross symptoms such as headache, backache, or anxiety states. Even should he apply the basically "wrong" method, that of relaxation, he experiences what appears to him miraculous results.

A lady continued with me after her former analyst had discontinued treatment because of her negativistic and aggressive attitude. She had originally started the analysis because of high blood pressure, a chronic pseudo-asthma, frigidity, and family difficulties. So great were her breathing difficulties when she started with me that she could scarcely speak. First, I decided to tackle her asthma and postpone work on the deeper personality disorder. After a few hours of reorganizing her breathing, she burst into tears of deepest despair, and with this she obtained her first relief. Three months later her asthma and high blood pressure had disappeared, and now after six months she has lost her frigidity. At present we are working on her self-consciousness. One experiment in particular brought home to her the mechanism of her armor. At a distance of about ten feet from me she was relatively at ease: upon coming nearer, she stiffened more and more and again lost the tenseness with distance. This reaction worked in an entirely automatic way. It was necessary to make her realize that *visualizing* the approach of somebody produced the same effect, and further, that she was not only stiffened but that she was also stifling something.

Besides Reich, there are a number of other schools that tackle the organism from the physiological functional aspect, or to speak in dualistic language, which do body-analysis. They are, like the purely psychologistically-minded, condemned to the Sisyphus work of the never-ending unfinished situation. They have it, and they have it not. A certain amount of integration is possible; they are justified in their work because it is correct, but they do not realize the onesidedness, the incompleteness, and therefore, the non-integrative nature of their work. Of course, they all claim, like many psychologically- or semantically-minded, that they deal with the organism-as-a-whole. All these movements, like the schools of F.M. Alexander, Elsa Gindler, and Jacobson of "you-must-relax" fame, will assist any kind of good psychotherapy. The greatest danger here is the same as with compartmental thinking and as with every non-comprehensive approach; namely, the avoidance of the crucial issue and the concentration on a dummy.

The person who shuns the solution of his sexual difficulties will often avoid the classical school. An analyst who unconsciously wants to exercise his lust for power will be careful not to assimilate the teaching of Adler or the Washington school. The man who does not want to face his inner conflicts will be attracted to one of the body-analytical schools. Thus, only a therapist with a comprehensive view will be in the position to spot and to tackle the central difficulties which the neurotic avoids facing.

Typical of the incomprehensive attitudes is the fetish of relaxation. Of course, a patient can go a long way in learning to relax, but he will become tense again in every situation where relaxation is not a figure, where he is confronted with some unwanted sensation, action, or emotion. It is not easy for our patients to learn that they are not required to relax deliberately but rather to become aware of the inner conflict of which the tension is only a part.

This brings us to the next step in integration. (As always, this subdivision into steps is artificial, and the different stages frequently overlap.) In this period the patient should get thoroughly acquainted with the structure of his inner and outer conflicts and the acceptance/rejection concept. In the previous period he should have learned that a permanent stream of consciousness is going on, except in sleep or trance. He has become acquainted with a multitude of processes in the outer and inner world. In the present period we examine these processes in detail. Which ones are spontaneous? Which ones has he invented in order to comply with the analyst's expectation or his idea of treatment? Is his attention erratic or does he give the processes a chance to develop and become complete? How does he avoid following up the processes? Is he escaping into intellectualization, into facetiousness, into the past or the future, into listening to outside noises, sleepiness, monotonous speech, etc? He is already aware of a certain amount of censoring and realizes primitive conflicts such as "This is embarrassing to tell," or "I should not think such things," "I want to relax, but can't," etc. The main difficulty lies in the fact that he mostly identifies himself with the censor. To him it is obvious that one should not criticize one's doctor, that people should have a good opinion of him, that it is permitted to hurt oneself but not others. However, by working through his muscular tensions, he is becoming much more aware of the structure of many conflicts; for instance, his efforts to suppress crying, anger, and so on.

The patient soon learns that the censoring is done by a very simple principle, by accepting and rejecting. He also learns by experiment to accept more of his drives and wishes. He realizes that by accepting and expressing his emotions he can get cathartic relief, and finally, that his ideas of accepting and rejecting are largely correlated to his pattern of orientation; namely, to his need for being accepted and his fear of being rejected by the world. He is astonished that in spite of his great need for approval, neither praise nor other tokens of acceptance have lasting effect but that *refusals* can worry and hurt for a long time. This apparent inconsistency results from the characteristic neurotic tendency to leave many situations unfinished. If he learns to listen to the figure-background language of the organism and to act according to this reliable means of orientation; that is, to complete the unfinished situation, then he will be able to restore the balance of his personality and pave the way for productive development.

Let us take two simple examples of unfinished situations: one has the urge to urinate or one has an important letter to answer. One can reject the urge for a considerable time but the conflict between retaining and letting go will cost more energy than finishing the situation which would not take more than a few minutes. The same applies to the letter. The answer can lie on your conscience for days and weeks while the actual writing may cost you no more than an hour. Rarely will the situation finish itself merely by the passage of time and then usually not to your advantage.

Sleeplessness is a frequent symptom of unfinished situations; so are dreams. Probably the most important part of the dream is its end. Often the dream works towards the solution of a problem, but the dreamer cannot even stand the awareness during sleep and prefers to wake rather then finish the dream. Therefore, he wakes up before his wife gets smashed on the pavement since in the dream she has fallen out of the window, or before he enters the vagina in a love-making dream.

The next phase could be called *topological* re-orientation and re-organization of language.

Topological orientation is concerned with three processes, introjection, projection, and retroflection. In this paper these very interesting concepts can be treated only superficially. Each really requires several chapters. All three phenomena are symptoms of a lack of integration. In reference to introjection I disagree with Freud who recognized it as a pathological phenomenon only in total introjection and considered partial introjection to be a healthy process providing the building stones of the ego. My own contention is that every introject, be it partial or total, is a foreign body within the organism. Only complete destruction as preparation for assimilation will contribute to the maintenance and development of the organism. Destruction does not mean annihilating but rather the breaking down of the structure of physical or mental food. Freud said that it is not enough to bring material into consciousness, it must also be worked through. According to my analysis of the alimentary functions, I formulate this insight in this way: It is not enough to bring up undigested material; it also has to be re-chewed so that the digestive process can be completed. This was true of the patient described earlier who annihilated the events he could not stomach by bringing them up in the consulting room. The cure involved resensitizing of the dead palate, becoming aware of the disgust barrier, remobilizing the clenched jaw, and investing his aggression in biting and chewing.

The topological aspect in regard to projection is obvious, but it requires special scrutiny. How is it that some part of a personality which should be experienced as belonging to the personal structure is disowned and treated as belonging to the outside world?

The child lives in confluence with its environment. It has not yet developed its contact functions. That is, it cannot differentiate between self-ness and other-ness, between subject and object, between projection and self-expression.

Confluence means the non-existence or non-awareness of boundaries; means taking one-ness for granted. Confluence in the adult is sado-masochistic fixation, disguised as love. Hatred is frustrated greed for confluence; contact is appreciation of differences. Boundary means contact *and* separation: it means individuality.

If the state of confluence does not develop into the ability to make contact, or if by later de-sensitization the boundary is breached, then the infantile projection mechanism remains. Self-expression does not develop, as it presupposes the recognition *and* manipulation of the boundary. With this lack of adequate self-expression, an emotion will not be expressed and disposed of by emotional discharge, but it will be projected and remain in emotional connection with the personality. The personality becomes depleted and the projected properties cease to be useful instruments in the pursuit of personal aims. The paranoiac remains connected with his persecutor through hate, the religious person with his God through awe. Whether aggression, initiative, or responsibility is projected, in each case the result will be a crippled personality. Many neurotics project tendencies to accept and reject and thus cannot integrate these functions into discrimination. They remain connected with these projected tendencies by greed and fear.

The projection mechanism is connected with the linguistic problem. Through the projection of initiative and responsibility our patients experience themselves in a permanently passive role. A dream *occurs* to them. They are *struck* by a thought. Speculations go through their minds, brains, or whatever vacuum they choose for their perambulation. More specifically, this refers to the patient who is not willing to identify himself with his activities, who talks about his hard luck, about fate; who is the victim of circumstances. If his language is reorganized from an "it" language to an "I" language, considerable integration can be achieved with this single adjustment. One has to start this linguistic adjustment during the work on the muscular armor. Not before the patient fully realizes that there are not spasms in the small of his back, but that *he* is contracting, stifling feelings with the help of certain groups of muscles, can he develop or regain his ego functions and make contact with his muscular activity. Only then can he release tensions deliberately, for conscious control is indispensable for experimenting with whatever amount of rejected emotions or sensations he can tolerate and integrate.

The unity of linguistic and structural reorganization is equally essential in the treatment of retroflection. Retroflection is, one might say, the daily bread of the psychoanalyst. It coincides approximately with what Freud called "secondary narcissism." My objections against accepting this term are several. First, the so-called primary narcissism is not a pathological state. On the contrary, the lack of it, the lack of self-awareness, is detrimental to the personality. Second, retroflection or secondary narcissism has taken on a significance far beyond self-love, while in the customary language a narcissist remains a person in love with himself. Third, a descriptive term like "retroflection" is preferable to a purely symbolic one.

Retroflection is characterized by the word "self." Self-love, self-control, self-punishment, self-destruction, self-consciousness, and so on.

In retroflection one part of the personality is split from the other but it remains in active connection. Object relationship is replaced by an "I and Self" relation. In active retroflection, a tendency, e.g., love, destruction, control, scrutiny, etc. is directed toward one's own person. On the other hand, in passive retroflection, the "I" replaces the missing active object; I pity myself because nobody else does it; I punish myself in anticipation of someone else doing it to me.

Once the patient understands this mechanism he is on his way to recovery. Instead of being in a clinch, both parts turn toward the world; contact and expression are facilitated. *Self*-reproach will lead to depression and impotent resolutions, while *object*-reproach leads to object *ap*proach, to having it out, possibly to finishing a resentment situation.

In the projection mechanism, desensitization is apparent; in retroflection the mal-functioning of the motor system is more obvious. As a matter of fact, the good response to treatment is a result of the fact that the retroflective process can be easily demonstrated. Whether the origin of the muscular suppression is the training in cleanliness or, as is more often the case, the hanging-on-bite, is immaterial. What is important is that a tremendous amount of motor energy is invested in the inhibition of catharsis and initiative. The muscular mal-coordination is precipitated into symptoms which then constitute the manifest problem; clumsiness, constipation, asthma, headaches, etc.

Finally, we have to mention another set of powerful processes, the emotions. Just as the visible manifestations of processes in the human organism received the name "body," just as the awareness of the orientation/manipulation functions were called "mind," so the totality of the emotions was called "soul." This term tends to disappear in correlation to the progressive degeneration of our culture cycle in general and to the progressive emotional depletion of the neurotic individual in particular.

This depletion leaves the individual and society with ever greater unsureness, with the need to replace the biological means of orientation by intellectual ideas, by moralism, and by perfectionism. The pleasure-pain principle represents the biological compass whereby the organism finds its bearings, away from the painful and toward the pleasurable situation. Admittedly, a primitive compass, but one which is absolutely necessary for the individual's survival. What is good and bad for the individual coincides less and less with what society determines as good and bad, and still less with the neurotic's moralistic notions.

Integration, in the final analysis, is prevented by the desensitization of the emotional barriers, especially the disgust, embarrassment, shame, anxiety and fear barriers. Indifference is the best way of avoiding these experiences. Once these barriers come into existence, the patient still will avoid the complete situation, namely the conflict between self-realization and the interfering emotions. The negative emotions are indeed essential for the dichotomy of the personality. We have not only the task to expose them, but we also have to turn them into co-operative energies. During this process we encounter a transitory phase. Disgust turns via greed into discrimination; anxiety via excitement into specific interest, such as hostility, sexual excitement, enthusiasm, initiative, etc; fear via suspicion into experimentation, that is, into widening the orbits of one's life; and embarrassment via exhibitionism into self-expression.

The treatment is finished when the patient has achieved the basic requirements: change in outlook, a technique of adequate self-expression and assimilation, and the ability to extend awareness to the nonverbal level. He has then reached that state of integration which facilitates its own development, and he can now be safely left to himself.

The changes which he experiences compare with his previous state in that he is now *actually* growing up while previously he tried to realize his infantile concept of an adult. Instead of taking his orientation from his desire to be accepted and his fear of being rejected, he is now doing the accepting and rejecting himself. Instead of living in oscillation between a jelly-like confluence with, and complete isolation from, his environment, he knows now that "contact" means acknowledgement of differences. Instead of experiencing himself as an outcast, he recognizes that he is a cell in the larger social organism, and that to be effective in this organism he must function to the best of his ability. He will integrate his interpersonal relations not by servile adjustment and sacrifice of his self-realization but by selecting contacts that make for a rich, productive existence.

Most of us realize that the science of personology is in its infancy and that much work has still to be done. The period of classical analysis is drawing to a close. In a few decades it will have a mere historical interest. The present period, which could be called "the para-Freudian interval," started with the dissension of Alfred Adler. It is characterized by a multitude of promising re-orientations, but also by a peculiar unsureness manifesting itself in a high degree of intolerance toward schools of different orientation. There must be a way to overcome this sterile isolation and mutual intolerance. There is a tie that can unite all of us: the frank acknowledgement that we know very little, that our orientation is as crude as the maps of the Phoenicians, that compared with other branches of knowledge we are *beginners* like Hippocrates or Paracelsus.

Have you ever been in despair when one of your patients had his vision blocked by his or your pre-conceived ideas, and didn't you wish then—to quote Freud—that he should display a more benevolent skepticism? I shall be very happy indeed if my paper has encouraged you to be benevolently skeptical towards both your own and my present convictions and to make the transition from any compulsive dogmatism to the experimental, insecure, but creative, pioneering attitude for which I can find no better example than the courage of Sigmund Freud.

Resolution

Frederick S. Perls

In our lectures and demonstrations I have presented gestalt therapy as a series of bits and pieces which you may find of use. I assume now that you know much and I can go beyond the categories, divisions, and pieces to explore the center point, the resolution of the closed gestalt. My ambition has been to create a unified field theory in psychology. In this lecture I would lead you from the play of opposites to the unity of resolution, so that you might experience the goal implied in gestalt work. This is the other side of the coin: unity instead of division; resolution, a coming home instead of wandering. As in all things the main barrier to resolution is ourselves, and particularly how we fantasize about ourselves and the world. In many respects resolution can seem so pleasant, mild and simple that we distrust it and by our questioning undo its peacefulness.

It is said we *have* a mind, that we *have* an id, ego, and so on. By projecting living experience into external categories we fantasy that we have grasped and can control something. I propose the idea of universal awareness as a useful hypothesis that runs counter to this tending to treat ourselves as things. We *are* awareness rather than *have* awareness. From our aware experiencing we can look on the rest of existence and suppose that there are varying degrees of awareness in all things. The flower that turns to the sun is aware of sunlight. The rock that falls experiences some difference between falling, hitting and lying still. In varying degrees, all things which are *this*

This paper was given as a talk at Mendocino State Hospital, Talmage, California, in 1959, as the conclusion of a series of talks and demonstrations, and is published here for the first time.

rather than *that,* function *this* way rather than *that*, are varying degrees of awareness.

Awareness, consciousness, or excitement are similar experiences. Man's awareness appears more comprehensive and hence more ambiguous than that of other things. The rock can only fall when it has no support: Without support we can project, repress, desensitize, etc. With the hypothesis of universal awareness we open up to considering ourselves in a living way rather than in the aboutisms of having a mind, ego, superego and so forth. Also by the hypothesis of universal awareness we open up to considering ourselves as intrinsically like the rest of existence. Starting from isness, this awareness here now, we consider ourselves as we are, living, here, varied and similar to others and the rest of existence. It puts us in a position to contact, to move over boundaries, to range across differences, to find resolution.

Whether our awareness is greater than or more intense than that of animals, bacteria, cells, plants or stars I do not know. We need to suspect the vanity of saying we are the most conscious. It seems clear, though, that our awareness is the most ambiguous. It seems to split, divide and conceal itself more easily than rocks and plants. Most of what we have talked about is this apparent tendency to divide into foreground (what we sharply experience) and background (what is less differentiated). Foreground is in dynamic relationship to background. Very simply, *what cannot be here, is there.* Background is all other; the world outside, meanings projected, other selves as dreams, our potentials, everyone and everything else. What cannot be here, is anyway and so is there; or, at least, *appears there.* If I cannot leave the room when I feel like it, I leave in fantasy. That way I can be here and there simultaneously. I can be kind and unkind, elated and depressed and so forth, simultaneously. It is partly the assumption that "I am this and not that" which is wrong, which creates a division, which we will need to amplify so that the missing part can also be conscious.

Actually our idea of the unconscious as being what is packed away and unused is wrong. What we do not know as ourselves is lived out anyway and can be seen by friends. It is as if we have a conservation of mental energy that corresponds to the conservation of matter/energy in Einstein's relativity theory. Nothing ever dies or disappears altogether in the realm of awareness. What is not lived here as consciousness lives there as muscle tension, unaccountable emotion, perception of others, and so forth. Nothing disappears, but much is displaced or misplaced. Boredom, for instance, which is a dreary state, also contains a drive to do something. The man dying of thirst has water everywhere except on his tongue. In gestalt therapy we are in the paradoxical situation of always dealing with a two-part existence, what is awareness here and now, and what this awareness stands in relation to. Foreground implies background. The background shapes foreground.

What cannot come forth here appears there as other. My rejected resentment turns up as your obvious faults. Most of therapy is finding these splits, and activating both sides. Any activating of both sides tends to gather them together again. Questions are created out of the suspicion of the answer. The question that is intensified collapses into its own answer.

It is partly the demand for differences, the questioning, that divides. What are you aware of now? This rather than that. Can you be aware of this and that? Well yes, but not with the same intensity. The demand for intensity, the questioning, the expecting of this rather than that, creates the foreground-background misplacing of part of ourselves.

In love and especially in orgasm it is as though we experience across the boundary of selves to a contact that leads to the confluence of orgasm, to unifying differences. Understanding, which is more than aboutism or bullshit, is also an assimilation of differences. But let us for the moment break out of the differences which our concepts, our psychopathologies, and our ways of thinking almost insist upon, and join in universal awareness, in the zero point of creative indifference, the resolution of the quiet center.

In taoism there is the yin/yang symbol which represents the interplay of opposites. The white half of the circle is growing darker, and the dark half is growing whiter. The two interact to make the round of existence. What is it like to experience both sides at once? It is ambiguous. Am I a strong heterosexual man or an effeminate homo-

sexual? A full awareness can experience both, and not need to resolve the difference Do I love or resent her? I can experience both
and this brings life and complexity to our relationship. Emerson said
consistency is the hobgoblin of small minds. Consistency demands
that we experience one or the other. Much of the time we experience
both sides, opposites. And this enriches the range of our possibilities.

In fact, the more you try to be just one-sided, the more the other
side is also experienced. If I must be strong and dominant in all
situations, I am forever watching for and experiencing potential
weakness. If I must be a very good saint, I become aware of evil
everywhere. If I am good, you appear evil. We don't hate or love the
world, only ourselves. Each is the all of awareness. Resolution is
closer to experiencing good *and* evil, dominance *and* submission,
topdog *and* underdog. The more we would tilt all power to topdog,
the more powerful underdog becomes. It is the effort to make a
topdog which creates the equally powerful underdog. At the point of
resolution topdog and underdog are both present aspects of the same
dog. You can enjoy the yin or the yang of opposites in this Chinese
symbol, or experience it as a unified balance, which we call, simply,
awareness. As the yin and yang interplay our consciousness is rich,
varied, changing, exciting, not quite predictable, surprising.

Although we are dealing with the resolution of conflict, to find
the satisfied and somewhat ambiguous center between opposites, I
would also like to resolve our conflict with conflict. Suppose, for the
moment, we could satisfy everyone's needs fully—a world of satisfaction. Would all action stop? Perhaps people would sit and sleep
for a day or two, but action would begin again. Here a man would
choose to build a needed workshop, a woman would make a dress,
and so on. Out of this renewed action would appear again conflict,
frustration, and difficulty. Though we need resolution for a time,
just as sleep makes up one third of life, still it would be boring
without action and conflict. Though we seem forever trying to put
out the fire of conflict, we do not really want to put it out altogether. Perhaps we just want to contain it, like a fire in the hearth. If
we didn't get thirsty we would fail to drink. But drinking enough is
very different from drowning. Conflict, the unfinished situation, is

itself a call towards resolution. The conflict we seek and respect is that arising out of the new combination of circumstances in the now. It is not an unaccountable replay reflecting what we dread and experience repeatedly. Therapy gets the individual past the dead replay to the new creative conflict which invites growth, change, excitement, the adventure of living.

There is but awareness endlessly coming forth. Beyond awareness there is nothing. At all points of discomfort it seeks to make itself comfortable. This one awareness appears to split into self/other so that in the trouble of search and finding, it can recall its parts and find itself intensely. Unquestioned, in peace, it finds itself as one. The apparent boundaries of me/you, mine/thine, become fluid, disappear and reappear carelessly. It is not wrong to question and divide, but it is even more complete to see that the question arises from its own answer and that the function of boundary and difference is to excite a contact resolution. The gestalt opens to demand closing and the energy towards closing is in the opening.

The unified field is satisfaction, the oneness of what is, isness. Question that this is so, and you create the split, the search, the apparent need that could again lead to unity, satisfaction, the closed gestalt. Deepen the split and it reaches across to find itself.

One symbol for this is the Buddhist mudra in which the thumb and one finger make a circle. Thumb and finger appear as two, making a circle, the round of existence. Yet these two are one hand, one life. The other three fingers represent the multiplicity of existence which is also one hand and one life. In most gestalt work we find and exercise the split, so that the parts of unity may come together. Yet, away from our own questioning and demands we can enjoy the unity of awareness in which the division within self disappears as do the splits between self and others, self and the rest of the world. One awareness. It is aware aliveness, experiencing conflict at all points that parts of itself have been displaced and growth is called for.

Somehow I feel mellower than usual today. This is a fitting place to end a series of talks. You have been a very receptive group and I have done quite well.

Invoking the Actual

Wilson Van Dusen

My theme is simple. The actual, existential, or real can be invoked so that it stands forth in its own apparentness. It is just as though one struck a bell with a hammer, and the reality of the bell vibrated in its uniqueness. The bell then calls out something of its nature. How different this is from most psychotherapy where one is not certain what is hammer and what isn't, where is the bell, and how can it be touched. I am thinking of ways of making the situation more concrete, and I will give concrete examples from my own experience. These examples will range from simple obvious ones to things that could be attempted and are yet mostly untried.

By the actual in psychotherapy I mean something with its own obvious nature so that when one runs into it you know you have hit something solid, living, critical. When the actual is involved you find it powerful, and therapy gets up and has body and moves. In simile, therapy is like my visiting your basement. As I go down the stairs in your place I find all sorts of odds and ends: dolls, bits of string, a collection of stones, children's books, a bent nail. In the corner of the basement I might find odd store dummies that look like mother and father. I may hear something alive, moving, like a rat. I go looking for this rat and he scurries away, defensively. The rat has more life than the rest. The rest is scattered bits of history or images of the self.

But in everyone's basement there is a lion sleeping. His snores fill

Reprinted from *Journal of Individual Psychology*, Vol. 21, No. 1, 1965, pp. 66–76, by permission.

the whole basement, sending life everywhere. I can locate this lion and awaken him. But, like waking all lions, one ought to be careful. He may be ill-tempered and hungry. So one awakens lions carefully, with due respect. Perhaps one's respect is so great Sir Lion isn't bestirred. This is wisdom in respect to invoking actualities. One can examine string and bent nails forever, but powerful living actualities are another matter. They have claws and teeth and uncertain dispositions. One invokes them, just as one calls upon heaven, with regard.

There are old, easily recognizable examples of this. The main one that comes to mind is the analysis of transference and countertransference. Instead of speaking of things removed, such as wife, and children, mother and father, one is suddenly speaking of us two here, how we feel about each other. This is a present actuality. One wakes this lion carefully. Best have some acquaintance before patting him on the head. Stroke the fur, speak softly, hope he had a recent meal. This is an invocation of the actual—what is actually going on now between us here. "Why do you keep coming to me?" "What do I mean to you?" "Should we quit seeing each other?" This stirs the lion.

I gravitate towards action and show no particular fondness for words. Often, when people speak at length to me, I tune out the words and study the music of the voice and the dance of their movements. From this I can see them better than I could from many words. In part this prejudice of mine may stem from ten years' work with chronic schizophrenics in whom words can be a morass that can swallow up an armored division without a trace. I would prefer the actuality of a little rat or even a store dummy or a bent nail. I am wary even of symbols, images, and mythologies produced by people. They are not usable coin to me unless they are translated into the actualities of a person's life. A learned therapist told a lady of my acquaintance that four in dreams means completeness and three is incomplete. All very fine. But what is complete and incomplete in your life, and does it look like the dream symbol? The word "death" is a long long way from the chilly feeling of "this is it, here I go," in one's personal death. Words are just brief sounds. Words and symbols are lifeless unless they choke up, frighten, bring tears, or alert like the actually numinous. The actualities I speak of are all visible and palpable.

The Force of the Actual

Let me give examples of invoking the actual. A pale young man tells me of difficulties with authority figures such as boss, father, teacher, etc. They could be spoken of because they were removed. But I am an authority for him too. Could we experiment and see what happens as we play with the authority role? What happens as I walk up to him? How does he feel as I stand over him and look down at him? It frightens him a little, yet he knows it is partially a drama that can be controlled or stopped. It cuts through circumambulations about the issues. The issue is alive here.

Fritz Perls once told me the following: "One young man was frightened of murderous thoughts. Of course it was others he killed, not me. Words are mostly about things and people removed from the here and now. But could we experiment with a little murder? His preferred mode was choking. Could he try choking me? He was reluctant to try. He warned me he might lose control. I wasn't particularly afraid since he was a small fellow. Reluctantly he strangled me a bit and then turned away in shock. It took a while to find out what had been invoked. He was shocked to feel overwhelming love for me. He wanted to touch and caress. In a few moments we had cut below aggressive issues to touchier ones of love."

Words play a role, but they need to be living ones of present actualities. A common problem is of the very passive patient. All he sees is that the therapist has all the answers. He asks should he do this or that? He thinks that the clever doctor will show him the way. My comment back is passive. "There it is again. You lean on me." He asks what do I mean. "You are leaning on me again." All very fine but he brushes it aside. Yes, but he again asks how he should live his life. "There it comes again. You lean on me." This invokes the issue of passivity. You call it by name, by the name which reflects its whole nature. This is perhaps what is meant in the Bible by calling the spirits by name. The one who really knows their nature can call them out. Eventually the patient gets the impression that I am talking about what he is doing at this moment. He becomes vaguely aware that perhaps he often does this same thing. We have a wonderful game going. Once we know what is meant we can even coin a symbol and represent his passivity by a gesture. He leans on me and I show this by one hand leaning on the other. He demands an answer and one hand leans even more aggressively on the other. It is important that the symbol be natural to the situation—preferably one chosen by the patient. One doesn't tease lions. It is done in the spirit of play and honest communication. I recall a session years ago where the actualities of a person's life were represented by a burnt match lying in a match box. All the words are forgotten, but the spirit of the situation is recalled. We had arrived at the wordless actuality of a man's life.

An example of this comes from a psychoanalyst friend of mine. He is a gifted man who had three classical Freudian analyses by men of the era and caliber of Fenichel. As with the Freudian drift of things, and as actually appropriate to this man, several years of conversation boiled down to issues of his potency or male adequacy. As they got down to cases, the issues evolved around the penis itself. Then my friend participated in the most remarkable therapeutic coup he had ever seen. In a mild manner the psychoanalyst asked his patient to produce his penis so that they might examine the offending organ. The patient couldn't believe his ears. The fool wanted to see the thing they had been talking about for a year. Well, with the organ in hand, the whole case shifted. He had been viewing his organ through subjective feelings colored with inferiority. The objective fact didn't look inadequate. A refreshing breeze of actuality had blown away some smoke of fantasy. My friend later became known for cutting through words to actualities. More than a penis was brought out.

With chronic schizophrenics a good deal of such ingenuity can be useful. I commented earlier how language with them can be a morass that swallows up whole batteries of therapists. I recently read an army manual on survival. To try to stand up in quicksand is deadly. To cross quicksand it is best to fall flat on one's face and swim across. Perhaps there is a vague analogy here for dealing with schizophrenics.

After a year I discovered that a schizophrenic was using words in an unusual way. He planned speeches for me. All went well if he could anticipate the conversation and work out all his ploys ahead of time. The usual psychiatric examination he had down pat so that nothing meaningful would be revealed by him. We shifted to more actual things. We walked together, examined his work, and looked into his locker. These patients often collect things in their pockets. With respect we went through the things he had with him. Here were all the items precious to him. I could handle these actualities of his life. He collected empty tobacco bags. He asked what happens to them when thrown on the ground. It was said with tears. For a moment it sounded as though he were speaking of the death of people. By saving them it was as though he were salvaging lives. Why string and rubber bands in his pocket? Well, should a situation arise he would be prepared to meet it. He collected hospital administrative bulletins found in garbage cans. If a question arose regarding some fact or figure about the hospital he might be able to prove his adequacy. He couldn't let anything new be thrown away. It was too much like a man going to waste in a mental hospital. He had pockets full of self-images.

I always feel like going out to meet any actuality that intrudes into the situation with the patient. One woman had killed her husband while in a distraught schizophrenic state. She had loud, nasty hallucinations plaguing her in spite of electro-shock treatment and ataraxic drugs. The day before, she had thrown a chair through a window because the voices seemed to come from that direction. With reluctance she revealed they were mostly pressing her towards a perverted sexual act with her son. The voices were unavoidable so we went to meet them. With her help we could deal with the voices. In fantasy she could try complying with them. As she approached them, they seemed to become more considerate. They also lessened in intensity. Finally they disappeared when she saw that she had been far from her son and the voices wanted her to express her love for him. One meets many devils in state hospitals. The more one flees them the more devilish they are. In fact, they seem to be an image of the patient. Their negative intensity reflects the patient's attitude. Consideration of them lessens their opposition until finally they fuse and become one with the patient.

One meets actualities one is afraid to invoke such as the sexual or aggressive. How can one go to meet obsessive sexual thoughts, for instance? Where they cannot be invoked directly, I am inclined to let them be enacted in fantasy. One woman was plagued by an attraction to older females. She felt a horrible homosexual possibility. She misinterpreted and blocked the impulse because it seemed repulsive. With nervous restraint she explored the drift of her feelings in fantasy. The fantasies rose from the pubic region to the breast. It became clear to both of us she was looking for a mother on whom she could again depend and be childlike. The homosexual issues had disappeared.

Over and over again it seems that these terrible demons of the unconscious reflect the patient's terror. Like well-intentioned masked actors at a dance, they scare the audience out of proportion to the real spirit behind the mask. Devils can be decent chaps made malevolent by frustration. They represent something that insists on existing in spite of any opposition and becomes negative with opposition. The patient's negativism is reflected in them, and a more cooperative attitude toward them is also reflected.

This use of fantasy to explore the real drift of the inner self reminds me of the impressive work of Desoille in his guided daydream. One is free to invoke anything in fantasy: parents can be killed, and cities blown up. If there is difficulty, fantasy armies can be rushed in to help. The fantasy world of some people is narrow and prison-like, but with help one can knock a hole in the walls and escape. Whenever the invoking is too much to represent in action, fantasy can be tried. This is not the hasty and socially contrived fantasy of an unpracticed person but an artful practiced fantasy which emerges from the other individual with its own definite form—a form reflecting the actualities of a life. Where one can't tap the actual bell one can try fantasy bells which have definite notes of their own. Most conversation is unbell-like in comparison. One woman represented herself in fantasy as a ruin. Later a beady-eyed vulture turned up to sit in her ruin. She asked why it couldn't be the blue bird of happiness. My answer was that the vulture more accurately reflected her situation.

Perhaps some therapists are blocked from the worlds of others by too rigid and limited a preconception of human worlds, where there are only a few primary dimensions such as sex, aggression, status, role, or introjected parents. The existential idea of being-in-the-world as a unique personal mode of existence permits unique worlds for each individual.

An example of uniqueness is that of a woman for whom Baldwin pianos were the hub of existence. Hers was a world of exquisite sounds and unpleasant sounds. There were no visible objects in it. When she met her lover he was playing the Baldwin piano. She had an exquisite hearing for nuances of overtones. Her thoughts were all of impregnating the world with this sound of the perfect instrument. She was a gifted pianist in part because she could feel sound better than most people. The usual therapeutic gambit of talking with her didn't mean much to her. Words weren't musical and the overtones of the air conditioner were unpleasant. We found a Baldwin on which she played beautifully for me, and as she played her lover seemed to enter the room. The issues around her lover came alive. *My* world was my office. *Hers* was the piano. We worked in her world. It is difficult enough to be in emotional trouble without having to fit it into the therapist's world and the therapist's way of doing things.

In psychosomatic disorders the intruding actuality is the bodily organ itself. Usually the sick person is far from some part of himself. One woman with chronic muscular tension was less aware of it than I was. A minister suffered little bouts of angina pectoris. Like clever therapists, some people have theories about their organs. Such theories do not impress me. I want to hear what the muscle says or what the heart says. It is slow work to get persons to become acquainted with a part of themselves. They speculate at a remote distance what it is all about. But I want the words of the heart itself. "Oh, I am bursting with anger and I hurt." As this becomes conscious the hurt anger can erupt in awareness rather than in the heart. I want the words which are beyond speculation, rumor, or theory; the words that are swept along by a torrent of feelings. These words are sacred.

They are the blood of the life. Being somewhat dense, I must see the blood. Theories about blood are too bloodless.

Invoking the real feelings of the other person seems one of the subtler arts. Here I study gesture and voice quality to absorb a sense of the other person. Where I see feeling I call it out. It is easy to see tears in another person before they are clearly aware of them. The eye reddens and looks watery while the voice trembles. Anger is fairly obvious. I don't hesitate to name a feeling by some name and let the other person perfect my understanding "You look angry." And the other person says, "No, I'm not angry. I'm frustrated." In this way the patient helps the therapist's aim. It makes a marvelous difference in a conversation to note and call out the feelings, rather than to chase the content of the words. The situation suddenly has a thump to it as though a solid actuality had been reached.

The Actual in Dreams

For some years I have experimented with detecting the actualities of dreams. A person tells a dream, says it sounds silly and he does not understand it. How can one penetrate this mass of symbols? I would like to have the person tell the dream slower, feeling his way along in its nuances. As this is done, the dream is acted out in gestures, voice quality and the subtle nuances of being present. Often I can just see bits and pieces. An engineer spoke of locking a bathroom door and crooked his finger over his lip. To my question whether the lock was the hook type he said yes. A woman said she was led by a blind cat in a dream and she seemed momentarily stupid to me. A stout man says he is in a hut full of food. He describes it by holding out his hands to the width of his body. I see the hut full of food. Upstairs in the hut a lion gnaws at a man. We speak of things that gnaw at him and he meets his lion. The dream is quietly re-enacted in the telling of it. By various maneuvers I try to make more vivid this enactment so that the dreamer can define for me what his own dream means.

Sometimes a bold approach works. The woman led by a blind cat looked up at me stupidly and said she didn't understand it. I said,

"There is the blind cat." She said she didn't see it. I said, "blind cat." She saw how she was being led by her own lack of understanding. Or there was a talkative man running on spoon-shaped bones. I clasped my thumb and fingers around my jaw and withdrew it to show its round U shape and he recognized the spoon-shaped bone he ran on. He talked a good deal and ran on the lower jaw when anxious.

On other occasions the enactment is more subtle and entangling. Often the dreamer will just feel towards me as towards the other person in the dream. These feelings must be called out to untangle this part of the dream. Invoking actualities of dreams is difficult, but it is a pleasure to see obscure symbols become transparently clear in the present real situation with another person. Sometimes it depends on unaccountable intuition. One alcoholic man spoke of dropping all his business papers in the mud. I felt confused and asked him if he also felt confused. We had both dropped our business papers (planned, logical, business-like thoughts) in the mud. As soon as we recognized this, the mud cleared. He then could give other ramifications of the dream thought. He had let his real estate business slide into ruin, but he said the dream papers could be salvaged and so could his business. The dreamer can often work out the remainder of a dream after one or two central dream elements are pulled into the light of day. Dreams are difficult to invoke because they are more concrete and present than our understanding of them.

Theoretical assumptions can be blinding. One psychotic woman produced no dreams or symbols for two years. Finally she had a little dream for me. In the dream she knew that only her husband's key could save her. She drew the key for me. It was a blindingly beautiful phallus. Freudian notions crowded my mind and we could make no use of this key. The sexual implications just didn't mean anything to her. She was middle-aged and long since separated from her husband emotionally and physically. In retrospect the symbol is clear now. The dream said "My husband's masculinity is the key that could save me." She was a woman who drifted helplessly without a man. Husband's key (not any man, but a husband) could save her. The phallic shape said masculinity more blatantly than I could understand.

Related Experiments

There are whole areas of invoking the actual that are already known. Play therapy is one example. Toys are actualities to children. The girl plays out her understanding of family life with her dolls. The boy assays the masculine role with his cowboy outfit. The child does not use the windy circumambulations of adults. "Bang, bang, you're dead." Morita therapy, growing out of Japanese Zen Buddhism, is an example of invoking actualities with adults. The emotionally disturbed adult is put through a regimen which bypasses words and brings the patient back into the actualities of life. They begin with bed rest, then light work and then heavier work in the soil. Only after this re-embedding in actuality are they permitted talk and visits with relatives. They claim success with this beautifully actual therapy.

Using this central theme as a model, one can think of a number of untried and half-tried experiments that are possible. Would delinquents benefit from a situation where they can practice making, enforcing and breaking their own rules? Let the issue be their actual self-regulation and let them practice with laws, courts, police and delinquency. An experiment similar to this is taking place in a state hospital. For every rule there is someone to break it. The Chinese say locked doors make thieves. It is necessary that mental hospital patients get out of bed and contribute a little work. Some stay in bed and this causes battles with staff. The more staff insists, the more enticing and justified it is to stay in bed. In one very pleasant unit where the women have their own living room, coffee pot and other comforts, they are assigned to groups. The groups rise and fall as a unit. If one member won't get up in the morning and do simple duties, the group gets five demerits on the bulletin board. Being crazy, but not dumb, the group catches on to the order of things and begins to take responsibility for themselves and each other.

An example is the catatonic who refuses to eat or move. This alarms staff who proceed to force food down via a tube. In the patient's mind this can justify all sorts of notions about a malevolent world. The psychiatrist spoke gently to the patient: "We will let you know when meals are being served down this hall only thirty feet.

When you want to eat you can go down there yourself. We won't force you to eat, as this is unpleasant for you and us." She said she never saw a patient miss more than three meals.

There are endless possibilities of experiments in self-government along the lines of Maxwell Jones' therapeutic community. One might almost define mental illness as an unlearning of responsibility towards one's self. In state hospitals we collect the world's most useless people. They are more useless than bums and hobos, who carry their own bedroll and manage to take care of themselves. Here I would consider using food itself as a reward with medical control to prevent anyone from being hurt. "If you will do this little bit of work, you will earn a meal. I do this because I think you will feel better if you are productive. If you do not work there will be no meal." But in such an experiment one has to deal with staff attitudes and the public. Some would cry cruelty, not realizing that letting a person slide into a useless life of playing with one's own thoughts may be the worse cruelty. Everywhere we have experimented with more responsibility for the patients, they have tended to take it and improve by it.

Summary

Anyone with a little ingenuity can think of similar examples. Summarizing, what actualities might be invoked? First, whatever insists on intruding into the situation with the patient. If someone insists on knocking on the door, one would do well to let him in and see what he wants. If the lady is preoccupied with Baldwin pianos— then to the piano. Second, I think it is valid for the therapist to invoke or call out whatever bothers him. Many therapeutic sessions are bogged down because the therapist is circumambulating about what bothers him. Whether or not it is objectively valid (the patient really *is* annoying) or only subjectively valid, doesn't make much difference. At times the patient will simply show the therapist to be mistaken, but the matter is then out of the way. If a lady is overly seductive, I call out this spirit. One can hardly seduce then. If someone is too loud or too soft-spoken or whatever, I call it out.

How one invokes depends on individual style and ingenuity. I doubt that there is a perfect way to do any of these things. What would suit me, would not be appropriate to someone else. Or said another way—what is actual depends on the two people present. I see the process as a give and take in which either patient or therapist may make the greater gains. There is no expertness in the sense of one knowing more than the other. Hopefully there is a greater ease and readiness to explore on the part of the therapist. Invoking the actual has many religious overtones for me. The actual is sacred because it is a life. While interviewing a nurse in a group she came to tears over her loneliness. The group became silent. No idle chatter. No clever theories what this "really" meant. No questioning whether this was real or not. Its reality flowed down her cheeks, and mine. It is holy, numinous and awesome. It is a life laid bare. This nurse made more real whatever loneliness there was in each of us. In the presence of the real I have no advice. One does not tell any respectable lion how to be a lion. He might eat me to show that his teeth understand my flesh. In these moments one shares the vistas of what it is to be human. The aim is to bring into actuality the central concerns of the life. With these realized, the person hopefully makes wiser choices.

For me, this is the area in which one person helps another. Whatever it is called, the actual is holy, and it has a most pleasing thump of the real when it is met. And truth *is*; it need not be invoked. Its reality invokes us. Like a dream more concrete than I can understand, it intrudes, stands forth, exists as the sacred *real.*

Wu Wei, No-mind, and the Fertile Void

Wilson Van Dusen

From the first not a thing is.
— Hui-neng

Though clay may be molded into a vase, the utility of the vase lies in what is not there.
— Lao Tze

At the very center of psychotherapeutic experiences there is an awesome hole. With Western modes of thought the hole tends to be seen as a deficiency which the therapist plugs by an interpretation of what it means. My point is quite simple. The hole is the very center and heart of therapeutic change. To my knowledge the only place its dynamics are adequately described is in ancient Oriental writings. From them one can learn to make practical use of this fertile void around which psychotherapy turns.

The void is not unknown in the psychoanalysis of the Western world. Freud discovered it in orality, regression, the going back to an infantile state. At a deeper level he once characterized it as Thanatos, the death instinct. Otto Rank put it in the womb. Pathology began by the trauma of leaving the womb. In Jung the void is not as clear, but in general it is found in the archetypes of mother, earth and origin of things.

What will be treated here as the void is seen by Western psycho-analysis as a going back, returning to the origin, as a destruction and

Reprinted from *Psychologia*, Vol. 1, 1958, pp. 253–256.

loss of ego development. The main implication is of a weakness so that one has to start over instead of moving on from here. The going back can be totally destructive as in chronic schizophrenia or it can be productive as in the so-called therapeutic regression in the service of the ego. The void is seen primarily biologically as a mouth or a womb.

Using the phenomenological method I discovered a world of tiny holes most of which were smaller than the orality of the Freudians. In the phenomenological approach one simply attempts to discover the world of the patient as it is for him without reducing it to any pseudoscientific categories (obsessional, anal, etc.) In a careful examination of the worlds of others I ran across many blank spaces. For a moment the patient couldn't concentrate, couldn't hear me, couldn't remember what he intended to say or he felt nothing. At first it appeared these holes or great blank spaces were characteristic of schizophrenics only. Certainly in schizophrenics the blank apathy can enlarge to fill their whole life space. But closer examination showed that these holes appear in all persons to a greater or lesser extent. More and more it came to appear that these blank holes lay at the center of psychopathology. The blank holes came to be the key both to pathology and to psychotherapeutic change. Though my knowledge of Taoism and Zen Buddhism is poor (grandmotherly, a Zen monk might say) it was these two that helped me understand the way in and out of the holes and their meaning.

First, what are the holes? They are any sort of defect: blankness, loss of memory, failure of concentration or loss of meaning. They can be of very brief duration so that the person is hardly aware of a lack of continuity to his thoughts or feelings. Or they can last for years as in the chronic schizophrenic for whom decades can slip by without being noticed. In the lapses of the schizophrenic they not only drop time, but when it is dropped, they can't recall what they intended to say, or they forget they dropped time. A common mild example is to be unexpectedly caught by the gaze of another person and for a brief moment lose the sense of direction. Or, when in a group, one may lose the thread of conversation and several moments later realize one's fantasies have wandered from the group. In the hole one momentarily loses one's self. What was intended is forgotten. What would have been said is unremembered. When you try to trace your way back to where you were a moment ago you have lost the trail. One feels caught, drifting, out of control and weak.

These holes and blank spaces are important in every psychopathology. In the obsessive compulsive they represent the loss of order and control. In the depressive they are the black hole of time standing still. In the character disorders they represent an unbearable ambivalence. In schizophrenia they are the encroachment of meaninglessness or terror. In every case they represent the unknown, the unnamed threat, the source of anxiety and the fear of disintegration. They are nothingness, non-being, death.

It is extremely important to know what people do when faced with encroaching blankness. Many talk to fill up space. Many must act to fill the empty space with themselves. In all cases it must be filled up or sealed off. I have yet to see a case of psychopathology where the blankness was comfortably tolerated. Even in very chronic and apathetic schizophrenics there is a filling up of the space. One examined a door hinge for an hour because not to fill his world with something was to die. This void is familiar and comfortable to the Taoist or Zen Buddhist. The pathology appears to be in the *reaction* to the void. Normal and often very creative individuals can allow themselves to become blank and think of nothing with an expectation that they will come out of it with an idea for a painting or other work of art. Many have deliberately used the void to find creative solutions to problems. The neurotic and psychotic struggle against it.

In large part the culture of the Western world fosters this struggle. In the West the world is filled with objects. Empty space is wasted unless it is room to be filled with action. This contrasts markedly with Oriental painting, for instance, in which empty space is the creative center and lends weight to the rest of the painting. Subtly the culture of the West teaches one to fear and avoid blankness and emptiness and to fill space as much as possible with our action with objects. Or we let the action of objects (cars, TV) fill our space. In the Orient emptiness may have a supreme value in and of itself. It can be trusted. It can be productive. The *Tao Te Ching* comments that thirty spokes make up a wheel, but only in the emptiness of its hub is its usefulness. Walls and doors make up a house, but only in the emptiness between them is its livability.

Following the lead of the Orient I explored the empty spaces. If the patient obsessively plotted every move and worried everything into existence, he was encouraged to drift. If he anxiously filled space with words, we looked for a while at wordlessness. The person who feared going down in depression permitted himself to go down and explore the going down. The findings are always the same. *The feared empty space is a fertile void. Exploring it is a turning point towards therapeutic change.* A case will illustrate some of these points.

The patient is a 30-year-old schizophrenic who has been hospitalized nine years. He enters stiffly like a wooden puppet, sits awkwardly and avoids my gaze. I leave him alone. His eyes fix on my bookcase and he stares emptily. After several minutes I comment that he is at the bookcase and I ask him what it is like. In no way do I attempt to move him from the spot he has drifted to.

Slowly he says he is looking at the top books. They are decoration. That is, they have no meaning. They are part of the bookcase, they are decoration in the furniture. This he says with no affect, punctuated by suddenly touching the top of his head and repetitive movements with his fingers. I try not to disturb his state. A slow exploration indicates that really the whole world is like the meaningless book-decoration he sees before him.

He accepts this as a black, hole-like world. In this black hole he can't think or remember and this threatens him. I'm a strange doctor not to fill up the space with questions to occupy him. In the nothingness he is nothing. When he touches the top of his head or his nose he exists for a moment, he felt himself there. Because I don't fill the void with questions he tries to remember what other doctors asked so he can ask himself these questions and answer them and thereby fill the void. A question should fill this empty space and move time on a bit. But he is dually threatened because he can't remember what he was trying to think of even though he repeated it over and over. It too went out of existence. Again the dull concern: "I must concentrate, hold my mind from drifting and find questions to fill my space."

I ask him if he will let himself drift. Because my request fills the void he complies. We are silent. In a moment some feeling breaks forth. He reddens and laughs. He can't quite tell me what happened. Usually, in the past, these were feelings critical of me. I speak of drifting in the hole. When he drifts he seems to stumble on something new. Once before he found strong sexual desire (which is quite unusual for him). In one long session he drifted into a fantasy of a violent rape attack. Today he drifted and ran upon the fact that there was something in his left side. Explored further it turned out to be a flat black oval mass (the nigredo of Jung). In subsequent sessions it changed and became a feeling of life in him. As the hour ended I asked whether he wanted to climb out of the hole. He said (with a trace more of affect) he would stay in it and see what else of interest might happen. I was pleased because he had discovered that of itself the void filled with new things. He didn't have to work so hard to fill it up.

The schizophrenic gives the purest example of the black void in human experience. Other disorders give examples of briefer and less empty voids. What I learned in these is quite simple. When we are threatened by the void and attempt to crawl out or fill it up by keeping our minds centered (the mind-dusting of Zen) the void grows and encroaches upon our will. When one sleeps in the void, allows himself to drift willy-nilly, he stumbles upon surprising new things in the void.

The complete dynamism is relatively simple. Let me use an analogy with night and day. The two alternate naturally and spontaneously. We do not make the night or the day. If we try to stay awake indefinitely and thereby deny the night we are dragged into fatigue and eventually sleep. (The schizophrenic by his constant plugging of holes is dragged into timelessness.) On the other hand we cannot sleep indefinitely. We will be thrust into wakefulness. (The alcoholic who tries to drink away his responsibilities is dragged into the wakefulness of a hangover.) The day wears on to night when all things rest. Out of the timeless black night a new day emerges. This is the cycle of the Chinese yin and yang. In psychotherapy all action is the day and all of the holes, the defects are the fertile void of night. The fertile void of night comes into psychotherapy so that we might dissolve a little and come out a little changed into a new day. I no longer fear the fertile void for either my patient or myself. The way to day is through the night. The night or the void is the no-mind of Zen. It is not nothing nor is it something. It is a fertile emptiness. The only thing I can think of that is kin to it in Christianity is psychological openness to grace.

In Taoism and Zen there is a healthy understanding and respect for this night aspect of life. It is used in painting, in the tea ceremonies, in wrestling, in the building of houses, and in flower arrangement it is the space around a graceful branch. It is known and respected in its permeation of Oriental life.

The patient comes to one because he fears the void. If he didn't fear it he would be a productive person and not need help. If the therapist also fears the void he will be unable to help the patient. For each patient the void has different meanings. For the compulsive it may be disorder, for some it is age and death, for the young woman it may be the loss of self in sexual climax, for the early schizophrenic it is the force destroying the ego. The meaning of the void and how it appears in the transference relationship must be discovered anew in each case. A common way to try to fill the void is to find *the answers* as to what is wrong. Not only is there the major void in the presenting symptoms but the many little ones that appear in the immediate relationship with the patient. The way out is through the voids. The fears that keep one from entering them can be explored. As these are studied the void becomes less fearsome. Finally the voids can be entered. In each case one comes out a little changed as in the case of the schizophrenic above who came out with more feelings than he had known in a long time. Often the therapist cannot predict the direction of change. It is spontaneous and natural. It is change from within the patient and not a change in any way planned by the therapist. When fully recovered, the patient not only no longer fears the void but knows and can use its productivity.

"From the first not a thing is." If a thing still is (if there is action or talk or the patient is toying with *the* answer) one has not yet reached the first which is the beginning. For literally at the first not a thing is. At this turning point one has no words, no actions, no answers. One may well not even remember.

In Wu Wei, the blankness, the state is characterized by total uncertainty. One doesn't know answers, one doesn't know solutions. Even the problems besetting one may be unclear. The uncertainty can be painful. "Somewhere in all this there should be a solution if I could only think clearly enough to find it" is the feeling. It is a void, no-mind, but it is certainly not empty. It is chaotic with possibilities. One feels helpless and waits. It is central that one's own will can no longer find the way out.

My apologies to the ancient teachers for a poor over-simplification of their work. But it must be done. Somewhere it is necessary to show not only that these teachings have practical value in psychotherapy, but that their relevance is ever-present.

The Phenomenology of a Schizophrenic Existence

Wilson Van Dusen

If I had to represent my own existence as faithfully as possible, I wouldn't describe myself as a case history because I don't experience myself as a case history. Rather, I would be inclined to describe the central theme or drama of my existence and then show its ramifications into details of my experience. My existence is more like a repetitive drama soaring and falling than it is a case history with its neat categories of early development, sibling relationships, sexual history, and so forth. My existence is here—now. I would have to begin here—now. Yes, this would be reaching a faithfulness to my experience.

This is precisely the difference between the phenomenological viewpoint and that usually taken in mental health. If a young person's existence is a lousy drag, it should be described as such rather than attempting a pious observer's outside viewpoint by describing it as an "adolescent rebellion against conventional mores." A phenomenological study is an attempt to represent or describe a person's existence adequately by a faithfulness to the very quality and experience of that existence. The point of view, the terminology, the emphasis in a phenomenological study is that of the experiencing subject himself. There are only a few such studies in the whole English literature, a strangely sad comment on the sciences which attempt to understand humans.

I will attempt to describe the existence of a young man named Jack here, a so-called chronic schizophrenic.

Reprinted from *Journal of Individual Psychology*, Vol. 17, No. 1, 1961, pp. 80–92, by permission.

First, a few facts about Jack. He is a 32-year-old tall slender male. His father was a dentist, and he is the middle of six siblings. None of the other members of his family have been hospitalized for mental illness. He had been hospitalized in state hospitals some 11 years and had not responded sufficiently to electro-shock, insulin coma, three types of ataraxic drugs, or therapeutic community and hospital milieu treatment to be released. I saw Jack for two and a half years. He partially recovered and left the hospital for sheltered employment.

The General Quality of Jack's World

There is a significant and pervasive quality to Jack's world which makes any well-ordered description of it a falsification. For Jack, existence is a falling apart, a fragmenting with the fragments fading and disappearing. He complains of this mostly as memory difficulty, but it pertains to all phases of his existence. His most common experience is to feel pulled apart into circumstances so that he cannot concentrate his thoughts, or experience himself consistently. Worst of all, in this state he must struggle very hard to direct himself. Every bit of routine helps. It lends an order to his existence which he can no longer maintain himself. Bear in mind the falsity of a presentation which seems to lend ordered relationships in an existence which is mostly a falling apart of order. It is more than just fragmentation. The very pieces fade as memory experiences. Worst of all, the falling apart and fading is himself. This falling apart is so confusing that the report below has taken two years of two hours per week sessions to piece it together.

The Central Drama. The central drama of Jack's existence might be called an heroic attempt at mind control which is constantly being threatened with dissolution of the very self which is controlling. It is very like someone trying to hold still a boat bobbing in a rough sea, only to find repeatedly that the self trying to hold the boat still has nothing stable to stand on and is itself bobbing and losing all sense of direction. I recently asked Jack if this was really the aim of his present existence, to hold his mind still. He said yes. I then asked what he would do with it when it was still, and he was embarrassed.

96

He hadn't had it still long enough to figure that out. What satisfaction is there in such an existence? Jack said it is the momentary victory when he was in control. At this he beamed. This was reason enough, even though his mind had been bobbing for over 11 years.

The bobbing itself is not so bad, even though he is so distracted as to lose any consistent sense to his existence. It is the failure encroaching on the very self that is threatening. In this failure he dies little by little. The dying is a failing and sinking of existence. Failure begets failure, and his whole existence is threatened with doom.

The sequence of events is often like this. Someone asks a question of what he felt or thought. (It is easier for him when a questioning starts from another person. *They* are then a stable ground.) What he felt or thought is always a moment ago, since where he is now is pulled apart into nothing. By such a question he has a chance to follow the other person and, at the same time, show his mental strength. He searches his recent memory for what he felt or thought. If he can come up with any plausible answer he smiles in self-satisfaction. He has done it—shown his strength. He has matched up to the questioning of the other person. But often, in the process of searching his own memory, he senses the falling apart into not remembering and not-being. He becomes confused in this searching, tenses up his whole body, and fights desperately to match up to the other one with an answer.

When there isn't a questioner, he does the same to himself. He calls it making a problem. "Those words written there. I must break them up into three-letter groups. Where it doesn't come out even, I must find a plausible way out." For instance to complete three-letter groups he will make a *w* into *u u* (double *u*). In this internal struggle failures are to be avoided ("perish the thought," he says) and successes held on to. Where there are failures, that part of existence is chopped off. For instance, he failed on the word t h i' n k i' n g. Thereafter he must avoid the word thinking. This heroic little game he plays results in a narrowing down of existence to those little parts where he can be victor. Because of failures, he has chopped off most of outside-the-hospital existence and almost every friend and acquaintance. He has a narrow little world from ward, to dining

97

room, to work in the upholstery shop, to the gym. By avoiding the gaze of others, he avoids many defeats in the risky world-with-others.

There are many disruptions to this existence. Curiously to us, most of these disruptions have the character of normal human experience. One of the most serious inner contaminations to the constant attempt at victory are sensory experiences. They range from such a simple thing as itching to lively images of interesting parts of women. Included in sensory interruptions are thirst, hunger, pleasure of any sort, and even the insidious temptation of smoking. His fluctuating mind will latch onto one of these sense experiences, and he will have to "perish the thought," and with it he kills off his own normal affect. When he succeeds, he feels a pleasant and momentary victory. In a way he feels he has put down the devil himself (he is Roman Catholic). As he goes into one of his more visible psychotic periods, the senses get the upper hand. He can't get food or women off his mind. They crowd him out of existence, and he becomes very confused. In one psychotic break he fought to not eat or drink, though images of these and sex crowded his mind. He could eat only when I ordered it because he hadn't given in then. I had taken the responsibility. All the way through his existence there is the striving to be one up, to match up, to be victor. He fears complete victory as much as failure because in the few cases he really knew victory he had fallen into an abyss of psychotic punishment. Both victory and defeat are dangerous. He is suspended between them.

There is no such thing as spontaneity in such an existence. Spontaneity always leads to sense experience which is a defeat to his whole purpose. It was many months before I found he planned our talks together. He memorized speeches ahead of time so as to be prepared and never be caught off guard (hence defeated). "I must anticipate. I shatter when I can't." His image of the perfect person is one who can anticipate everything and handle everything. "I need to kill or fill up time because in the blankness (of spontaneity) I can't anticipate." Once he spoke of optimism and I commented on the physical tension he showed. He said, "I tried *to put* as much feeling in it as possible." In other words, optimism should be said with feeling, so he worked to put in the right amount. Everything must be planned or it gets out-of-hand. His whole world hasn't enough control in it. Once he said, "I try to keep my energy consciousness up. When it sinks I replace it with activity." Some of this activity is very stiff catatonic gesturing. Anything that spontaneously occurs is immediately doubtful. Once he became enthusiastic when he spoke of working. This was thrown into a doubtful questioning as to whether this energy force was his, or was it a coincidence. In this way the enthusiasm perished in the questioning. Most of his internal gymnastics he described as, "I made a problem to ward off the unknown, uncertainty of blank spontaneity." To help him in this, his locker is filled with somewhat academic paperbacks such as *Faster Reading Self-Taught* or *The Family Medical Encyclopedia* which he thinks he ought to master. He never does because of the constant falling apart of his experience.

This constant attack on the nature and sequence of his own experience is like one constantly attempting to lift himself by his own bootstraps only to find he is pulled to earth and defeat. He can have no clear stable center to call himself. "It's like I am hardly clear what I am to myself." When he is dashed into defeat, there is too little self left even to acknowledge the defeat. "When I slip it is beyond me to admit it." Because he is always distracted and destroyed as a self, he can't always look at his own thinking enough to see logical fallacies. When asked on the Wechsler Adult Intelligence Scale why does the state require a license in order to be married, he answered, "Because a systematic procedure has been established." Of course, the licensing is the systematic procedure, so the answer to "why a procedure?" amounts to "because there is a procedure."

"The day covers up despair. I'm not living in a world of any kind now. I'm suspended in ether," and he laughs at this. "You don't have the passion or thrill of individual things. Life seems dull. When you talk to people, you don't respond as well. It's hard to gather your thoughts." Objects become meaningless decoration arranged around him. His mind stops and goes blank. He looks for something to fill the blankness. He grabs for a cigarette, and there is a little life. Then he fights this temptation. "I'm always following myself around instead of going where I want to go."

Gestures, clothes and property. Most of Jack's movements are awkward, as though he doesn't know where to place himself. There is a pervasive weak quality. I often feel he has come for a handout, though he doesn't have the courage to ask for a dime. At other times he looks like a prostitute who has been turned down so often she no longer can make advances. He moves stiffly or with a tremulous inadequacy. When he lights a cigarette, he may gaze at the match or cigarette for a few seconds as though he had gone blank. His fingers are often extended and stiff. When he sits he slides down in the chair, with sprawled long legs in his ill-fitting cheap hospital clothes. He has good clothes, but he manages to find the poorest, faded, ill-fitting ones. When he dresses well, he is less psychotic.

His gaze is almost always averted from others. As he poses problems, he looks to the ceiling for solutions. He has several kinds of grin. One is a wise "I know what I am talking about" one, which is often donned rather mechanically when he is suffering blankness. Another one is more weak and sickly in appearances. It says, "Don't hurt me" or, he called it, his "please-pass-me-grin." The expression of his face and the placing of his hands reflect the drama in his inner life. His hands drift into his crotch and when found there are jerked into a stiff aloofness from this dangerous area. His facial expression is often out of control so he has to readjust it. "It is as though I am always behind myself and having to catch up." He often sticks his tongue out a little bit as though feeling his lips though he is unaware of this. In part his control of his own mind reflects in stiff arms, hands, shoulders, and neck. He has some feeling that if he let go this control he might go blank. Knowing the language of these gestures has been of considerable help in following his inner experiences, since he is often slow and faulty in describing himself. It's hard to describe what is going on when your experience is falling apart and fading. Many of his gestures are quite on the fringe of awareness. They may have to be pointed out repeatedly before he even notices them.

We once went through the many things in his pockets to see what he saved there. He keeps a notebook with rather formal notes as to when his mother wrote and when he answered. It also has addresses and scraps of academic information he felt he should know. He also had two oranges, string, papers out of garbage cans, scraps of upholstery, empty tobacco bags and the like. Very seldom does he show emotion, and when he does he soon has it under control and killed. He did show emotion about the papers, scraps and tobacco bag. The papers were from hospital garbage cans and gave various bits of information about the hospital. When memorized, these would help him to answer the questions of others so he wouldn't be defeated by not knowing. String, rubber bands and scraps enabled him to be ready for emergencies. "You never know when you will need them." The scraps were new material. With tears in his eyes he said that something new should never be thrown away. It must be seen by someone and preferably used before it could be discarded. I had the feeling then and many times since that he feels like an unused scrap. He doesn't *want* to be thrown away. He has referred to himself as a can on the shelf of a state hospital. In the tobacco bags was the problem of life and death. They are made, emptied and thrown on the ground. With tears he asked what happens to them when they are forgotten and go into the soil. He was saving their lives by keeping them in his pocket.

Interpersonal relations. Interpersonal relationships, to Jack, are primarily a battle of wills where one proves superiority over another person. This fight for supremacy is in the glance, in questions and answers, and in being informed and able to anticipate the other person. It takes very little to defeat Jack on all of these scores. Everyone else's glance is steadier. They have the questions to pose which puts him on the keep-up-to-them end of the situation. They have more education and experience and are faster in social repartee. Dominant self-assured males are particularly crushing to Jack. He studies how to avoid them because their dominance threatens his very existence. "I always have to rush to catch up to others. In this way I abandon myself to the opinions of others." People with strong opinions nearly crowd him out of existence.

He has some means of protecting himself from this devastation. "I'm slow and careful not to expose myself. Or I masquerade as a competent, intelligent person." It took me some time to find out that when he looked wisest he was often most blank.

"I conducted myself as the competent, unquestioned, without-social-ties individual in contradistinction to the proven member of the group who *knows* what is going on. I didn't want to be found a stupid dummy. As it worked out they didn't go after my hide where they could have. And so it was I was able to bluff my way as an equal to some of these fellows who are a few grades above me.

"This is where comes in the problem of the adverse effects of such things as loneliness, strangeness in one's environment and the emotional feeling of non-acceptance. And when a person is not accepted, his sense of responsibility usually declines, when he becomes frustrated. After that, he may indeed also lose his self-respect. I want to admit, in a burst of honesty, that I have often been sick while I've been here. I'm thinking in particular of strangeness. Much value, I believe, is put on a person's ability to have the courage to express himself without fear. A tendency to withdraw; seek shelter and pawn off attention to neighbors; become insignificant, unnoticed; in short, to evade responsibility; to get 'lost in the crowd'—these are bad for him. So, if he has that sense of individual reaponsibility which is necessary, he has something. You're going to have to 'reach for yourself.' "

These very literate descriptions of his experience are rare. I've received only four in nearly two years. They are usually written when he is on the upswing and in a clear period. When he slips into blankness he doesn't write.

The joke. There is an even darker side to his social relationships which I was slow to discover. It enters, for instance, when the other party slips or makes a mistake. This usually pleases Jack considerably. The listener might have trouble following Jack's train of thought because Jack will often speak in such general terms one doesn't know if he is referring to himself or the universe at large. When the listener becomes confused, Jack's face brightens. He has won a point. This extends to the whole matter of hospitalization. Repeatedly I've gotten the impression that he has defeated mother, father and siblings by being the mentally ill one. It is as though he says, "See, they have to come to see me."

Some of the most hilarious jokes between us pertain to his riding along on the state. We described this as his being a bum riding along in the state's box car. To repeat the joke I need only say click-click, click-click (the sound of time passing or the click of the tracks) and he laughs out loud, as is rare for him. The other day he didn't feel like talking to me or anyone. We sat silently. He would chuckle when my chair squeaked (my weakness showing). Finally, I just made a sound of sucking. He saw my point and laughed till his face was red and his eyes running tears. The joke? The hospital is a breast. He is sucking on it by becoming passive and incapable of anything better. It is so funny because I've caught on and Jack is suddenly exposed. It's hilarious. By his behavior he quite passively defeats everyone. That's why his enigmatic laugh. It's only serious when he tries to get out of his passive dependency and finds he can't. Then he becomes frightened. Jack has said, "I had it tougher as a boy than I have it now. There's a routine here so you don't have to think. They make it too easy for you." On the one hand one feels Jack is in a trap. On the other hand, one feels Jack has designed the trap, and it closes on us too. He has one-upped us. Don't we care for him?

Jack's Own Account

The following is Jack's longest and finest written account of his experiences. It was one of the many periods when people began to talk as though he was recovering.

"*Questioning.* I find now that the questioning experience is more so a less harrowing one than it used to be. Or rather, the visits with my psychologist. It was always (almost always) difficult after I'd started to make my way to his office. Has my confidence grown? I remember the importance I attached to these visits, my own marked un-self-assuredness and uncertainty. Often there was the polite conformity and readying before the meeting.

"One thing it did for me was to arouse my self-awareness. I wanted to, very much, please. As little as I knew about what *I wanted,* yet I was pretty aware of the person-to-person relationship. This is much. And since, I believe, my relationship to people in general has definitely known an actual, undeniable improvement. However, during this time, preceding visits also, was the presence of conflicts. They, too, were aroused. Many were questions about myself. What was I? Was it okay for me to be here, and would I pass? After I came out that door, would I make it down the hall and slip upstairs to my room, or would I be intercepted and stared out of existence on the way? Did I have the date for next time down so I wouldn't forget it? Did what was discussed here jibe with what other people knew me as, or, had I learned something new; something different? If so, what would be the significance in relation to them (other people)?

"*Reflection on lostness (blankness).* Had I been stunned or shocked into netherness today? Did I know what it was that caused this state? WHAT was it I can't remember? WHAT WILL HAPPEN if I don't? God, this has happened *so many* times already, I fear the end if it happens this time—the end. I don't feel so good right now, 'cause I haven't been able to concentrate on the job, I'm moving pretty slow, there doesn't seem much to inspire me. So, I perform lazily, maybe take it out on a cigarette, which also hides my weakness in that while I'm smoking I can discipline my facial expressions, all the while the morality of it is wrestled over, and other matters or ideas are first hog-called pleadingly then dispelled as invaders.

". . . . Wha-a-at would happen, now if I (gulp), if I . . . . ? But, no, I can't. I couldn't do that. And he might . . . . 'cause he's not going to let ME get away with . . . . But maybe I can use a new twist. Yeah, some sort of sharp new twist. One of the conventional ad-libby impersonations, or sympathy stories (something like the rationalizations as to why I'm here in the hospital) might do it, or a probe started by him, or both of us might start me off in a hopeful enlargement. If interrupted, okay by me. I got many techniques, too, you know. There's a return to questioning. Otherwise, blankness will work. He'll let off when I go blank. That suicide. That ill cry. Or the simply helpless. *Honestly* helpless. This, I think is the most unrehearsed . . . .

"Or, BANG! Another time I would idealize. Put on my (ahem!) dubious armour of profound religious fervor and virtuism. Clad in this, I could proceed unquestioned until, well probably until it began to feel too tight.

"I know distinctly that; formerly, all the time, I was, in actuality, a shriveling, cringing coward-baby (although never required to acknowledge it outwardly), a trembling spineless BUM, hopelessly succumbed to his disrespectable fate, with little or no active hope, and immersed in his comfortable situation, actually a hideous pig pen and he a pig, which pig pen he cursed as the cause of his trouble (silently, never aloud), while yet languishing like the old Romans. During years of hospital life, this animal is what I actually was. It describes me. It's what I wanted to be, and it I was. Typical demeanor was a timid, over-cautious, egoless, nameless, cringingly hopeful handout-seeker walking along trying for an invite, scarcely daring to use the eyes directly. Or walking along, trying to find the guy who "blessed my household" by inviting me in his household last. Or get a "buddy." I used to do the same thing when I was young. It grew with me as I grew up, and in grammar and high school, was definitely a part of me.

"I guess at first I swore to do something about it, but when I tried I found obstacles, began putting it off, and so it overran me. The rest is ugly record. I had ceased to care. Others lost their meaning for me. I looked at them for as long as I dared. After that, they just weren't there. And my life since has been nothing but a pretense, a lie. I've not been something human, but something inhuman. I hardly dare guess how much of what I've seen is true. I honestly hope a depression never again affords me delight, as they have done, or a sense of achievement or "suffer's satisfaction" (martyr).

"More than once, oh, oh, how many times I edged my feeble way into a discussion (me, not quite committed or sure if I really wanted to be in *this* group—actually beyond mercy and afraid of and incapable of, begging) during the course of which many times I died to myself, unwilling or unable to free myself in any way. No self-respect. A moral coward. Same deal with waiting for a door to be opened or service to be done by authority.

"I just walked into the day hall. Started to sit down to enjoy a cigarette after my (fast) meal. Television on. Comes "A girl, with the Million Dollar Legs." I get up to leave the room. I removed myself from them and the TV, lest I become intoxicated with joy. Might not such ungrateful indulgence, particularly on the part of me, the self-conscious lucky-one (for lack of a better word) be greatly punished if I got drunk on sense pleasure, or social pleasure of the group? Might I not even be returned to the "dark hole," to insanity?

"At this time, I'm kind of trying to recuperate after a somewhat rough day, upset in other words. And it has frequently seemed that in such situations, when I felt my power after the initial successes in dealing with and being with other people, I wished to spend my newly inherited fortune slowly, not in lavish spending. That fortune was ME. So what did I do? It had come free. And in the matter of taking things it is hard for me to decide. I doubt if I can refuse any more. I've been so weak I'm a trained bum. Here my motive is hate. I hate the group or the TV (although I desire these things) because they make me take what I don't want to take. How will I atone and pay for my gift if I yield to this? I've yielded in conversations so many times, and at these times I never even did get a chance to assert myself. They tricked me into thinking they'd accepted me, but actually I was outnumbered from the start, used as a fool, and crushed by the big monsters. Result: I hate groups. Solution: Don't mix too much. Enough to escape criticism, and that's it. Besides, they've noticed your improved ability, so are expecting more from you, but before they expect too much, undershoot yourself. But the main thing is don't yield. Likewise with women.

"Anyway, it is a strange thing, to WIN. To walk into that day room with confidence of being a winner provides its own misgivings. The old forces of non-existence strike. You want to fight regression. Or to "storm" boldly (in my case), proceed (feeling good, now) into a more personal situation, i.e., one in which I'm armed with more ego-support, wherein the confidence-ego is vs. the timid ego . . . and, very recently (but not really recently, for I've done it regularly, for years, and even since childhood) my reaction (or decision) would be not to realize the blankness of the environment (the room, the group, others). ME, *my* blankness, were one and the same being, but frown and sigh inwardly, virtually collapse mentally, and panic-stricken, withdraw, disappear to my room, and freeze, become cold and remote, rather than wriggle into the womb-like atmosphere there to rest up. My rationalization would be, I can't atone here, so better to flee elsewhere. It's not running away, for me, for although I don't know what would be better, I'll find something more worthy, something better. *Anything* would be better than this.

"Also, there is the case of the ego-erection. Probably, my marriage in the church of this hospital, my marriage-acts in the day hall of the unit, and the consequent illegitimate children are unwanted (children) born during a moment of impulse. But, let's not reject them, shelve them. Why not give them a chance to live, and with them myself? There is meaning behind the bad-marriage erections. The woman *does* think of other things than just the marriage act. Here that paradox is."

The Inversion of the Drama

There is a drama within this drama which turns it inside out and reverses all of its features. The inversion of the drama seems to have to come from an outsider. Jack can't or won't do it himself. It comes when one encourages him to give up trying, drift in the blankness, or let go of all thoughts. On someone else's direction he will do it. There are two major kinds of experiences when he lets go and drifts. Both of them appear quite normal. In the first he rediscovers his own sensuality. In the void he has sexual feelings; he will visualize a seductive woman, or he may simply experience sensual pleasure of less threatening sorts. All of these imply defeat to him, so he struggles to kill off the sensations and pose a problem to himself to get back to his usual condition. In these experiences he seems to rediscover himself as physically real for a short while.

The other experiences in the void are even more striking. In them he forms impressions of what he is. They are impressions such as "I'm a weak jellyfish," or "I'm a sniveling coward afraid of others," or "I play this game of mental illness because I have no courage to do anything more." The comments all look to be objectively accurate. That is, they are what most people would say if they really knew him. They are just the opposite of any pretense. They get right down to business and seem to be genuine revelations of what he is. *All that occurs in this void is the opposite of mental illness.*

The ordinary Jack is all social pretense. In the void is the undoing of all pretension. The ordinary Jack is always striving to be on top. In the void this seems foolish. The ordinary Jack is effeminate. In the void he is strikingly masculine. The ordinary Jack is somber striving. In the void he laughs and is carefree. What emerges from the void is the opposite of the schizophrenic Jack. I've called it his normal mind, but the ordinary Jack rejects that. What is ordinary is his constant striving to control the mind.

It is impressive that what appears to be the very kernel of the schizophrenic pathology, the blankness, the falling apart of existence is itself the entrance to a fertile void which contains his normal side. By fertile void I mean the fertile core of experience which is revealed when one is emptied. This normal side of Jack would live in his body, enjoy it and reflect more as others do on himself. I don't know yet how to bring about an inversion that would bring this inside out. At this point the usual Jack doesn't think too much of the other side. It looks too much like common clay and defeat to his whole elaborate structure. So he avoids it.

Outer aspect—the usual Jack: Hang on, keep up a good front, look intelligent, find others' weaknesses, overcome one's weak drifting mind in order to taste the sweet moment of victory which is mind control. Above all, reinforce one's self as a spirit over the body and the whole world.

Middle aspect—the change: But I am suffused with blankness. I hate it. It pulls me down from victory. It says I am all front.

Inner aspect—the hidden: I can't force my will through the blankness. I must give up my will. When I do, I feel my body and myself. I feel my vanity, my stiff face, my stomach is scared, and masculinity stirs in my genitals. Here I am alive. I want to work, marry and do something useful.

Conclusion

Most psychiatric description appears to assume from the outset that certain aspects of people's lives (for instance, love and aggression) are central, and in concentrating on these it seems to prove its own thesis. For me, the beauty of phenomenological description is that it seeks to uncover a world of experience just as it is. What is central in the description is whatever is central to the person living the life. One can have the subject himself examine and pass on the description, for, after all, his is the last word. Jack modified words here and there and emphasized points. His corrections were incorporated. This isn't entirely fair in this case because the very coherence in the description is greater than his ordinary experience of himself.

Uncovering the world of the other person is itself psychotherapy because, as we learned together, Jack's own experience took on more meaning, order and ramifications than he had known when we began. In the last six months our conception began to unify under the theme that he was a bum riding along on the state, a half-drunk failure meditating on the meaning of it all. The bum combined both the outer drama of moral weakness and the inner man grounded in sensuality. He later recovered sufficiently to leave the hospital to work as a gardener for an institution. He lived outside the hospital for the first time in 11 years and worked at his first paying job. He is still a socially impaired individual who continues to take a low dose of stelazine. But the study of his world brought at least a partial social recovery.

The most curious aspect of his existence for me is the way in which his pathology appears to be an attempt to maintain a superiority over his own experience. In his subjective experience he must control all impulses so that almost every spontaneously arising experience is already suspect and must be stamped out or converted into something more acceptable. This inner struggle toward a position of superiority over himself reflects outwardly in his marked sensitivity to inferiority-superiority in social situations. Whatever is contrary to this aim is cut off or avoided, including reality. In this effort to superiority he is always in the has-been, trying to keep up with dangerous spontaneous developments.

The whole of this hypercontrol is beset by a falling apart of existence, an encroaching blankness and taking away. Yet, when we explore the blankness, give up and enter it, here is his most normal and reality-grounded thinking. In the center of pathology is hidden normality. How to use this center, I am not certain. In less serious cases it appears therapeutic for the patient to give up the self, enter the void, and learn what he really is. It is as though the pathology that haunts the schizophrenic contains his true self. No wonder he can't get rid of it. But, I don't yet know how to make the productive descent into the heart of pathology. At least, I suspect pathology shows us we cannot assert ourselves against our own nature.

The parallels with Adler's description of schizophrenia are striking. There is the same striving after an impossible goal with its concomitant distance from others and reality. Superiority and self-esteem are maintained at the cost of the world of others and even at the cost of control within his narrow world. Adler described the narrowing of life space, the use of weakness as a weapon to attain hidden ends, and Jack's way of shifting from facing situations to battling pseudo-problems. The main and practically only difference I can find from Adler is the rather surprising finding that in giving way to the encroaching void Jack runs into his normal self.

But even in this regard Adler at least dropped a hint when he advised depressed patients never to do anything they disliked. If they replied there was nothing they liked to do, then, he suggested, they should stay in bed. In this way he tried to relieve the patient's ordinary tension and striving, thus going "to the root of the whole trouble."

Perhaps it should be expected that pathology shows one is in flight from one's self. And hidden in the pathology is the very pull back into one's self. If one must be superior to one's own impulses, than a pull down into impulse is to be expected. In a way, chronic schizophrenia is an over-playing of ordinary life, and in its drama it may serve as a caution to us.

I once remarked to Jack that his existence looked to me like an endless play with himself. He smiled and answered quickly, "That's right. It ends up in my own pouch. Nothing lost and nothing gained."

The Perspective of an Old Hand

Wilson Van Dusen

The essence of what Fritz Perls showed us is that a person's disorder is present and any way of getting it to enact itself will illuminate both therapist and client. Fritz ably demonstrated several ways
of getting the issues to show themselves. Other therapists have more
or less imitated the master in this.

As an old man, who fears he has worked in a profession which
borders on empty magic show and self-deception, I am concerned to
advance beyond anything we've been shown, so that we might one
day be as proud as brick-layers who can rightly say "there is my
work," a work that is mute testimony to skill for many years. Up
close to the therapeutic process we are elated over our impressive
demonstrations, and put aside and forget failures. I think it almost
humorous when I see that a colleague has issued a tape of a successful session. How much was not issued?

Are there ways that we could further the lines shown in gestalt
therapy and go beyond imitating the master? I believe so. Gestalt is
basically a way of activating the subtleties of a life and getting them
acted out so that the life might be seen and understood more clearly.
Therapy is remarkably like TV detective work, where the crooks are
concealing and obscuring at every turn. It seems to me 90% is finding
out What Is Going On. The 10% Changing This Pattern almost occurs
of itself if the 90% is done well. Are there other possible ways of
illuminating What is Going On beyond those ably demonstrated by
Fritz? Yes.

After working with Fritz in gestalt I spent some years living in Synanon-like communities of people who were working hard to undo drug styles of living. Working with much more difficult and devious a client, they were often much faster than any therapist. Why? Mainly because they lived with their "clients" and had heavy indictment material. They knew what each other did in the most subtle and intimate circumstances. Moreover they used this indictment material in a clever way. They didn't just blow up at their fellows in the community at every turn, they saved it and then dropped the boom on them at the most effective moment, when everyone else was sitting around. Nor did they fear to use anger, shouting, and exaggeration in this therapeutic moment. In a TV drama sense it would be the same as not only catching the crook with his hand in the drawer, but also closing the drawer on the hand while discussing his behavior.

Therapists who see clients for an hour or two, now and then, are at a severe disadvantage. Would not any of us, as clients, tend to dress up and put our best rationalization forward? I would like to see any method which gets heavier, more factual information on the client and then confronts them in the most effective way possible. It would be possible to contract with the client that we would like to learn as much as possible of their real life before we commit ourselves as to what we see. Then we could spend much time with the client, dine with him and family and friends, walk with him, spend half a day going thru his personal possessions, and interview old girlfriends, fellow employees, enemies, etc. We could gather much more outside information. Just as an example, I was impressed by the case of a very intelligent friend who became an alcoholic. Like all alcoholics he reported to the therapist that he drank only a 6-pack a day and thought his wife unreasonably alarmed. If the therapist knew what his wife, 12 kids, and friends did he could have acted much more forcefully when this clever fellow turned up for therapy. How much more effective a position the therapist could have been in if he knew at least as much as everyone else knew. This very verbal, intelligent man who said he restricted himself to a 6-pack a day was in varying degrees of drunkenness all the time, was called a lush by his sons, took an axe to the walls of his house when confronted on his drinking by his wife, manifested child-like dependence on her in her absence, etc.

Suppose the therapist had taken the weak initial contact to get a contract to gather more information and then, when sure of his case, had called a general family meeting to confront the client in the presence of all those intimately concerned with his behavior. Because of a real threat of violence a policeman might also be called. One can picture the power of such a session. The therapist is heavily armed with facts from all. All those concerned with his behavior are briefed and drawn into the drama.

This alcoholic's trump card was that he would go berserk with violence against things, but by implication against the wife and children. No one was ready to call this card though the older sons had considered arming themselves with clubs. Armed with clubs and a policeman at the door it is my guess this very weak man would cave in. If he didn't, some lumps on the head would also be therapeutic. Then some new contracts might emerge. It was a big thing to him that he was *paterfamilias,* master of the house, though secretly the kids called him a drunken lush and avoided him. One contract might be that one drink and he was not *paterfamilias*, and no one had to pay any attention to him until he was again cold sober. With thirteen vitally interested helpers other useful contracts would emerge.

I see this as a simple extension of gestalt therapy: getting it out in the open. But contrast this with the usual situation. Contrast the few bits of information even a good session yields to visiting the home, talking with family and friends, going through personal things, etc. Contrast the dribbling out of the therapist's reactions in the usual session to this gathering of a whole case before the detective shows how the murder was committed and who is guilty. Contrast the usual client versus therapist bout, to client versus therapist, family and friends. Contrast the weakness of the usual therapeutic pussy-footing to this. If for no other reason, the therapist needs to know much in order to act with a sufficient and useful boldness. I saw this when Fritz, working with a colleague of mine, would come out with a right-on perception of my friend, only to have it turned aside and dismissed by him. With a greater certainty Fritz and all of us could have acted with much more bold and confrontive gusto.

My point is simply that we have been shown that the truth can be made to act out and show itself to us. Yet, the greatest respect to Fritz would not be a slavish imitation, but ever seeking other ways to get the truth out. And, being an aged skeptic, I'm not even totally impressed when the client weeps and confesses all and gives me a feather of victory for my cap. Changed behavior is the aim, and besides the client's happy report of change, what of those concerned others and the children? I once worked two years with a schizophrenic who carefully rehearsed what he would say to me (reported in this book as *The Phenomenology of a Schizophrenic Existence*). I finally reached the guy in two sessions. In one session I was on LSD and in the other I was curious enough to go through the things in his pockets and in his locker.

My point is that we should consider any way that helps discover the client's real existence. Seeing the client in an altered state of consciousness is another way, i.e. drunk, on drugs, in hypnosis, meditating, etc. I worked a long while with women on a hospital ward only to find amazingly clear and simple aspects (missed before) when I danced with them. For a long while I longed simply to get the person in their usual pathology and just slow down the process. For instance, the one who wants to quit smoking: light up here, smoke slowly, very slowly; what is going on? In a hospital setting I would like to give an alcoholic booze slowly, demanding consciousness for every sip.

In a mental hospital we had many chronic patients called sitters, because that was all they did. I've almost never seen anyone accomplish anything with these people, including Fritz. The hospital administration frowned on an experiment I would like to have done on these people. Their lives were the epitome of dependent uselessness. With patient kindness I would like to have restructured their environment so that no work, no eat. The simplest things to do would be at hand: empty this ash tray and get this food. It would have tested if their stomach was as mad as they. I wouldn't have starved them to death, just close to it. The administration wasn't afraid of me, but of public reaction. It was permissible to restrict patients to 1000 calories a day on a diet, so I proposed to work with fat sitters. But even this wasn't permitted. It was better to have thousands of sitters wasting centuries than to confront public reaction, if any.

Perhaps we therapists are tacitly afraid of confrontation ourselves. Perhaps training as therapists should include judo, tai chi, or survival training in the woods, to shift us into a capacity to confront life and death before we take on puny clients. I can see the true therapist breaking five boards in a judo chop before turning to gently confront the new client. Of course it is paradoxical. The one with the greatest power can afford to be gentle.

Although I've seen impressive sessions in my hands and others, I remain relatively unimpressed with psychotherapy as a whole. The more one looks beyond the impressive tears of the moment to the total life, and the reactions of concerned others, the less one is impressed. Though Fritz showed me for the first time that what I wanted to see was really before my eyes, still even Fritz failed with my average client, the chronic psychotic. I have suggested, but certainly do not delimit, ways that we might further illuminate and thereby improve lives, that we might one day be as useful and secure as bricklayers.

Saying Goodbye

Stephen A. Tobin

I find that most patients have failed to say goodbye and finish some relationship that terminated in death, divorce, ending of a love affair, or in some other way. This "hanging-on" reaction occurs with missing persons who were of strong emotional significance to the patient. The relationship does not have to have been filled with love. In fact, *most* such relationships were characterized by much fighting and resentment rather than by love.

The adaptive reaction to the loss of a loved person is a fairly long period of grief followed by renewed interest in living people and things. The adaptive reaction to the loss of a hated person presumably would be relief. The hanging-on reaction is to inhibit the emotions triggered by the loss and to keep the person present in fantasy.

In this paper I shall discuss the causes of the hanging-on reaction, the symptomatic results in the hanger-on, gestalt therapy techniques I use in working with patients to say goodbye, and a sample of such work.

Causes of the Hanging-On Reaction

One cause of the hanging-on reaction is the presence of much unfinished business between the two persons long before the relationship terminates. By "unfinished business" I mean the inhibition of an emotion that was experienced at one or more times during the

Reprinted from *Psychotherapy: Theory, Research and Practice*, Vol. 8, No. 2, Summer 1971, pp. 150–155.

relationship. A simple example would be the employee who feels angry towards his boss but, because he is frightened of being fired, decides not to express his feelings. Until he expresses his anger in some way, he is left with the physical tension that results from the impasse between the physical excitation of the anger and the inhibiting force that suppresses the emotion. He may try to deal with this unfinished situation in indirect ways, e.g., by having fantasies about telling his boss off or about the death of his boss in an accident, or by taking it out on his wife and children when he goes home that night. No matter what he does, he is tense and anxious and has a nagging feeling of not having done something he should have done. Until he finds some *direct* way of finishing the business of his anger towards his boss, he will be unable to relax or involve himself fully with any person or in any activity. In addition, his relationship with his boss will be strained.

This is, of course, a minor situation that probably wouldn't cause much difficulty. Most of the people I see in therapy have accumulated many unfinished situations of great emotional intensity. For example, one man as a child was continually humiliated and rendered helpless by his father. To express his rage toward his father would have meant his own destruction. Today he continually attempts to finish this situation by provoking authority figures into attacking him and then attacking back.

The Freudians have discussed such neurotic behavior and have coined the term "repetition compulsion" to describe it. They have not, however, dealt with the physical changes that take place. In addition, Freudian therapy, with its stress on thinking and its endless why-because games, reinforces hanging-on to the past rather than encouraging letting go of it. Behaviorism, on the other hand, while working towards the elimination of outmoded response tendencies, does not give the client tools he can use to prevent future hanging-on reactions.

How do people stop themselves from finishing situations? First, the vast majority of people start in early childhood to suppress painful or overpowering emotions by chronic tightening of their skeletal and smooth musculature and by inhibiting their breathing. This results in a partial deadening of their bodies; by the time they are adults, they have limited sensory awareness of their bodies. Since all feelings are located in the body, they are unaware of their feelings. This lack of awareness makes it impossible for them to finish emotional situations. Even if they do become aware of their emotions, they are apt to suppress them; their minds tell them they shouldn't be angry, shouldn't express love, shouldn't feel sad. So they turn off the messages their bodies give them and the emotional excitement then turns into physical pain, tension, and anxiety.

A second way people stop themselves from finishing situations is by placing great value on some of the secondary gains they get from hanging on. If the present is unexciting or if they feel incapable of getting involved with other people, they can relieve their loneliness by thinking about past relationships. While one might imagine that these past situations are pleasurable, more often than not they are negative. Hanging-on to resentment, for example, can be used to enable one to feel self-righteous or self-pitying—characterological ways of being many people are willing to settle for. Resentment can also be used as an excuse for not getting close to the object of one's resentment.

For example, a woman in a therapy group talked continually about what an awful mother she had. Whenever anyone else spoke of his mother, she would very dramatically start to recount the "terrible" things her mother had done to her. When I asked her to imagine her mother in the room and to talk to her, she would blame her mother for ruining her life. She would not, of course, ever confront her mother directly with her resentment; her excuse was that she didn't want to hurt her mother and, "It wouldn't do any good anyway." Her real reason for not confronting her was that she didn't really think she had the resources to change her existence, and her mother served as a ready excuse for her failures in life. Another benefit of her game was that she could project all her own undesired traits on her mother; when I pointed out that she resembled her description of her mother in many ways, she would shudder and plead with me not to say that because she hated her mother so much.

While her complaints to the group afforded her some expression of resentment, the situation was still incomplete for her. She still harbored resentment and hatred which appeared even when she was not speaking of her mother—in her tone of voice, her posture, and her gestures.

Self-righteousness, which is a particularly prevalent side-benefit of hanging-on, is common in those patients who evaluate every conflict between themselves and others in a good-bad, right-wrong fashion. They think that the only way to resolve a conflict is for one person to admit that he is guilty or bad or stupid. Since admitting to these judgments is humiliating and degrading, many people hang on to their resentments hoping that the other will see the light and humiliate himself by admitting he was wrong.

So we see that even before termination of a relationship, there is often a great deal of unfinished business. Matters become more complicated when one of the persons leaves and the relationship is ended.

Hanging-On After Termination Of The Relationship

The unfinished business can be between a parent and child, between spouses, between lovers, between friends, or between any other two people who have had an intense, long-standing relationship. There is much unfinished business within the relationship while it lasts; when the relationship ends—through death, divorce, one person moving away from the other, etc.—the relationship itself becomes unfinished. The individual is still carrying around much accumulated unexpressed emotion: old resentments, frustrations, hurts, guilts, and even unexpressed love and appreciation. The presence of these unexpressed emotions makes it difficult for him to finish the relationship simply because the other person is no longer around to hear them. One of the ways it can be done is for the person to express his feelings in fantasy to the one who is gone. I find, however, that few of my patients have done this. There are a number of reasons why they have not.

First of all, some of the ways in which people prevent themselves from finishing things discussed in the previous section are also used to prevent themselves from finishing the relationship and saying goodbye. Many patients have been unaware of what they felt at the end of a relationship. For example, a young man in one workshop was almost completely unaware of the intense guilt and grief he felt about his sick pet cat whom he had had to have destroyed.

People also get much secondary gain from not letting go. The woman who is fearful about attempting new relationships with men can use her attachment to her dead husband as an excuse for not getting involved.

Many Americans have simply lost the ability to let go of dead relationships because of their fear of intense emotion of any kind, particularly when a death has occurred. The mourning process, which is recognized as natural and necessary in other parts of the world, frequently does not occur in the United States. The Kennedy wives were praised for their lack of public emotion after their husbands were assassinated. In contrast, the widow of Tom Mboya, the African politician, was shown in a national magazine attempting to throw herself on her husband's grave.

Another example of this inability to do what is necessary to finish dead relationships is the individual who has been jilted. Instead of venting his feelings of hurt and anger, he is apt to keep them to himself so as not to give his jilter any "satisfaction" for rejecting him. The adaptive reaction to divorce would be for each person to express his lingering resentments and to go his separate way; instead, most divorced people continue hanging-on in a kind of guerrilla war, particularly when complicated alimony and child settlement agreements are legally enforced.

Another reason for my patients' inability to say goodbye is their unwillingness to experience the pain they would feel if they did let go. Probably as a reaction to American Puritanism, which taught people that life was supposed to involve nothing but pain, we have become a nation of people who believe it's wrong to feel any pain at all. As soon as most people feel anxious, they take tranquilizers or smoke pot; as soon as they come into conflict with others, they try to end the conflicts as quickly as possible by either avoiding the others or by trying to overpower or manipulate them and "win." Rather than letting go of dead relationships, most people avoid their emptiness and loneliness by "keeping busy," by finding a new relationship as quickly as possible, or by pretending that the dead person is still around.

Finally, many people avoid saying goodbye because they feel that letting go, particularly of the dead, is a dishonor to them. Most of my patients no longer believe in a life hereafter, and they often feel that the only kind of immortality possible is to be remembered by the living. They don't realize that had they really had a meaningful relationship with the person when he was still around, had they really said "hello," they would have been continually enriched and changed through the relationship. The lost person then would *really* have become part of the one who is left and live on in a much more meaningful way—as a part of that person's being—instead of as an introjected lump of dead matter that comes between the person and his world.

Results of Hanging-On

Physical symptoms are one result of hanging-on. Some patients have identified parts of their bodies as representatives of the persons who are gone. Two women I saw in therapy kept their mothers present in the form of ulcers. Another example is a young woman with whom I worked in a weekend workshop who had chronically cold hands, maintained an attitude of contemptuous aloofness towards others, and literally would not touch others. Her mother had died when she was three and she became aware during our work together that her cold hands were both links with her cold, dead mother and also symbolized her mother. When she was able to say goodbye to her mother, her hands suddenly warmed up and she was able to make meaningful contact with others for the first time in her life.

Other people identify their whole beings with dead people and appear to be walking zombies: their voices and faces are expressionless, their movements are controlled and mechanical, and they report feeling physically numb.

Secondly, those who have refused to say goodbye usually exhibit emotional symptoms. For example, those who have identified with dead people are emotionally dead. I am not referring to depressed persons; these people feel neither depression nor anything else. There are also, however, many persons who, because of incompletion of the mourning process, become chronically depressed in an attenuated way. They are gloomy, apathetic, and have little real interest in life. They have been depressed for such a long time that they frequently are even unaware of their depression.

Another common emotional result of the hanging-on reaction is a whiny, self-pitying attitude towards oneself, and a blaming, complaining attitude towards the person who has gone. The whiner often uses the lost person as an excuse for his inadequacies: "If my father had loved me more, my life wouldn't be such a mess now." The obverse of the whiner is the person who blames himself rather than the dead person and feels guilty: "If I had been nicer to my father before he died, he would have been happier and I would be better off now. Now there's no way I can make it up to him."

A third symptom is an inability to form close relationships. One who is continually fantasizing about the past or is having relationships with people who are gone, has little time for those still around. He does not see or hear or feel in the present.

I have found that the more a person is able to finish things in a relationship, the more authentic that relationship is. What happens, however, in most intimate relationships is that, after a while, there are so many unexpressed resentments and disappointments that the people in the relationship cease really seeing or hearing each other or feeling *in the present.* In contrast, those people who can say "goodbye" when they part temporarily are better able to get fully involved with each other in a fresh, meaningful, realistic way when they next meet.

Thus, in a very important sense, saying goodbye to the dead parent or the divorced spouse is an identical process to expressing feelings to another person and to letting him go during a temporary absence.

Working With Patients on Saying Goodbye

The first step in helping the patient who is hanging-on to say goodbye is *to make him aware of hanging-on* and of how he is doing this. Usually something the patient says or does in group or individual therapy makes me suspect that he is in conflict about some unfinished business. Sometimes it is a dream in which the dead person appears, sometimes a gesture. For example, a few patients have looked up when speaking and I found out they were looking up at "heaven." Sometimes the patient appears so lifeless that I have a hunch he has identified with a dead person.

I then ask the patient if he has some unfinished business with someone who is gone and, if the answer is affirmative, I ask him if he wants to say goodbye. Most patients at this point will say that they do; if they openly state they do not wish to let go, I will just work with them long enough to get them aware of their objections to saying goodbye. If they still insist, after finding out their objections, that they don't want to let go and are in no conflict about this, I stop at this point. If a patient does wish to work on saying goodbye, I then proceed to the next stage.

Working Through the Unfinished Business

The second step is, I take an empty chair and place it in front of the patient and ask him to imagine the dead person sitting in it. I next ask him what he experiences as he imagines the dead person there. Whatever the emotion or thought expressed, I ask the patient to say that directly to the dead person. Frequently patients experience resentment at not having been "loved enough," or guilt about not having been kinder to the dead person before he died. After he has said what he wants to, I ask him to switch chairs and become the dead person. Frequently the patient will spontaneously say something; if he does not, I again ask him what he is experiencing, this time as the dead person. When he replies, I ask him to say that to himself sitting in the other chair. The dead person as imagined by the client may feel anger for the lack of kindness in the patient towards himself. The dead person may become defensive at the resentment expressed by the patient, and give excuses for the lack of love. After the dead person has had his say, I ask the patient to switch back to playing himself in the first chair, and he is asked to reply to the fantasied dead one. When the patient gets into the two roles completely, I ask him to let himself switch back and forth as he finds himself changing roles.

In almost every case there is much emotion expressed—anger, hurt, resentment, love, etc. When the patient seems to have no more unfinished business, I ask him if he feels ready to say goodbye. Frequently patients say they are ready to say goodbye but are unable to do so when I ask them to say it directly to the imagined dead love-object. At other times they say goodbye but it just doesn't sound convincing. In either case, I help them to become aware that they are not ready to let the dead go, either because of a fear they won't be able to find living people to relate to, or because they have more unfinished business. I do not push or encourage the patient as long as he is willing to take responsibility for his hanging-on.

If the patient is ready to terminate the relationship, however, there is usually some explosion of emotion. Usually the patient completes the mourning process and cries; occasionally, however, the emotion is one of great relief and joy at the dead weight that has been eliminated. When this kind of work occurs in a group, it tends to be a very moving experience for me and all the other people present. Typically, feelings of greater group closeness, warmth, and a kind of profound, religious love of all of life are expressed by all the people participating as observers of this work.

I have done no systematic study of the follow-up effects, but my impression is that the results are long-lasting: little or no thinking about the dead person, a feeling of more energy, and increased interest in life and other people.

Clinical Example

The following is a re-creation of some work I did with a woman with whom I had had no previous contact, in a weekend workshop. The woman, whom I shall call "Mrs. R.," was a married housewife in her mid-thirties. She spoke in a very mechanical way, sounding like a child who was reciting a poem she had been forced to memorize but didn't understand. In her relationship with her husband and children she played the part of a masochistic martyr, controlling them by showing how much they made her "suffer." Our work on her saying goodbye to her dead mother started during a dream in which her mother appeared. While working on the dream, her voice and demeanor suddenly changed; she began to cry and sounded whiny and complaining. I asked her if she had some unfinished business with her mother, and she said:

Mrs. R: Well . . . if only she had loved me, things would be different. But she didn't and . . . and I've never had any real mother love (crying).

S (Steve Tobin): Put your mother in that chair and say that to her.

Mrs. R: If only she had cared for me, I'd be much better today.

S: I want you to say this to her, not to me. Can you imagine her sitting there in front of you?

Mrs. R: Yes, I see her as she looked when she was still alive. Mother, if you had only loved me. Why couldn't you ever tell me you loved me? Why did you always criticize me? (almost a wail, more tears)

S: Now switch over to the other chair and play your mother. (She moves over to the other chair and doesn't say anything.)

S: What do you experience as your mother?

Mrs. R: I-I-I don't know . . . I don't know what she would say.

S: Of course you don't know. She's not around any more. You're playing the part of you that is your mother. Just say whatever you experience there.

Mrs. R: Oh, I see. Well, I don't know what to say to her.

S: Say *that* to her.

Mrs. R M (Mrs. R as Mother): I don't know what to say to you. I *never* knew what to say to you. I really did love you, you know that. Look at all the things I did for you, and you never appreciated it. (voice sounds defensive and whiny)

S: Now switch back and reply as yourself.

Mrs. R S (Mrs. R as Self): Loved me! All you ever did was criticize me. Nothing I ever did was good enough! (voice beginning to sound more whiny) When I got married to J. you disapproved, you were always coming over and telling me what I was doing wrong with the kids. Oh, you never came right out and said anything, but you were always making snide remarks or saying, "Now, dear, wouldn't it be a good idea to put another blanket on the baby." You made my life *miserable*; I was always worrying about you criticizing me. And now I'm having all this trouble with J. (breaks down and starts to cry)

S: Did you hear your voice?

Mrs. R S: Yes.

S: What did you hear in it?

Mrs. R S: Well, I guess I sounded kind of complaining, like I'm feeling sor—like I'm feeling mad.

S: You sounded more like feeling self-pity. Try this on for size: say to your mother, "Look what you've done to me. It's all your fault."

Mrs. R S: Look what you've done. Everything's your fault.

S: Now let yourself switch back and forth as you find yourself changing roles.

Mrs. R M: Come on, stop blaming me for everything. You are always complaining about something. If you had been better—if you had been a *decent* daughter, I wouldn't have had to criticize you so much.

Mrs. R S: Oh, oh, (under her breath) Damn. (She's swinging her right leg slightly.)

S: Notice your leg.

Mrs. R S: I-I'm shaking it.

S: Exaggerate that, shaking it harder.

Mrs. R S: (shakes leg harder, it begins to look like a kick)

S: Can you imagine doing that to your mother?

Mrs. R S: No, but I-I-I-I'm sure feeling pissed at her.

S: Say this to her.

Mrs. R S: I feel pissed off at you! I hate you!

S: Say that louder.

Mrs. R S: I hate you! (volume higher, but still some holding back)

S: Louder!

Mrs. R S: I HATE YOU, YOU GODDAMNED BITCH. (She sticks her leg out and kicks the chair over.)

S: Now switch back.

Mrs. R M: (voice sounds much weaker now) I-I guess I didn't show you much love. I really felt it, but I was unhappy and bitter. You know all I had to go through with your father and brother. You were the only one I could talk to. I'm sorry . . . I wanted you to be happy . . . I wanted so much for you.

Mrs. R S: You sure did! . . . I know you did love me, Mother, I know you were unhappy (voice much softer now, but sounding real, not whiny or mechanical). I guess I did some things that were ba—wrong, too. I was always trying to keep you off my back.

Mrs. R M: Yes, you were pretty sarcastic to me, too. And that hurt.

Mrs. R S: I wish you had told me. I didn't think you were hurt at all.

Mrs. R M: Well, that's all over now.

Mrs. R S: Yeah, it is. I guess there's no use blaming you. You're not around any more.

S: Can you forgive your mother now?

Mrs. R S: Mother, I forgive you . . . I really do forgive you. (starts crying again, but not in the whiny way of before. She sounds genuinely grieving and cries for a couple of minutes.)

S: Now switch back.

Mrs. R M: I forgive you too, dear. You have to go on now. You can't keep blaming me forever. I made my mistakes but you have your own family and you're doing okay.

S: Do you feel ready to say goodbye now?

Mrs. R S: Yes. I-I think so (starts to sob). Goodbye, Mother, goodbye. (breaks down, cries for a few minutes)

S: What do you experience now?

Mrs. R: I feel better. I feel . . . kind of relieved, like a weight is off my back. I feel calm.

S: Now that you've said goodbye to her, to this dead person, can you go around and say hello to the live people here, to the group?

Mrs. R: Yes, I'd like that.

(She goes around the room, greets people, touches some, embraces others. Many in the group are tearful. When she reaches her husband, she starts crying again, and tells him she loves him, and they embrace.)

Wholeness and Self-support

Stephen A. Tobin

"Time's up," I said. Jim hesitated a moment, then slowly got up. I also stood. Instead of moving toward the door, Jim looked at me. Then he smiled, walked over to me, and hugged me rather woodenly. He then stepped back and said, "I've been thinking of going to Colorado for a while." He looked at me searchingly and I felt uncomfortable. I imagined he was waiting for me to give my opinion about his going to Colorado. "Are you asking me if I think you should go?"

"Yeah, I guess I am."

"Jim, it doesn't matter to me if you go to Colorado or not."

"Yeah, well ... you know, I don't think I *really* want to go to Colorado at all. I feel more like going to the beach right now." Another searching look.

"I don't care if you go to the beach, either."

A disappointed look now. He backed away, said he had to be going. He wasn't through yet, though.

"You know, I just about decided to stop screwing around. I have been thinking about going back to college, maybe medical school."

"Look Jim, I really don't give a damn what you do; it just doesn't make any difference to me if you go to Colorado, medical school, or Disneyland. You're still trying to get me to approve of your decisions, to support you—"

"Yeah, yeah, you're right," he interrupted. "Well, guess I'll be

Portions of this paper originally appeared as "Self-Support, Wholeness, and Gestalt Therapy" in *Voices, the Art and Science of Psychotherapy*, Vol. 5, No. 4, Winter/Spring 1969–1970, pp. 5–12.

going." He again started edging towards the door. "Oh, look, I hate to ask you, but I'm broke and don't have enough gas to get home. Could you lend me a buck?"

This dialogue is from a recent session with a young man I have been seeing in group therapy and infrequent individual sessions for about a year. He had a great deal of previous therapy before coming to me, about ten years of analysis and analytically-oriented therapy. Despite all the "insight" he has obtained, he still regards himself as "sick" and leads a chaotic, unrewarding existence. Instead of making his own decisions and supporting himself emotionally, he continually attempts to manipulate others into taking responsibility for his life.

Although the analysts could make a convincing case for unresolved oedipal conflicts within Jim, such an explanation is irrelevant to Jim's major problems, which are existential. Underlying his continual need for validation from others are feelings of incompleteness, of inadequacy, of being split up into many parts.

I believe that the desperate search outside oneself for self-esteem gratifications seen in Jim is also the major symptom of our culture, affecting the successful and well-functioning as well as the failures and "mentally ill." The basic feeling of worthlessness found in most people much of the time is, I believe, the motivating force behind the politician's striving for power, the businessman's dishonest practices, the black militant's hatred of "whitey," and the welfare recipient's attempts to cheat a humiliating, infantilizing Establishment.

As Fritz Perls has pointed out, any system of therapy that does not result in the patient's being able to provide his own validation as a human being is incomplete. The purpose of this paper is to discuss certain features of this ubiquitous problem of our times.

The emotional state of one who needs to manipulate others into validating him can best be described as a feeling of incompleteness. I find that when I myself am unable to provide my own self-esteem supports I feel empty, worthless, tense, and vaguely dissatisfied. I am partially unaware of what is going on around me, and have fleeting, scattered thoughts about things I "should do." I sense that I am *missing* something and think I must search outside myself for it. In the past I attempted to fill myself up with material objects, with praise from others, or by doing work I imagined would bring me prestige or power. Even major achievements, however, only made me feel worthwhile for a very brief time, and then I usually became depressed.

This pattern I have noticed in my own life has been reported to me by many other people. For example, a physician I know imagined that he would feel complete when he had established a successful practice. After eleven years of college and specialized medical training, and another four years of building up his practice, he had achieved his dream. He had "arrived," but, as you may have already guessed, his achievement left him feeling empty and despairing.

A sixty-five year old patient of mine had come to me after fifteen years of analytically-oriented therapy. She had hung on to unsatisfactory relationships with her therapist and her husband because she felt basically worthless and empty, and believed that someday they would give her what they had previously been withholding. She would then, she imagined, feel complete and whole. When I spoke with the ex-therapist I learned of his part in this neurotic relationship: as he spoke of her, his pessimism and his opinion that she could never stand on her own came through his technical description of her "case."

Jim, the patient I described earlier, is luckier than the physician and the elderly patient, for he is dealing with this existential problem while still young. If he were unfortunate enough to be "well-adjusted" to our psychotic society, he would probably have started on the same path as the physician, only to realize years later that what he was searching for all that time was something that only he could give himself.

The opposite of incompleteness is a state in which the individual feels complete within himself and functions in a wholistic fashion. Behaviorially, wholeness is a state of being in which an organism functions in a congruent way. Plants and animals are usually whole within themselves; even when they are in conflict with the outside world, they are generally functioning for themselves in a way that is in their best interest.

A newborn human being is whole emotionally and physiologically. When a baby experiences pain, its entire body will move in an undifferentiated way. If he's happy, he laughs with his whole being. As the baby grows, however, he begins to become more differentiated: his range of emotions increases and he can perform more varied physical and intellectual activities. He learns to move just one limb at a time, to differentiate sadness from anger, to distinguish between past, present and future. It is this tremendous differentiation that makes man so adaptable. Often, however, this differentiation develops without integration, and with this differentiation comes his greatest curse as well as his greatest benefit: he becomes split up and, in our culture, rather than being for himself, he soon becomes against himself. Rather than using his abilities to get what he wants from his environment, he tortures and tears himself apart with warring wishes, demands and "shoulds."

The most destructive split within Western man is the one that is created during childhood between the controller and the controllee, or, in gestalt therapy jargon, between the topdog and the underdog. The topdog is the "shouldnik" or conscience that is constantly blaming, scolding, threatening, and making promises of rewards that are never kept. For example, my topdog told me that I could relax and not do anything for a while after I finished my last paper. As soon as I was finished, however, he said "You're really going strong now; why don't you just start a new paper right away?"

While most people's topdogs are known to them, they are relatively unaware of the tactics and styles of the other part of the split in their personalities, the underdog. The underdog is the sneakily rebellious part of the person who tries to defeat the topdog by playing helpless, making excuses, ignoring the topdog, etc. My underdog didn't say to my topdog, "Go to hell, I'm *not* going to do any more writing now." It said "I can't write any more now, I'm too tired. I'll do some writing tomorrow." As is usually the case, my underdog won out, albeit sneakily; my last paper was completed over a year and a half ago!

This particular split is something I have found in all the clients I have ever seen. It is so prevalent that most philosophers, theologians and other scholars have made the mistake of believing that it is necessary and inevitable. The Bible, for example, places great emphasis on the original sinfulness of man and on the necessity of his continually attempting to control and atone for his sinfulness so that he can attain salvation. Freud believed that there is an inevitable conflict between society and individual needs (reflected in superego-ego-id conflicts) that requires man to exert the greatest efforts at control and compromise. Even existential philosophers, such as Sartre, seem to think that there is an inherent split in man that makes a hopeless, endless quest after a being he can never attain the only recourse for man. What Sartre doesn't realize is that hopelessness is merely the other side of the coin of hope, and that both are looking toward the future and intellectualizing about life.

In contrast to this Western idea of the inevitability of being split up, Eastern religions and philosophies say that man can achieve wholeness. One of the major purposes of meditation in Zen Buddhism is to achieve wholeness both within the self and between the self and the rest of the universe.

I also believe that man can achieve wholeness. I don't think very many people achieve a continuous state of wholeness within themselves, but I think it is possible for all people to do so on a moment-to-moment basis. In fact, I think that this achievement of wholeness, of internal harmony of body, mind and spirit, may be man's most important task.

At this point I want to say something of how I experience wholeness on the infrequent occasions that I do. I am sensorially aware of the present; I see, hear, smell, touch, and feel without the intrusion of thoughts. I use thinking only when a conflict is experienced and for the purpose of considering various alternatives for resolving the conflict. I know when I have found the best solution: my feeling of completeness returns.

I am aware that, as Steve Tobin, I am alone in the universe. I am not *lonely,* but realize the inevitability of my death in a much more profound way than I do when I am feeling incomplete. (In fact, I would say that I don't really believe I shall die when I am feeling split, even though I "know" it intellectually.) I realize that no one is more of an expert about what is right for me than I myself am. I also realize that I don't need power, prestige, love, or lots of money; these things will not make me feel any more worthwhile as a person.

Paradoxically, I feel a sense of community, of being a part of the entire universe. Since I am not observing myself, I have no sense of "I" as separate from the universe. I have a sense of the unity of the universe, and see myself as neither more nor less important than any other part of the universe. This feeling of no sense of self seems to contradict the feeling of aloneness I described in the preceding paragraph, but I do not experience any contradiction when I feel whole.

Freedom is a very important part of the experience for me. I realize that I had innumerable invisible, enslaving bonds between myself and others that I have dissolved, at least for the time being. I am also free in the sense that I know I can make my own decisions, that I am not enslaved to the past, to expectations of the future, or to any other person.

I also feel very much alive and am in touch with all my emotions. Sometimes these are painful, sometimes they are joyful but, whatever the emotions, I have no need to avoid them. Experiencing "pleasure" is unimportant to me, and I find myself becoming annoyed at anyone attempting to attenuate my painful feelings by comforting me.

Finally, and most importantly, I find I can really become involved with people in a non-defensive way. Since *I don't need* anything from them I can risk asking directly for *what I want* from them, even though refusal might be unpleasant. I find I can really see people at these times, instead of viewing them only as potential enemies or as potential helpers.

In many ways I am a very pessimistic person. I don't have much hope for man in general; I am afraid that we shall blow ourselves or pollute ourselves or over-populate ourselves clear off the planet. When it comes to individuals, however, namely my patients, I have a great amount of faith and trust in them. *My trust is that, if they take a stand on what they are doing, whatever it is, and do it openly and directly and completely, they will do the "right things" for themselves and others, and they will be more alive and whole.*

I trust people's natural functioning—their impulses, their feelings, and their senses—but I do not trust their judgments and their theories about themselves, about life, and about other people. I trust that if they do what they *want* to do, they'll do what fits them and what is growthful for them. I don't trust them if they do what they think they "should" do.

How do I and the patient know when something fits him? To answer this, I'll first say how most people keep themselves from finding out what's right for them.

One way is to base their decisions on rules and moral standards, for instance, deciding to suppress anger toward others because "that's not nice," not crying because "that's weak," etc.

Another unnatural basis people use for making decisions is their rationality. For example, one patient tried to decide whether or not to ask his girl to marry him by writing a list of her virtues and comparing it with a list of her vices.

In contrast, the natural way to make decisions is to base them on one's whole being, on logic *and* feeling *and* morality *and* on one's senses. For example, I decided to divorce my first wife after my left arm, which had felt dead and lifeless for days, livened up when I thought of divorcing her. I used my mind to think of various alternatives and my body told me what was right for me.

A common attitude that is unhealthy and accepted by most people in our culture is that life is to be lived *for* something else. Most people don't live just to live; they continually do things for future goals; for material, intellectual or spiritual success; for posterity; for retirement; or even for the betterment of man in general. Nature is regarded by these people as something to be used and conquered; similarly, they regard their own natural selves—their feelings and their bodies and their senses—as less important than their mind's fantasies and ideals. They assume that they have to be split up, controlled and half-alive if they are to exist in our society.

Since persons who practice psychotherapy are part of our culture, they generally accept these cultural attitudes about life, man and nature. Freud thought that there was an inevitable conflict between the demands of the id—which he conceived of as completely amoral, alogical, and unrealistically oriented towards immediate gratification—and the very existence of society. He thought that in order for the society to continue to run in a relatively smooth fashion, certain ego defenses are absolutely necessary.

Most therapists and patients implicitly agree in their philosophical assumptions about life, nature, and man. In some ways they reinforce each other's beliefs and restrict therapy. The result is that the patient does not grow in ways he might be capable of growing.

I do not believe that man's purpose should be to live life for something else such as for some future good, a job, a cause, or for anything else. I really don't have any shoulds about the purpose of life. I do have preferences, however, and my preference for my patients is that they learn how to be as alive and aware and as free as possible.

I'm sure many therapists would agree in the abstract with this preference. I think, however, that many would disagree with certain specific choices I would suggest that patients make. For example, I believe that sacrificing the present for some uncertain future good is deadening and is a bad choice for most people. I think that abusing one's body for some financial gain—for instance, doing therapy for sixty hours a week to make a lot of money—is a neurotic, deadening choice. I think that merely putting up with a current hardship because this will enable one to get to heaven more easily is a deadening choice.

I don't mean that I believe people should impulsively do whatever they feel like doing on the spur of the moment, or that they should never do anything that is difficult. I do believe, however, that, in any conflict situation, there are choices that lead to greater deadness and stagnation, and choices that lead to greater aliveness.

The alive person functions in a wholistic manner, being congruent in his use of his mind, his body, and his senses. He trusts his natural functioning rather than placing his trust in outside ideologies or specific authorities. He feels free, realizing he always has choices, and therefore feels personally responsible for what happens to him. He exists sensorially in the present: seeing, hearing, smelling, and touching, using his computer only in the service of his senses and his body. He views himself as a process rather than as a fixed "thing" and he can flow between contact and withdrawal, activity and passivity, loving and hating. He is aware of death as a reality and accepts its inevitability rather than fearfully fighting it all the time.

In contrast to the alive person, the dead person functions in a disconnected manner, his mind and his body being at odds rather than being congruent. He is apt to develop such diseases as hypertension, ulcers, colitis, asthma, and perhaps even cancer because he listens to and trusts his "shoulds" and his computer and what "experts" tell him rather than his natural functioning. He feels trapped and sees himself as a helpless victim of outside forces, and feels he is not responsible for what happens to him. He is always fantasizing about the past or the future, and consequently has largely lost the ability to exist in his senses in the present. He views himself as a static "thing" and becomes upset when he finds himself behaving in a way that he did not predict. He thinks he has to be the same all the time and generally tries to have a consistent "character." He tries to deny death as a reality and, when he can't, tries to protect himself against it, thereby never taking any of the risks of living.

While most of the people I know fall more towards the dead end of this polarity, I make the assumption that it is possible for anyone to become more like my description of the alive person. This existential-humanistic assumption of gestalt therapy is what makes it unique as a therapy and distinguishes it from therapies which reinforce the splits in their patients rather than healing them.

Now, what are the implications for therapy of these ideas I have about life? First of all, I refuse to help anyone become more dead. If a client complains, for example, that he gets in trouble with friends because he is too blunt and honest with them, I do not automatically assume that there is something wrong with him, and that he has to learn to "control" himself. Perhaps he needs new friends who would welcome his honesty. In any case, I would want him to consider all the possibilities that are open to him. If a person is experiencing despair because he has achieved a great deal, yet finds his life meaningless, I will not work with him on finding hobbies or new achievements, which would probably result in a further deadening of himself and even greater despair in the future. Rather, I will suggest that he stay with his despair. What generally happens is that he comes up with some new ways of experiencing the world rather than continuing to look into the future for fulfillment.

Many people, of course, are not interested in becoming more alive and more real. Instead, they want to be able to play their old games with greater payoff and, when I refuse to play with them, they leave therapy.

I believe that people are happiest when they freely make choices about what they do. For example, I have been faced frequently with the following conflict: I hear of an anti-war meeting and tell myself I should go to it to support the movement against the Vietnam war. I really don't want to go, however, because I imagine that the meeting will be, as I have found most such meetings, boring. I further imagine that, if I attend the meeting, I shall either start thinking about other things and not really hear what's going on, or I shall make my body strained and tight as I force myself to attend to the speeches. If I imagine just skipping the meeting, I feel guilty.

Rather than blindly doing either because I thought I "should," I have generally made the choice to skip the meeting and to do something else for the peace movement, such as donating money. Such a choice has always satisfied both my conscience *and* my own physical and emotional needs.

In dealing with patients, I try to get them in touch with the ways in which they generally try to resolve conflicts and, if possible, alternative solutions that would lead to greater freedom and aliveness and wholeness.

Because most therapists are themselves split up into warring parts, it is difficult for them to provide an environment in which their patients can begin to experiment with making their life decisions in a more organismic, wholistic manner.

In order to create a climate in which a patient can achieve a sense of wholeness and the ability to provide his own support, the therapist should be able to support himself or at least be aware of how he is incomplete. Without awareness of his own incompleteness, therapists are apt to become involved in a variety of mutual manipulation games with patients.

For example, the therapist who needs to have his patients admire him, agree with him, and ape him is easily trapped by the person who plays the "good patient." The "good patient" picks up the therapist's jargon very quickly. He is particularly obvious in group therapy, where he plays the role of assistant therapist.

Therapists who view themselves as "healers" of sick persons tend to be vulnerable to patients who play the sick role as a way of manipulating the environment. These patients never really want to "get well" even though they pretend to put complete faith in the "doctor." Most therapists see their clients as sick and helpless to varying degrees and needing their advice and guidance. They worry a great deal about what catastrophic effects their interventions and behavior will have on their fragile little "sickies."

This attitude is, in reality, a disguised authoritarianism. It is part of our authoritarian culture, in which all persons are trained from birth to look to others for support and validation. With this kind of background almost none of my clients are able or willing to take responsibility for themselves when they enter therapy with me.

Some clients are very direct and open about wanting me to support them, and leave therapy when I refuse. They see themselves as weak and helpless and as unable to stand on their own two feet. Many therapists buy these self-views and believe that if they support the client for a while, they will eventually be able to wean him. I'm sure this is sometimes true; I have had patients, however, who had finally left therapists very little changed after ten, twelve, or fifteen years of being supported. It has been my impression that these therapists were authoritarians who needed to have dependent, submissive patients and, without being aware of it, didn't really want them to grow up.

In contrast, the therapist who does not *need anything* from his patients realizes the patient is just as autonomous as he is and therefore is just as responsible for his behavior. Not needing anything, he sets the patient free. He is only responsible to himself, not the patient. In a very fundamental sense, he doesn't care *about* the patient, although he may care *for* him. He responds to the patient as he is right there in front of him, not as the patient says he is outside the office or as he intends to be in the future.

I take the position that each person must find his own way in life, that, although he can learn from others, he is ultimately responsible for his own behavior. I don't see myself as a "doctor" who can "cure" my patients or as a judge who can tell them what they should or shouldn't do. I don't know more about the patient than he knows about himself. Hence I do not and cannot take responsibility for his behavior, growth or lack of growth. Of all the tenets of gestalt therapy, this is perhaps the most important, the most difficult to comprehend, and the most controversial. The word responsibility is much used in our culture and usually is synonomous with "duty," doing something one really doesn't want to do. *That type of responsibility is completely the opposite of what I mean by responsibility.* In my opinion, the most irresponsible thing a person can do is to try to force himself to do something that he doesn't want to do, *out of duty.*

To me, responsiblity is freedom, the ability to respond in a variety of ways to a given situation. Stated another way, responsibility is the ability to make choices. Of course the number of choices a person has open to him is always finite; he always has limits. Within these limits, however, he is free to do what he wants to do. If he chooses to do what his computer tells him (making decisions solely on the basis of logic) or what his judge tells him (making decisions solely on the basis of morality), then he is being irresponsible. If, however, he attempts to do what fits his computer *and* his judge *and* his senses, then he is being free and responsible.

Let me give an example of irresponsible behavior. A patient is very unhappy in her marriage. She is depressed, physically run down; her children are unhappy because she is unable to give to them; and her husband is unhappy because he isn't getting what he needs. Yet she refuses to consider divorce because her thinking tells her divorce is bad. She is being irresponsible to herself for not listening to what her body, her children and her husband are telling her. If, of course, she disregarded her moral precepts and impulsively got a divorce, she would still be making an irresponsible choice, for she would still be disregarding a part of herself.

Now for an example of responsible behavior. A woman is having an affair with another man and is considering divorce. Despite the fact that the relationship with her lover is more satisfying to her than her relationship with her husband, she does not feel right about getting a divorce, splitting up her home, and ending the relationship with her husband. She realizes that she has never really confronted her husband with her dissatisfactions, and decides to end the affair, despite the pain that choice gives her, and to begin to work on the marriage by becoming involved with her husband in marital therapy.

The problem that most people have concerning freedom is that they either tell themselves they have no choices, or they resent and refuse to accept their limits. Rather than work with the alternatives available, they do nothing, and complain about the alternatives that are not available.

For example, I do not have the choice of being a major league baseball player because I am too old and do not have the physical ability, but I could be something other than a psychologist if I wanted to change my occupation. Or I could decide not to work at all at a job and grow my own food to feed myself.

A black man with little education may not have the choice open to him to become a clinical psychologist but he might have the choice of being a postman or washing cars. "Some choice!" you might say. Well, in my opinion, the recognition that he does have some choices makes him better off *existentially* than the wealthy white executive who thinks he can do nothing else but hang on to the job he has.

I find that most patients attempt to avoid the freedom of taking responsibility for what happens in therapy by placing me in the role of topdog, and then trying to manipulate me into providing support, guidance and comfort for them. I never, however, give to patients the kind of support that implies that they are helpless and weak and need to be coddled. I will, however, express warmth and pleasure towards them when I feel it. This results in the reinforcing of their openness and steps toward growth, but it is not intended by me as support or as a way of manipulating them to grow.

While patients sometimes ask for support directly, they usually ask for it indirectly in ways they are unaware of. I realized, for example, after a long time with one patient, that after every statement he looked at me and began nodding his head. I would nod my head, he would feel supported, and then continue talking. When I stopped nodding my head, he became aware of how he was using me to validate his statements.

The way I usually deal with patients' indirect attempts to get support is to refuse to respond to them. I typically find that patients have a whole repertoire of measures to manipulate support from the environment. For example:

P: I don't know what to say. (a long silence)

P: I-I don't know what to do here. (a long silence)

P: (tearfully) I can't ever find anyone to rely on.

T: (sarcastically) You poor thing.

P: You son of a bitch!

T: (chuckling) You don't sound so weak and helpless now; in fact you sound pretty powerful. Do you know what to do now? Or do you still think I have to guide you by the hand?

P: No, I know what I want.

T: Could you imagine asking for it directly instead of trying to manipulate me with your helpless act?

P: Yes.

With this patient I was quite blunt. I sometimes attempt to "show" patients how they are trying to trick me into supporting them, but I usually find this ineffective. They want to be given something—*anything*—by the therapist, and will even see an interpretation as advice or guidance. For example, one patient played helpless with me for months and always managed to frustrate himself and me in each session. We worked on this for months without any change until I refused to do anything with him until he took a stand. There were many sessions during which I just ignored him and read a book.

So far I have mostly discussed how patients avoid taking responsibility for themselves in therapy and avoid being free. How do they assume responsibility for what they want? In my opinion, they do this by asking directly for what they want from me. This is the essential feature of self-support and self-responsibility: *discovering what you want and taking steps to get it. If you want something that someone else can give you, taking responsibility is asking them directly and openly for what you want.*

I am coming to realize that there are no such things as neurotic "problems." Instead, there are just neurotic styles of living. Therefore, I am taking the content of my patients' "problems" less and less seriously. I am finding that even when they resolve a conflict and are feeling content and happy, they are not satisfied, but immediately find some new way to make themselves miserable. The following is a typical example.

Pt: Oh, I'm so mad at that place! I wish I didn't have to work there any more!

Steve: You tell yourself you *have* to?

Pt: (sarcastically) Well, I don't if I don't mind starving.

Steve: Could you imagine getting another job? One that you would like more?

Pt: No, I really couldn't . . . I probably wouldn't know what to do with myself if I didn't have that place bugging me.

Steve: Okay, I want you to pretend you've just inherited a million dollars. You don't have to work at all.

Pt: (with a big sigh) Ohhh, that really feels good; I really feel relieved.

Steve: Okay, stay with that and tell me what happens.

Pt: Well, I would take a trip around the world, buy a bunch of new clothes—

Steve: (interrupting) You've gotten out of the fantasy. You're saying "I would" rather than "I am."

Pt: Oh, you're right. Okay, I'm taking a trip around the world. On a nice slow boat. Nothing to do except relax. I'm sitting on the deck of the boat. Looking out over the ocean. I feel so relaxed, not a care in the world. (A long silence ensues. Then the client starts to appear restless.)

Steve: What's happening now?

Pt: I'm starting to feel antsy. I'm getting bored. Oh! Why that's ridiculous! I'm thinking about that goddamn job again.

Steve: (laughing) I guess you better give your million dollars away and go back to your job.

Pt: (looking at me, surprised) You know, I don't think I'd know what to do with myself if I had what I say I want.

Steve: I don't think so either. Would you be willing to take responsibility for that? Instead of always complaining about your job? Admit you like it?

Pt: No. (laughs) I think that part of the fun is that I get to complain about it. (then ruefully) But I really don't enjoy myself there. It really does make me miserable.

If this woman had been willing to stay with her restlessness while having her fantasy, she would probably have begun to become aware of emptiness, loneliness, and fears of getting close to others. Instead, she ran away into her "conflict" about her job.

This hanging-on to misery and conflict is, in my opinion, one of the most prevalent but least understood features of modern man. I find it over and over in clients who have been in therapy for years, both with me and other therapists. I think it is so prevalent that it may even partially explain the seemingly impossible nature of our quest towards world peace. People who have spent a lifetime being in conflict both with themselves and everybody else in their environment are incapable of doing without it, even though it does make them tense, anxious, frightened, and unhappy. Having a peaceful world with no conflict between nations might be intolerable to many people, for it would force them to face their own emptiness.

The way most people try to deal with their misery is through the use of hope. They are always working towards the future, hoping that things will either get better by themselves or they will be able to "improve" or grow enough so that they will no longer be unhappy. One of the steps most people have to go through in successful therapy is to give up hope. Most people are unwilling to do this at first because they then become depressed and despairing. When they have given up illusory beliefs and ideals, hopes for the future, covert ideas of immortality, etc., they have nothing left—or so they think.

Many existentialist philosophers have seen modern man to this point of existential despair, but they have stopped there. They seem to believe that the ultimate awareness is to see the universe as ridiculous and man's plight as absurd. I see this as the ultimate result of basing one's existence on concepts, on beliefs and on ideas; in short, on one's computer rather than on one's senses and feelings. The man who says that the universe is meaningless and absurd is almost as misguided, in my opinion, as the man who says that it's meaningful. After all, what meaning *could* the universe have? If I eat a good meal or read a good book or listen to some fine music or have an exciting sexual experience, what *meaning* could that have? To say that the universe is meaningless is to assume that it could have a meaning other than the satisfaction of the experience itself.

You may be asking, at this point, if you give up the idea of the universe having a meaning, on what can you base your existence? *In my opinion, the only thing that you can base your existence on beyond hope, beyond thinking, is your own organism: your eyes, your ears, your bodily functioning, your emotions.* Until you wake up and start using your organism, you must stay with and face your despair and hopelessness. If you are willing to do this, you usually explode into some real way of existing in the world. This is what living in the now means.

It is, of course, impossible for anyone to live completely in the present and not look toward the future occasionally. But all of my more successful therapy sessions result in the patient's "waking up" to the now, what Fritz Perls used to call a "mini-satori." The process from half-awakeness to waking up is usually as follows. The patient comes in and plays his usual games with me and/or himself. These games are ways of avoiding pain and also indirect ways of trying to get what he wants.

For instance, the patient who avoids his emptiness and loneliness tries to keep my attention on him by chattering about his past week. By a combination of working with him on becoming more aware of his games and my refusing to play the games with him, I help him get in touch with the ways he frightens himself away from trying to get what he wants directly. If the patient sees the foolishness of his games for the moment and stops playing them, he arrives at a state of impasse; he is too frightened to take the step of doing what he really wants, but no longer is able or willing to use his usual methods to defend against what he wants. He is frustrated and paralyzed. If he is willing to stay with this impasse, he generally starts to feel despairing, empty and lost. I still refuse to "help" him beyond encouraging him to stay with his experience. The result is always some kind of explosion: into grief, joy, love, or anger. At this point the person is whole. After the explosion, the feeling of wholeness, of not being in conflict, remains, at least for a while. Here is an example of such a process:

Pt: I feel stuck, I don't know what to do.

Steve: Stay with that, let yourself feel that.

Pt: Okay, I can't do anything else anyway . . . I feel like I'm at a dead end, no place else to go . . . I think I want to stop working now. I don't know what else to do. I guess I'm just stuck.

Steve: I think you want to get away from being stuck. You want to avoid the feeling.

Pt: Yeah, I guess you're right . . . I-I really feel lost.

Steve: Close your eyes and imagine yourself literally lost.

Pt: I'm out in the desert.

Steve: Keep us in touch with what you experience.

Pt: It's night and very cold. There's nobody and nothing around. I feel scared.

Steve: Stay with that; let yourself be afraid.

Pt: Now . . . I see some eyes looking at me. It's-it's some kind of an animal . . . or person. Both animal and human. A face moves back and forth . . . towards me like this (gestures towards him and away from him). It's frightening. It has its teeth bared—looks ferocious. Long hair, evil, nasty looking. It wants to eat me up I think! I want to run away!

Steve: Okay, let yourself run.

Pt: Okay, I'm running away, I can't see where I'm going. I stumble, I'm falling down. I hear that thing behind me. It's going to eat me up!

Steve: Can you let it?

Pt: Oh, I can't! I'm scared, petrified! But I can't get away. It's getting closer and closer. It's got its teeth in me (patient writhes around in pain) . . . chewing me up . . . I'm gone. I'm dead. (a long silence)

Steve: What do you experience now?

Pt: I feel ... peaceful. Quiet. Calm. Relaxed. I just want to sit here and enjoy it.

Steve: Okay, do that.

Pt: (After several minutes) I'm beginning to feel some trembling in my body. I want to open my eyes. (looks around the room) Oh! Things look so bright, so clear. The colors. So vivid! (looks at me) I see you. I think I've never really seen you before. You know what I mean? (Patient moves around the room, looking at other members of the group. Everyone is transfixed.)

For a moment, we are all alive—really alive—and we know, all of us, what it means to be alive and joyful and whole and a part of the universe.

Thou Art That: Projection and Play

John B. Enright

"You're projecting!" is a frequent comment in therapy and encounter groups. Whatever else the response to this ploy, it is usually valid to say, "Of course." The practice of experiencing my own feeling or potential for action as being the property of someone or something "out there" instead of my own is universal. Sick or well, we all do it frequently; the "sick" differ only in doing it more tenaciously. The purpose of this note is to describe a method of harnessing this basic human process; instead of wasting energy opposing or criticizing it, to "go with it" as an exercise that can enhance awareness and develop feelings and perceptions more vividly. It is not a new technique. Artists—particularly Japanese sumi e painters—have used it for centuries. I have run into it as a parlor game, and even seen it referred to in a Reader's Digest article. Fritz Perls developed some variations at some length in *Gestalt Therapy*. Somehow, however, therapists and group leaders have overlooked its simplicity and power. I have used this method perhaps a hundred times in an extensive way, and in a partial way many more, and feel ready to present some concrete instances of its use, and a few of the endless number of possible variations.

In a therapy or encounter group, I usually introduce the exercise during a pause or break by suggesting that each person look around the room and pick an object that stands out vividly for him. Everyone then spends a couple of minutes working by himself *identifying*

Reprinted from *Psychotherapy: Theory, Research and Practice*, Vol. 9, No. 2, Summer 1972, pp. 153–156.

with his object, i.e., making statements as though he *were* the object; describing it, but saying "I" instead of "it." When most seem to have stopped this process I suggest that everyone go back into the exercise and say one or two more things. More often than not, the point of stopping is just when the person is getting close to something particularly interesting. Almost always, a few people in the group get quite excited by what they have run into, and share their projections with the group. Surprisingly strong feeling and involvement is developed within a minute or two by the exercise; this can happen even in first meetings of groups up to 200 in size. A woman, for instance, identifying with a beam in the ceiling, became very distressed as she heard herself say, as the beam, "I'm very old-fashioned and uselessly ornate . . . I have a heavy load to bear . . . and I'm not getting very much help; the nearest other beam is a long way away, and I have to carry this part of the load alone." Being close to tears, she asked to stop at that point, but an hour or so later was able to report many important connections with, and some new realizations about, her present life situation. Another woman, identifying with a bright colored section of the wall, became quite depressed and cried when she realized that she, as the wall, was unfinished at the top. She had the courage to stay with this painful perception, and within a few minutes was joyful over the fact that this gap actually left her free to grow and be finished in her own way. A man, identifying with a loudspeaker, commented that although he talked a lot, he initiated nothing, but only passed on what others said. I always do the exercise along with the group, frequently with quite involving results for myself. On one occasion, I was not enjoying a group I was working with and rather resented being there. I "happened" to choose a large candleholder, and the following sentences came popping out: "I'm beautiful and sturdy, but have no candle at present; I'm empty. My job is to give light, but I'm not doing it right now." When the group and I stopped laughing, I was freer to get down to work without resentment or distraction.

If the reader has not stopped and tried this experiment already, I suggest doing so. However there is something about the enhancing effect of a group, and seeing someone else use the method well, that makes a group a better setting in which to begin. It is not possible to convey verbally how intense and involving this simple exercise often becomes.

Frequently, when a person begins to "run down" it is possible to manipulate his object or the situation in some way to keep the flow going. One woman, working with a pot with a lid, kept emphasizing how heavy and tightly closed her lid was. I reached over and touched the lid, intending to lift it. In a panic, she leaped on me, and tore my hand off the top; For a moment she really was that pot, and no shrink was going to get *her* lid off! A furled flag can be unfurled, a chair sat upon, a light dimmed or brightened, while a person is identifying with it, and dramatic changes in affect and perception may result.

After a few people have shared their projections, we often begin to run into the "rehearsal" effect: those who have waited too long lose some of the spontaneity of their choice. At this point, I often bring out a box of toy figures and objects, and suggest that people come up one at a time as they feel ready, select one that stands out, and work with it. Since they do not see the objects until after committing themselves to work, rehearsal is not possible. Any toy or object is a candidate for the box. I continually have to replenish it, as people frequently ask to keep a figure that was particularly meaningful. On one occasion a psychologist became quite excited by this technique when it was presented at a seminar. Having no time to get to a toy store, as his group met in the following hour, he used the objects from a Stanford-Binet kit, with good results.

Again, the variety of response to these stimulus figures is endless. My favorite is still the sour and self-critical man with a toy buffalo. Suddenly, as the buffalo, he was strong, noble and protective of his herd. After a pause he noticed a small bit of plastic sticking to the rear leg and commented, "Even my shit is useful; the Indians dry it and use it for fuel." A woman using a toy gorilla was describing her strength until she noticed a slight defect in the back, and gasped with horror, "I'm wounded!" and went into a very intense death fantasy.

These last examples point up a crucial way in which this method differs from most fantasy and dream techniques. The object provides a recurrent "nudge" into areas that might not emerge in pure fantasy. As person B observes A working with his object, it is obvious to B that A is selecting quite idiosyncratically from the possibilities of the object, missing some "obvious" features, and choosing very peculiar ones that B would never have dreamed of. Person A, however, experiences himself not as choosing, but as being compelled and pulled by what truly seem to him the objective features of the object. He can resist saying what he sees if he feels disturbed or threatened, but he does not feel a choice in seeing it. The subjective experience of doing the identification experiment has been compared with being on a roller coaster; once on it, you go the route, with all its twists and turns and ups and downs. Frequently, after a glance at his object, a person will cease looking at it, and instead work with his fantasy of the object—looking away or closing his eyes as he works. Thus one man, as a toy sports car, was going on about how flashy and elegant he was. Noticing he was looking off into space as he talked, I suggested he get back to simple description. As soon as he again began looking at his toy, he seemed startled, and started talking soberly about all his nicks and scratches, and wondering if he had been in an accident.

When a person begins to slow down in his identification process, there are many ways to renew the flow, usually growing out of the particular way he has talked up to that point. I may suggest he say something to the group as his animal or object, or perhaps wave my magic wand and allow him to make one change for the better in himself as the object. If a person comes to hate the object (himself), I may suggest he choose another, and then create a dialogue between the two. Many times, a person becomes fascinated with another's choice; he may pick up and carry on when the first person has finished. On a few occasions, the whole group has worked in turn with the same object. Very quickly, the group members learn not to speak up when someone else is working, recognizing that their perceptions, completely valid for them, can only be an interruption for someone else. In one group the phrase, "that's *your* gorilla, not mine" became a shorthand term for telling a person not to confuse his process with another's—in the current slang, not to lay his trip on someone else.

Several times, after most people have worked individually, group members have begun to interact from their toy object roles. This has led to very humorous and unlikely but quite productive confrontations. (I was amazed how much a golf ball and a scorpion had to say to each other.) Long-standing group problems have been solved in minutes with this exercise. One quite firm, independent woman had stayed on the fringe during all her time in the group, and people had given up pointing this out and trying to reach her. She chose a toy Mack truck, and was very pleased with her strength and ability to carry a heavy load. Then she noticed her cab had room for only one person. Her distress and loneliness stimulated by this perception were so touching that several people in the group opened up to her, and her relation to the group underwent a permanent change. Another time, two alligators had a forty-five minute conversation about life in the swamp. One emphasized how powerful and dangerous she was; the other, how vulnerable—alligator shoes being popular then. The assumptions of these two people about life and themselves became clearer than hours of ordinary conversation could have made them.

The above examples are only a few of the possible ways to develop this method in group work. Others keep spontaneously happening; there seems no limit to a group's creativity. Besides suggesting innovations and variations in this exercise, about all the leader has to do is make sure people stay in the identification mode. Slipping into referring to the toy as "it," or making a statement that assumes a point of view outside of it are resistances that must be pointed out—or at times, in gestalt style, accepted as a message from the whole person that he feels threatened and wants to stop working.

The technique is harder to introduce in individual work, but can be equally powerful there. One rigid, compulsive woman with a miserable marriage was once an uncharacteristic five minutes late to a session. She had been so taken by seeing some seals play by the beach that she had stopped to watch. As she described them, I suggested saying "I." Within a minute she was in tears, as she touched the long buried, thought-to-be-dead, playful part of herself. The seals became a touchstone of therapy for her. Many times as she described some miserable impasse, I had only to ask, "What would a seal do in this situation?" and she knew immediately how to free herself from her self-limitations.

Not surprisingly, some people "click" with this method more than others. Those for whom it works well often begin to use it at home and in the world as a way of tuning in and finding what is going on with them. Thus one chronically depressed lady became aware how frequently she was noticing the lily growing out of her compost heap, as she worked in her garden. Realizing this was a good time for the identification exercise, she began with, "I am a lily growing out of a garbage heap . . ." The feelings of hope and renewed life she got in touch with heralded a real shift for the better in her mood. I use the technique constantly myself to find out what is going on; and not just for "information," but because the awareness breakthroughs are often intensely pleasurable and rich. As a side effect, I find myself far more responsive to nature and poetry than I was before.

I have at this point no elaborate theory about what happens in this process. In myself I note that what seems to come out when the experiment works well is a feeling-ideation complex that has been developing strength and pressing for awareness. (Often I have been quite restless just before trying the experiment.) The object, the perception "out there," becomes an organizing focus for this complex of feelings. I saw my distressing feelings of deadness and sterility first as a tree branch, broken off in a storm, and another time my feelings of increasing focus and direction as those of the leading goose in a migrating flock overhead. As him, "I always know what direction I have to go in; nothing can turn me the wrong way." The sense of pleasure and relief at this complex emerging into awareness is very strong, even when the feeling is a negative one in some way. Paradoxically, I have found that if people keep "trying" to make connections of self and object as they work, the experiment remains superficial. *The more totally I can lose myself in the object, the more deeply I find myself at the end.*

In addition to the individual gains in awareness through this method there are some very positive side effects on the quality of group interaction and process. A group that has shared this experience a few times often develops a vivid and metaphoric "in-language"

("There's your damned elephant again.") that is quite expressive and exciting, and even those individuals who don't happen to work well with this technique are affected by this. As people get in touch with hitherto dormant and buried parts of themselves they become more vivid and differentiated to others, and less locked into their social roles. Even bitterly antagonistic spouses who are usually far too defensive and frightened to listen to each other in ordinary discourse, find they can hear each other empathically when the partner is deeply into a projection. In some groups, the "that's *your* gorilla" experience has generalized. Somehow, as a person works intently with the gorilla it becomes possible for me, the observer, to know deeply that he is *really seeing* what he says, and that it is *really different* from what I see; he is not simply describing ineptly the "objective reality" that I can see so clearly. We really are different, and that is O.K. A by-product of this realization is often the ability to let another person be. Most of us reserve the right to judge another constantly when he is expressing himself in language or social behavior. We feel quite free to say, "What you really mean is . . ." or "You should . . ." When he is deeply involved in expressing himself in the identification exercise, however, it is clearly intrusive and irrelevant for me to say, "But this object is really . . ." or "Your gorilla should . . ." Learning to let him be in this domain sometimes generalizes, and it can give him the ultimate human gift of letting him be, in his uniqueness, in life as well.

For me, however, the greatest effect of this exercise on a group is simply the over-all sense of excitement and playfulness the method generates. The realization that fun can be profound, and profundity fun; that we can laugh till we cry and cry till we laugh in the same few minutes; that knowledge of a highly useful sort can be generated by such light-hearted sport, helps a group move rapidly away from a heavy, problem-centered orientation toward something much more rich and full. The split between "learning" and "living"—so frequent in life as well as in groups—is well on its way to being healed by this attitude. It hardly matters what else a group does if it can achieve that integration.

Body Work

Barry Stevens

gestalt is —
like circulation of the blood is.
we can interfere with this natural functioning
we cannot improve on it,

William Harvey discovered the circulation of the blood. Five hundred years later, his discovery was accepted. Gestalt has been re-discovered throughout the history of man, and ways to remove our interference with natural functioning keep appearing in new forms. Fritz called himself "a refinder of gestalt." Gestalt therapy includes the tools that he invented, or improved on, to help release us to natural functioning and through this release to have some experience of what gestalt is. Only experience can do that—my experience of me. The gestalt process can never be put down on paper. Coherent descriptions are bound to be misleading.

Learning how to decontrol my body—not just "relaxation"—is one of the ways of arriving at some understanding of natural functioning and getting in touch with how I interfere with it.

I ask the person who is willing to explore his body to lie down on the floor on his back. "Pull up your knees until the soles of your feet are flat on the floor. Now wriggle around a bit to make yourself as comfortable as possible. This is just a beginning position which seems to work out best. You don't have to hold to it. In fact, don't hold to anything."

Dennis did that and said, reaching for a pillow, "I want a pillow under my head. My head hurts where it touches the floor."

"A pillow's all right," I told him, "but I'd like you to first try doing without it. Get in touch with the pain in your head, from inside, gently—like getting acquainted with it. Stay in touch like a spotlight that doesn't push anything around and doesn't keep anything the way it is. 'Stay in touch' means so lightly that if somewhere else in your body calls—any kind of pain or tension or discomfort—you can move to it, as easily as moving your eyes from a window to the door. Let the pain be. If it becomes more intense or less intense, let that happen—or any other changes. Let be what is.

"We are controlling our bodies all the time. *This* is simply de-controlling—letting my body do what *it* wants to do. My body knows better than I do what is good for it. You don't need to give me a running commentary on what goes on. Say something once in a while, so that I can track you."

Often, simply getting in touch with unpleasant body sensations diminishes them or releases them. A rapid heartbeat slows to its normal beat. A headache disappears—sometimes quickly, sometimes more slowly. Pains in the lower back, where it presses against the floor, may recede and seem to go somewhere else. Whether they actually do go somewhere else, I don't know. People quite often report this movement of pain, and this is what it feels like to them. It doesn't matter if this is "true." What is important is to move with the pain, let my inside focusing flow easily to wherever pain calls. "Staying in touch with the pain" means always staying with it so lightly that I can move easily to or with whatever else appears.

Sometimes the person immediately reports one place where he feels pain. Sometimes two pains in different places are reported. Then, I ask him to see if he can discover which pain "calls the loudest." Doing this, he is paying more attention to his body and what's going on there. Sometimes he chooses one. If they seem to be of equal strength to him, I tell him to pick one—it doesn't matter which.

From observation of myself, it seems to me that this dissolving of pain happens when I focus on it because I have stopped thinking about it. My experience is that when I fully focus on any place in my body, my thinking stops. This may happen only briefly at first, and some people of course have much more difficulty then others. When my heart beats rapidly as I take the hot seat, or lie down on the floor to get in touch with my body, the connection with my thinking is obvious. That other discomforts too are connected with my thinking is not so obvious. It becomes obvious to me when I learn to de-control my body. After all, *how* do I control it? With my central nervous system, directed by my head.

When some pain or tension does not disappear easily, I suggest, "See if you can explore it—gently, not pushing it around, like getting friendly with it—and see if you can discover what wants to happen there and let it happen. See if some movement grows out of the pain or tension. It may be some very small movement that you can be aware of that is not visible to me. It may be large movement that I can see. Let it do whatever it wants to do."

When no discomfort seems to appear, I suggest exploring. "Look around in your body, from inside. Begin anywhere and move any-where. Make this exploring slow so that you can be in touch along the way, discovering what is there." Rushing is not exploring. I must go slowly, and take time to look around. Then I see things that I haven't noticed before. I'm paying attention.

Basically, those are my beginning instructions, although even those change through being in touch with *this* person and what's going on in him. It is just as important that I move and flow with him as that he does this with himself.

I strongly recommend that anyone who wants to guide someone else in this body work first do it many times himself. I gain trust in the process in this way. I am familiar with the territory, and even though someone else's territory is not always like mine, still there is familiarity. I recognize something of where he is. Then, my spacing of what I say, the length of the pauses, the order in which I say things, and other variations come from *my* sensing with *this* person. A guide through any wilderness may meet with unexpected circum-stances, something that wasn't there before, but it helps if you have a fairly solid knowledge of the ground through having been there many times.

My sensing is not perfect. I still interfere with my own process. But being more aware of my sensing contributes to the flow of the instructions that I give, and to the natural movements of the other person. Also, when I interfere with myself I can be aware of that and let it go—not try to correct it, but just move on, with the interference gone. Rigid copying of someone else's instructions blocks the flow. There is no "One, Two, Three" in gestalt. There cannot be. Gestalt is not rules. What happens in the person who is learning to decontrol his body does not go by rules. Almost everything is unexpected, even when I have done this hundreds of times—with myself and with others.

That our bodies work to heal themselves of injuries, disease and so on is accepted. We try to provide the best conditions for this healing to take place. De-controlling my body permits better circulation of my blood, which is a part of healing. That what we call mental or emotional difficulties can work to heal themselves is much more recent knowledge, and not so widely accepted.

Dennis, who first wanted a pillow for his head, later became comfortable without it. This in itself is an accomplishment: to discover how I can let myself be comfortable without manipulating the world (bring in a pillow) to *make* me comfortable. Put the other way around, I discover how I make myself uncomfortable lying on a wood floor.

Dennis moved easily with what was going on in his body, reporting occasionally what was going on now. Then he sat up, arms around his legs, and said "I feel vulnerable."

"How do you experience 'vulnerable'? What is the feeling of that in you?"

"Squashed," he said. This surprised me, and I learned again the wisdom of asking the person, not assuming that "vulnerable" means to him what it does to me. Perhaps he didn't know the feeling himself until directed to look for it.

"Let yourself be squashed." Let be what is, and don't tell him how to do it. His feeling of being squashed is his, not mine, and also is *in this moment*. Another time may be different.

Dennis rolled over on his side, pulled himself into a ball, and squashed himself as tightly as he could. Then he sat up. "I feel light—when I was a boy, I used to pick up dry cow turds—so light. I feel light like that." Tears began to drop from his eyes. "My tears are for having lost that lightness for so long."

He went on talking, about how he hates to say goodbye. He had told us earlier that when he came to Shura he wanted to enjoy driving through Colorado, but all the time he was thinking about the place he had left. As soon as he got here, he was sad that he would be leaving at the end of the week. He said that he did this *all* the time. Now, still sitting on the floor, he re-lived some events of his childhood. His family moved often, because of his father's business. "They were always unhappy about moving. I guess that's where it came from." He said he was through, now, and got up. Dennis went to the kitchen for a drink, came back and sat on a leather cushion. "I feel so *solid* sitting on this cushion!" he said, with obvious good feeling. Later, he said "I'm still astonished that when I *squashed* myself, I felt *light*!" . . . As I observed him sitting on the cushion saying "I feel so solid!" it seemed to me that he had gone from "light" to the kind of "solid" that has lightness in it, where there had been only heaviness before.

It seems to me that something similar happened to me when taking Joe Kamiya's alpha wave testing. I am in a dark room with nothing calling my attention except what's going on in me. I am observing what happens in my head, and checking that against the score that lights up every two minutes. There is nothing else in my world. In focusing on this, I exclude all the thinking-about that usually goes on in my head. Afterward, when I went on a bus through San Francisco, I was still disconnected from the past, from memory, from habitual reactions. Everything and everyone looked fresh and new—as indeed they always are. No annoyances. Being delayed on the bus didn't matter. I wasn't going anywhere—even though I knew that my direction was to Lafayette and "home."

Krishnamurti has remarked that any rhythmic sounds will do as well as a mantra—coca cola, for instance. It doesn't even have to be that. When Steve becomes aware of thinking going on in his head, he says Blah blah blah blah blah (silently or aloud makes no difference).

I tried this, and while I'm focusing on saying blah blah blah blah blah I cannot find any thoughts in my head. While I'm saying it, I become more aware of everything around me and inside my skin.

For thirty years or so, I've heard now and then that at this time we are moving toward "conscious evolution." I had some high-flying mystical notions about that at the time—concepts (fantasies) of what we would arrive at. I do not now see moving to another concept as "evolution"—that's just replacing one fantasy with another. Clearing my mind of all fantasies, I experience myself and the world in a different way, sometimes beyond my own believing. It seems to me possible that this conscious evolution may be moving in the direction of giving up our thinking-about, and arriving at whatever we do.

Differentiating between thinking and feeling is powerful because of its accuracy. In encounter groups some years ago, I saw people quickly learn that in the groups it was right to express feelings and wrong to express thinkings. As a result, people said "I feel . . ." for what was thinking, and confused each other and themselves even more.

I tell people doing the body work to notice when thoughts come in, and gently re-focus on the comfortable or painful place in the body, from inside. When I am fully in touch with somewhere in my body, my thoughts disappear. Even when this happens only for an instant, I have discovered that something is possible. I have so far not found anyone who need fear to give up his thinking for a while—it comes back all too easily. "When thoughts come in, gently re-focus—like a spotlight that doesn't push anything away. If you have a lot of difficulty with thinking, let me know and we'll try something else. Let me know of any other difficulty too." When a person "can't stop thinking," I suggest that he get in touch with his breathing, just for a moment, and then let himself go back to his thoughts. Repeating this for a while often makes it possible for the person to ease into spending more time with his breathing, and then switch to being in touch with other things going on in his body. With some people, I repeat much more often, "No straining, no pushing, no *trying* in that sense."

I do not generally call a person's attention to his breathing. When decontrolling takes over, the person's breathing changes, often going through as many changes in movement as other parts of his body do.

When I get in touch with pain or discomfort anywhere in my body, very often the unpleasant sensation disappears—whether it's a headache, rapid pulse, pain in the neck or tension somewhere else. Often I say more than once that "staying in touch" means lightly, like a spotlight that doesn't push anything around, and so lightly that I can hear if any other part of my body calls, and let my focus move there. Lightly, like a cloud: No jumps, jerks, pushing, persevering, or holding on.

When I say that I do something "often" (especially with some people) I mean that I say it again but with spaces between, and repeating when my sensing indicates it may be needed. My head is no good for telling me *when*. My head can only be guided by rules or by how something went some previous time. My senses tell me *now*. They are incapable of doing anything else.

In the beginning, I keep more closely in touch with the person (by reports from him) and repeat instructions—softly, so they are not intrusive, not calling the person away from what he is doing. When I can see that the person's body is in charge, doing its own doing, then I simply sit or walk around, only occasionally checking to see that this is still true. Once the spontaneous exercising of the body begins, it almost always continues. In most cases, too, the person indicates when he is "finished" for the time being—when he wants to stop. My body is not interested in overdoing. I know this stopping place as spontaneously as the movement happens.

Sometimes I say to a person "You choose your own stopping point" so that he is free to continue longer if he wishes, and at the same time recognizes that he makes this choice from himself. Some people—even if they are simply lying on the floor and letting go a little with no obvious movement—keep on until someone says "Stop," unless told to do otherwise. With such people, I point out at the beginning that they can stop whenever they want to.

I know of only two ways that people can get into trouble doing this body work, and both of them come from thinking. A young woman who had been doing very well with the body work, and enjoying it, said "I see black." "Stay with the black," I said. She got into a good deal of distress and we stopped, to find out what was going on. From herself, her inner knowing—or memory—she saw what had happened. "I thought about black, and got scared. I went into all sorts of fantasies about black." (Death, funerals, black void, and so on.) She had slipped out of being simply in touch with what was going on in her, and into thinking-about, bringing in memories and associations—and she scared herself. I can scare the hell out of myself with my thinking. In fact, I don't know anywhere else that fearfulness comes from. When this young woman had got clear on how she had scared herself and produced her own terror, she pointed to the place where she had been lying down and said, out of her experience before the scare, "I still like that spot on the floor!" She had felt very good there.

When fearful thoughts come in, and the person expresses them, I point out that these are thoughts, and ask them to re-focus in their bodies, to really stay in touch with what is going on and let it be. When my thoughts disappear, my fear does too, and the image changes of itself.

The other difficulty that comes from thinking is that when I let my body be, it exercises itself in many ways, with frequent changes, nothing going on too long. If I like one of these ways especially, and *think* "This feels good. I'll do it some more!" then *I* am doing it—taking instructions from my head, and the movement is not free. I *overdo*. My body is sore afterward, and I don't feel good. In the same way, if I *make myself* yell, or make myself continue yelling, my throat becomes hoarse or rasping. Spontaneous yelling, happening of itself, is free and easy and my throat is easy, too—both then and later. Another thought that produces pushing is "I want to get through everything (all my troubles) right now! If I just keep pushing, that will happen." This is not infrequent, in spite of my instructions not to push.

It is my responsibility to tell people to report any difficulties they may get into so that I can clarify what's going on, and guide them. With some people I do this much more often. I cannot be responsible for what the other person does. The situation is the same as when a physician prescribes a drug to be taken in certain doses and the patient takes either more or less. That is *his* responsibility.

A young man who was with us last year tried the body work. When he began to let go, soon his belly started jumping, then pelvic pushing. This continued longer than the spontaneous movements of any body that I have observed. I asked if he was pushing and he said yes. I warned him; he continued. He thought of it as giving birth, and wanted to push through—as if he pushed enough his own birth would be complete. In the days following, he reported that the belly jumpings still appeared. I was not *thoroughly* clear about this at that time.

He was the first person who reported this continuation, and I err on the side of questioning what I know—sometimes this works out well, sometimes it doesn't. The same is true of those who don't question, who are *sure*. They think they know: I think I don't know. Both come from thinking. When I get rid of my thinking, then I know when I know and when I don't know. This happens more than it used to, and I work consciously in this direction. At such times I am accurate. Beautifully accurate. I spent a good deal of my life wondering if I were crazy or not. Now, I know when I'm crazy and when I'm not.

My senses and my own experience and the young man's admission of pushing all came together. I wondered (thinking about it) if there might be something I was missing, and so on, and fouled up both of us to some degree. The young man wrote me several times—at intervals of a month or more—that he still had the belly jumpings, that his pelvis jerked too, and that to his friends it looked like the sex act. I wrote to him reminding him not to push, and telling him not to accept interpretations from himself or anyone else.

He came back this year, and said that though he still had the belly jumpings, they didn't come as often and were much milder. When he lay on the floor again, this year, they started up and he pointed to them with his finger. This time, I told him they were coming from his head, so let them go and get in touch with somewhere else in his body. This time, the work went very well. He was also in fine shape in other ways: He was open with regard to changes in his parents, and so on. He was no longer the Angry Young Man, turning any other emotion into anger. He had also let me come down from the pedestal he'd put me on, and saw me as a person. Whether more firmness a year ago would have changed the belly jumpings then, I don't know. It's never possible to go back and do things over in another way. Too much has changed in the meantime. It wouldn't be the *same* beginning. There's nothing to do but pick up from here, where I am now, where you are now. Wondering if things would have come off better if I'd done something else is just getting myself into another fantasy. This fellow got into spontaneous body movements now, and that is good.

Thinking in gestalt body work is the only hazard that I know. My body is not interested in hurting itself, and it doesn't hurt me. More and more it seems to me that *thinking-about* is the only hazard for the whole human race. Thinking in connection with action may be all right. I'm no longer sure that it's *necessary*. I am fully convinced by the evidence—observing what goes on in my head—that mostly my thinking is garbage, and not helpful to me at all. I spend some time in groups directing people to pay attention to their thinking, in specific ways. This is so closely related to gestalt body work that it weaves itself into what I'm writing now, but I'll do that separately.

"You don't need to give me a running commentary. Say something once in a while, so that I can be in touch with you." This makes it possible for me to track the person and know if he is genuinely letting his body go, or doing things in his head. I listen for the times when he is reporting from his head and point this out: "That's thinking. Get in touch with your body again." When he does this, he observes in himself what happens. "I'm afraid," "I'm blaming my mother," "I don't like this numbness" are examples. *Any opinion* comes from my thinking, and "good" can get me into trouble as well as "bad"—as in the overdoing.

Numbness is not a bad feeling when I am not afraid of it. No feelings then, are bad. They simply are. Yielding to what is. Quite a few people are astonished to discover that when they get in touch with the pain, first the pain no longer bothers them, then it disappears.

We are controlling our bodies all the time. This body work is simply decontrolling—letting my body do what it wants to do. My body knows better than I do what will make it comfortable.

In my experience of doing gestalt body work with several hundred people over a period of several years, I find two extremes—with all sorts of variations in between.

One of the extremes is Laura. I spent half an hour with her one day and at the end, she was no more in touch with her body than in the beginning. As far as I could tell, this was zero in touch. I called it off then, as the group session had run overtime, and I was tired. Next day, I worked with her for about forty-five minutes, and at the end she was at least somewhat in touch. Early in this session, Laura said that her mind was on top of her head, and she was blaming her parents. I asked her "What does it do for you to blame your parents?" She seemed not to understand the question. I rephrased it. She said, "When I blame my parents, my mind on the top of my head goes away." I asked her (neutrally—neutrality is most important) "And you don't want to try another way?" She was quiet for perhaps fifteen seconds, then said "Yes" and her yes clearly meant that she was willing. From that point on, she began to get out of her thinking sometimes, and in touch with her body. She began to have feelings that weren't thinkings.

The previous evening, she had taken the hot seat with Steve and got nowhere. On the evening after the body work she took the hot seat again, and released a great deal of emotion. She also clearly moved a long way from her solid blaming of her parents. She developed some understanding of her father, and displayed some affection for him. At the end, she was close to acceptance of him, and willingness to let him be. Not quite, but close enough so that it seemed likely that more would follow.

At the other extreme was Arthur, who worked with Steve first, in the hot seat. "It won't work" characterized everything he said. No use doing anything or trying anything because it won't work. He hadn't been able to take a job for three years. Out of something that Arthur said, Steve suggested that he be a corpse. Arthur let go of himself a great deal, let himself lie more loosely in the chair. As a corpse, he "didn't have to do anything or say anything" and he felt comfortable. Later that evening, Arthur put his head on my shoulder, held my hands in his. He was trying to get in touch, and desperately feeling nothing. "I'm dead." His fingers moving around mine felt as if they were made of metal with hinges at the joints. Stiff and cold, moving without feeling. No flesh, no bones.

The next day, when he lay on the floor to try the body work, he said "It's that being a corpse ... (that makes me want to do this)."

Almost immediately, spontaneous movements took over. His arms crossed, his hands pulling at his cheeks. He was in an agony of pain from tension that was visible and audible, sometimes expressed in words. His cheeks felt numb and he pulled at them. His muscles were tense "like violin strings." He heard violin music. The floor under him vibrated. The ceiling was low over his body. He was a branch tossed around by other branches in a storm—no trunk, no roots. On and on—tossed from one torment to another without let-up. "I'm crunching myself up and backing up to an abyss," he said in terror. I intervened, giving him a pillow and suggesting that he crunch the pillow. He did this for some time, timidly, and became more quiet. Afterward he said, "I felt some power, crunching the pillow." Whether it would have been better to let himself back over the abyss, I don't know. There's no way to do it over and find out.

When I asked him to come back to us, he looked at me (no one else) and was afraid. I asked him if he could see me and he said that was "in and out." I told him that if he could not see, this was all right: it happens often when people have been deeply into fantasies, sometimes when people have been meditating for too long. No need to be afraid of it. For a long time, he looked at me with suspicion. Then he reached for my hands and held them. His hands were soft and warm, his fingers the way that I expect fingers to be. He said, "I'm afraid you're expecting something." He looked really afraid. I said, "I'm expecting nothing: I'm just here with you." He looked as if he'd had still another jolt of scare, pushing him more deeply into it, and said "Now I'm afraid of that."

Those are just glimpses, collapsing an hour or more into a page or so. When Arthur had eased off some more, and became aware of other people in the group, he said, astonished, "On the moon—or Mars—but all that happening *in me*!?"

Asking him to come back to us at the time I did was sensing. I can't give any reasons why. If he had indicated going away, I would have let him. In fact, he showed no sign of moving away, and held my hand very long.

When Arthur got up from the floor, he sat in a rocking chair, quiet and limp. "I'm wobbly," he said, "and it's all right, now." He let his head wobble a bit. He sat for long periods of silence, then said something, then silence again. He was simply saying some things from himself, including us, but whether we heard him didn't seem to matter. (The night before, he said many times, "No one listens to me.") "I saw all my prejudices." Long pause. I don't know if the next sentence referred to the previous one or to something else. "I knew it," he said. "Now, I see it." The night before he left here, he said "I don't want to leave"—with warm expression and without demand or appeal.

I'm *not* presenting this—or anything else—as a "cure." I'm simply describing something that can happen with gestalt body work.

Between these two extremes of Laura and Arthur are so many other people whose work has been unique and rewarding—as well as many who are much closer to Laura. If in reading about some of the people who came through uniquely, you begin to think that this always happens, go back and read Laura again quite a few times.

A woman in her fifties came to a workshop. A man who works with bodies immediately observed "There is no connection between her top and bottom." In doing the gestalt body work, the woman observed this for herself. She discovered a wide band around her waist, like an oversize cummerbund, an area where there seemed to be nothing. She felt nothing. Continuing, she re-lived being a small child, tied to a leg of a heavy table with a towel, her arms tied behind her back. Her mother had tied her there and left her. I don't remember the sequence of events now, but this woman got her top and bottom together, with no empty space between. She also discovered that sex was important to her because she had little or no feeling in her genitals and thereabouts. She said, with humility, "I saw this in others, and didn't know it in myself." She also said, "I can't think! I can't think about anything at all!" I told her to enjoy it while it lasted. She could speak, and make accurate (intelligent) observations *now*. She could not *think about* anything, the way that we usually do—bringing in memories, association, explanations, future concerns, or logically "Putting things together." The chatterbox that we usually think of as our "mind" was silent.

In my group at Cowichan when I was in training, a young Chinese said that he wanted to do something, but not talk. I suggested that he lie on the floor and try the body work. Very shortly, he was thrashing around violently, rolling his head and eyes, his tongue lashing out and gulping back as he sucked air. This went on for some time, and then he began shaking. Fritz came in and sat down. He put his hands on the man's knees (his feet were still flat on the floor, knees up) and told him to lift his hips and let the shaking get into his pelvis. Later, Fritz asked "How old are you?"

"Four."

"Is your mother with you?"

"No. I fell in the rice drain. My brother pulled me out by one leg."

I use that tip about holding the knees to let the shaking get into the pelvis. Once, it was necessary to have someone hold the man's shoulders in place too. Rich had been working on a dream and gaining insights. He began to shake strongly. Lying on the floor, his shaking became very intense, and I asked a man to hold Rich's knees. His shoulders then slid back along the floor, so that he was flat again. With one man holding his knees in place and another holding his shoulders in place, the violent movement included his pelvis, which also swung from side to side. I asked how old he was. He said "Sixteen." Occasionally I ask that question. Any routine is anti-gestalt. When I am not thinking and this question comes to me, I ask it—without looking for a reason.

Some people who lead gestalt groups do so mechanically, going by rules. Any new rule just puts a different monkey on my back. "Avoidance is bad" is one of the rules. Leaders who see "avoidance" or anything else as if they'd read it in a book, pounce as soon as they see it. People do that outside of groups, too. Sometimes avoidance is good, is part of the person's natural ebb and flow, and should not be interfered with. It seems to me better to err on the side of waiting than to pounce. If the avoidance is habitual, it will come in again. Sometimes by going on with it, the person becomes aware of what he is doing without having it pointed out. In any case, no pouncing. That comes from the head, with ego interest. It's better to be aware of this, and say what is going on in me. But this is tricky too. If I merely say the words, no change has taken place in me. If I pay attention to what I'm doing, stay in touch with it and know what I'm feeling, then something changes.

I return to Rich. His body release was very strong and continued for a long time. I don't know how long, actually. Twenty minutes or more comes to mind. When it was altogether over, he sat on the floor leaning against the wall, looking limp. Before I left that evening, I asked him if he was all right. I didn't want to leave him without being sure. He assured me that he was. I was not as sure, but he insisted and I left—knowing that he was in the home of friends. About an hour later, Rich was knocking at my door, close to frantic. Something else had started churning up. He lay on the floor and immediately began writhing, yelling and so on. Then he was in a crib, having a violent tantrum. His mother had left him and gone to her bed, crying because she didn't know what to do with him. He saw his father's hand flip the light switch as he left. His father didn't know what to do either. Child Rich kept calling to his mother, saying what he couldn't when he was a child, "Mommy! Don't worry! I'm all right, Mommy!"

That's what I remember of what went on, for probably about an hour. There were soft pauses at times when he was at ease, and then into turbulence again. At the end, he felt finished. He felt relieved, and content. He was also in no shape to drive, and phoned someone to drive him home. Before he left, he said that his friends where I had left him had started asking questions about what he'd gone through. This made him frantic, and he came to me. By the time he got to me, there was nothing for me to do but be with him, and hope the neighbors would not intrude. His organism did everything.

A year or so later, I saw Rich again. He said, "I want to tell you something. Always, when I talked with my mother on the phone, she worried about me, and I kept telling her not to, and she went on worrying. After that time at your house, when I talked with her on the phone, I just said 'I'm all right!'—and she accepted that. Later, I went to see my mother and she said that she wanted to talk to me, but I wasn't to say anything to her because she was too sick. She told me that she wanted to buy a house for me, and I was to get a job . . . all that stuff. When she stopped talking, I left, but then I went back and said, 'Mother, if you weren't in shape to let me talk, you shouldn't have talked to me.' And she said, 'You're right.' "

In a weekend group, I did both body work and hot seat work, letting people choose their own way. A woman, probably fifty or so, chose the body work, saying with panic "I've been dragging my left leg around for so long, I can't go on doing it any more!" Tears. She came out of the body work saying to her left leg "You belong to me!" When she got up, she walked easily. I know absolutely nothing more than that about her. Sometimes understanding comes through, sometimes it doesn't. Again, I'm not talking about "cure." I don't know what happened after that. I do know that she discovered that she is capable of walking on both legs, without dragging one around.

It seems to me that this must work in the same way as my knowing that at 72 I *can* walk easily. Sometimes I drag, feel weary, think (sic) "Yes, I'm old. That's what you have to expect," and so on. Then I become wearier and wearier, and less able to walk. Then I recall the feeling of walking easily, which I have come upon many times in different ways: with Ilana Rubenfeld guiding me by the Alexander method, with Al Huang through t'ai chi (or as he calls it now, *wu chi* which means before the form), through hot seat work with Fritz. I know that something is possible. I dump my thinking— and my weariness—and walk easily again. If I *make* my body do things again, out of reasons in my head, then I am in trouble again.

I use the body work quite often, to loosen me up when I've tightened myself by controlling. This happens best when I am alone in a room, with space to lie on the floor. On a mattress is less productive—although in bed I can use it to release my thinking and go to sleep. I get into it more easily and more deeply when I can let sounds happen without my worrying about anyone worrying about me. What happens is never twice the same. I don't always make noises, and not the same noises when they do come. I keep getting more deeply in touch with my body, knowing it better, and I'm impressed by the variety of connections that come through to me. My body is not bound by methods or systems in setting itself free, and when I leave it to its own doing, what it does changes constantly. I notice how my thinking tries to "make things even," demands "symmetrical," and my body disregards this. My left foot, for instance, does a sort of cake-walk on the floor. I think "My right foot should be doing that, too." My right foot is staying in place, flat on the floor. I have a thought to move it. But when I get in touch with my right foot, which automatically withdraws me from my thinking, my right foot says clearly that it wants to do something else. I let my right foot do it—while my left foot goes on cake-walking.

I have been releasing my body in this way for about seven years—sometimes quite frequently, sometimes infrequently. Sometimes I do not have floor space or aloneness. Sometimes I get over-involved in whatever else I'm doing. This is when I would do best to take myself out of what I'm doing and let my body go. Too often, I don't do that. Sometimes I get tied up in my head and forget what is possible.

Several years ago, I was asked to show some Fritz films. I said yes. Then I was invited to dinner "with just a few people—five or six" before showing them. I said yes. Instead, 20 people crowded into a small room for supper, all gabbling. I uptighted myself. Uptight is rigid, body movement is difficult, and I get tired. Then the films. Then questions. After that, a ride down the mountain to where I lived. I went to sleep without doing the body work and woke up stiff, and unable even to do things that I wanted to do—answering letters, clearing up potting mess from the day before, and so on. I sat down with a cup of tea. I went round and round in my head with the same old story: "Well, you got into those things yourself. You knew better. Now you have to waste a day recovering." I wasn't beating myself over the head about it, just reviewing what had happened and the consequences. Going round and round and round with the same stuff. I may have had some notion that by doing so, I was accepting it. I was tired, tired, tired, and expecting to live with that until tomorrow. For two hours, I did that. When my body is tight, my thinking is tight too, and very limited.

Then I remembered. I lay down on the uneven brick floor. This was sharply painful to me, at first. Then I began decontrolling my body. After about fifteen minutes, when I wasn't quite through but had arrived at comfortable, friends came and invited me to go to the lake with them. That sounded appealing. I almost said Yes. But then I noticed my happy wanting (lively attraction) to do the things around the house that I couldn't do before. Now, I could. I said No to the invitation and enjoyed the rest of the day thoroughly, feeling *with* whatever I was doing, and happily seeing things getting done as if by magic—with no "I" in the doing. Like being a breeze or a cloud or a tree.

The first time that I got into body de-controlling, in 1955 before I knew anything about Fritz and gestalt, I got scared and didn't do it again. I'm not quite sure how I got into it (I was doing a lot of experimenting at the time) but I'm pretty sure it was this way: I had been sick for a couple of years, living alone, spending at least 95% of the time in bed. Medicine helped to keep me from becoming an idiot, a vegetable, but I wasn't getting well. It seemed to me that exhaustion was a major interference. So what was exhausting me? I watched for everything that tired me, and did what I could to eliminate it. Then one day I became aware that something that happened earlier in the hospital was still tiring me. What on earth could I do about that? I fantasied it happening the way that would have felt good to me, and felt relieved—sort of happy, too. So I went through the fantasy again, and again, and again, brought in more details to relieve me. I don't remember now just what happened. I do remember having a thought "Thank God I'm alone! If anyone saw and heard me they'd think I was suffering and would try to stop me."

I wrote to Aldous Huxley about it. He wrote "Deadlines are confronting me on every side . . . hence the delay in replying and the inadequacy of this note to all but your remarks on the pseudo-sobbing, shaking and twitching, resulting in a sense of liberation and openness to healing. This is a phenomenon I have observed in others and experienced in myself, and seems to be one of the ways in which

174

the entelechy, or physiological intelligence, or deeper self, rids itself of the impediments which the conscious superficial ego puts in its way. Sometimes there is a recall of buried material, with abreactions. But by no means always. And when there is no such recall, many of its beneficent results seem to be obtained when the deeper self sets up this disturbance in the organism—a disturbance which evidently loosens many of the visceral and muscular knots, which are the results and counterparts of psychological knots. Disturbances of this kind were common among the early Friends—and led to their being called Quakers. 'Quaking' is evidently a kind of somatic equivalent of confession and absolution, of recall of buried memories and abreaction to them, with dissipation of their power to go on doing harm. We should be grateful for the smallest and oddest mercies—and this quaking is evidently one of them, and by no means the smallest."

I surely didn't understand all of that, but it sounded reassuring. I didn't know what "abreactions" were and asked the doctor. He told what he had *seen* when a man who had been in a mine explosion later re-lived it, this time letting loose what he had repressed at the time—possibly as a matter of survival, so that he could do what he needed to do. The doctor made it sound scary. I was afraid to go into that alone.

After that, once or twice when I was desperate I got into the shaking and moaning and so on. But I didn't know how to let it be in motion when I wasn't desperate. Later I learned how to do that from Fritz. Now, I don't get desperate, and I can de-control quite easily. Having done this lying on the floor at times makes it easier for me to do it some even during the course of whatever else I'm doing, and to a degree in public too. Huxley's letter is completely clear to me now, and though he uses different words, he's saying the same thing.

I remind the people I guide into the body work not to look for "meaning," which is thinking again. Once, as I was lying on the floor, my mouth changed to what felt like a large oval, showing my teeth. I thought "What's going on? Do I want to bite someone?" It didn't seem so. I let go of meaning or explanation and let happen. Liquid seemed to seep out of the corners of my mouth, then trickle, then stream, and then the liquid became blood and tears. This was all feeling. I let it flow. At the end I felt released—as if all the blood and tears that I'd held back had flowed out of me. That meaning came to me. I couldn't have found it by looking for it. I don't know if it's "true" except that the experience is true, beyond question. No need to question. Happiness was present, and a sense of purification. Had anyone *seen* me, they surely would have "seen" me suffering.

When I let my body be, free to do its own doing, my breathing always becomes deeper, stronger, and sometimes it becomes very strong indeed. I feel it like a figure eight lying down—my chest expanding, then flowing down into my belly like down a slope, my belly expanding (while my chest is contracting) and flowing downhill into my chest again. When this happens, I also feel my breathing in places where I am not usually aware of it—in my back, in my legs, sometimes in my feet. When a young woman was rolfed in my living room, she said, happily, "I can feel my breathing in my legs!" I have not yet had this feeling going altogether through my shoulders, up my neck, and into my head. It seems to me this is a possibility—like small bubbles all over and everywhere in motion. I'd like to spend more time exploring this way. That I don't is my own doing. Nothing is in my way except what I put there.

In guiding people into gestalt body release, I don't say what to look for, other than any present discomfort, or what to expect. I don't know what to look for or what to expect. A Chilean psychiatrist said "Oh! I have this bad place in my back and I thought I had to live with the pain for the rest of my life. Now I see what I'm doing!" I didn't know she had a bad back. A Frenchman released his left side above the waist and said, "I had an injury. Now I see how I've been holding it in." He looked very happy, stroking the place that he had been able to release.

A woman who was working very well, going with the flow of her body, feeling good doing that, said "I feel I'm being pulled into a corner." I suggested that she let herself be pulled into a corner. Instead, she got up and had a dialogue with her little-girl self about being afraid. The dialogue seemed superficial to me, and it ended very quickly with "Neither of us is afraid." She was satisfied. I let it go. My experience is that I louse up whenever I have goals, either for myself or others. The next day she said, "I'm owning my anger. I've never done that before. I'm doing it now." She worked in the hot seat way, and soon was a little girl standing in a corner with her father yelling at her. She became her father, doing the yelling, and movement continued from there.

With someone else, it might not have gone that way. Perhaps they would have closed off. Let each person move in his own way, in his own time. I'm not so wise that I can know what someone else should do—or when they should do it. I may express something that goes on in me, "I imagine that you do not want to go on" or whatever, but not as pushing or dictating to the other person. People choose to come to me. They also choose when to stop. When stopping is what's happening, I let that happen too. Doing this in groups helps me to live this way more myself wherever I am, in whatever I'm doing. This seems to me a better way to live than by manipulating myself and others. I feel better. More ease, less conflict (with others and within myself), and much less suffering.

An Australian, 6' 7" tall and standing very straight, discovered through the body work how he squashed his spine to make himself look shorter.

Sometimes it seems to me that "nothing has happened" in the other person. Then, six months or a year later I meet them and they tell me with excitement what happened, that is continuing now. A woman who did nothing in the group wrote "I've been doing the body work and it works!"

Sometimes, a person who has blocked in the hot seat asks for the body work and starts moving. A therapist who blocked repeatedly, after some body release began talking and heard himself. He saw his conflict clearly, instead of through a fog, and arrived at knowing what he wanted to do. He went back home and did it.

Whatever is, is—and by getting in touch with what is, something changes. A woman said "There's nothing between my shoulders and my head. My neck is gone—just space."

"Stay in touch with the space."

I don't remember what the space changed to, but it changed quite soon. Everything does, when I let it.

In the workshops this summer, Steve started the day with group people doing wu chi—the t'ai chi essence that preceded the form. We learned this way from Al Chung-liang Huang. From wu chi the group moves into working on the place, mostly outdoor work, and carries over what they can from wu chi into *how* they do their work. One man discovered the tightness of his body through this, especially his arms and shoulders. He released them very much, and a good deal of his torso, through the body work—most vigorously, and without after-effects. His body stretched enormously, and in odd and changing ways, clearly spontaneous. A few hours later, he told me that he hadn't got his legs released and he'd like to do that.

In the evening, lying on the floor, his feet raised in the air (spontaneously) and began pedaling. Then he said he wanted to kick. I put a heavy pillow against the wall and he kicked hard. Then he said, "I'm seeing faces—lots of faces—all the people who have pushed me to do things. I want to kick them. I HATE them!" He went on kicking. Then one face came through most importantly—an athletic coach. Jim stood up and stomped the pillow until he was used up and sat down. I asked him if he wanted to talk to the coach, and he did. In the dialogue, Jim said (as a boy of sixteen or seventeen) "I only go along with athletics because I want the attention of the girls," and the coach said, "I don't like it either, but it's the only way I can be close to some people." Clear understanding in Jim, all anger gone.

From this dialogue, he went into one with the woman he has been living with, and saw clearly that he would never go the way that she was pushing him—and that she would never go the way that he was pushing her. He saw how each was hoping the other would change. This wasn't altogether new to him, but it was the first time he had seen it clearly, uncluttered by fantasies.

There are people who get nothing from gestalt body work. A very confident and beautiful woman came to a group "for" her husband—"because he needed it." She was no part of it herself. With the body work, she did lie down on the floor. She lay there smiling for a while, said how comfortable she felt, got up, smiling, and saying "I didn't need it at all." It seems to me that I was remiss in not saying something to her of what went on in me. I don't know if it would have made a change in her, but it would have made a change in me. But mistakes are mistakes and all of us make them and best let them go—especially when we can't do anything about them. Al Huang says, in teaching wu chi, "If you make a mistake, don't try to correct it. Just keep going and you'll be doing fine again." If I'm trying to correct the past, how can I be present?

I am interested in acquainting some people with this way of de-controlling *so that* they can go on with it themselves. Whether or not they choose to, is up to them. Learning to do things myself is important to me, largely as a matter of convenience. When I'm not dependent on someone else, I don't have to make appointments (therapist, masseur or whatever), don't have to fit their time and mine together, am not frustrated when I cannot be with them at the time I need them, and so on. This applies whether the person is a paid professional, an acquaintance, or someone close to me. My time and theirs just don't always come together.

I went to Fritz to learn from him, and what I learned from him I can now do myself—for myself. A year after Fritz died, I noticed that I was irked by something he'd said about me in a group that wasn't true. I had just worked in the hot seat, and what he said was minuscule to me, then and in the days later. A year afterward, it was still miniscule, but now I was being bugged by it. I started to write a letter about it, to clear me up (an old pattern). Then I put down the pen and pulled up a chair. In less than five minutes of dialogue I realized—all through me, completely, not intellectually—"I haven't forgiven him for making a mistake!" All my body was free and loose and warm with forgiveness, then. Ever since, what he said has been a dead memory. I can recall it, but there's no life in it at all. Like a very small piece of paper blowing by in a wind. As soon as I've noticed it, it's gone. I thought then, "Dear Fritz. He gave me trouble *and* the means to get myself out of it." I share what I have learned so that others can learn and do it for themselves. People who want things done *to* them don't get much out of being with me.

I fall into many of the traps that other people do. After my first session with Al Huang, I thought "Oh! I've got so much from being with him! I want more! How can I be with him again soon?" Then I realized "I'm not *using* now what I learned from him this time!" I got busy, and then it was easy to live with not knowing when I would be with him again. A year later that happened easily—without force or pushing—as if the gates had opened and I flowed through. Since then, when we go our separate ways my feeling is that he is moving off in his direction and I am moving off in mine and when our wu chi circles come around and meet we'll be together—and the rest of the time we won't. Getting out of my head through body work places me in this stream or flow where everything comes and goes and meets or doesn't meet. *Using* even a small bit of what I have learned makes a change in me. Learning more and more in my head and not using it has no value—except to impress others, and that for me has no value.

In groups, these days, usually I start out with what is so simple— and extremely difficult for some people: differentiating between what is obvious and what is fantasy or imagination. It's so basic to be clear about the difference, and it saves lots of explanation later on to be clear about it in the beginning.

Two people sit facing each other. They take turns saying "It is obvious to me that . . . your hair is brown, you have a mole on your cheek, you are smiling, your fingers are twitching." If they say things like, "that you are nervous, that you are happy, that you are friendly"—*any* kind of interpretation—this is pointed out. What is *obvious* are twitches, smiles, and so on. Then, if they haven't included themselves, I remind them that what is going on inside them is obvious to *them,* although it may not be obvious to the other person. Then they also say things like "It is obvious to me that . . . I am speaking very rapidly, breathing rapidly, I'm nervous doing this, I'm feeling friendly toward you, I don't want to go on with this," or whatever is happening in themselves. When people do this *really,* they become comfortable with each other and themselves much more easily. At the same time, they get in touch with the difference between what is real and what is fantasy. They discover how what they imagine gets in the way of their really being with another person.

Of course some people try to be "good students" and get a good grade, and fail to get in touch with anything. Usually this comes through to me by their manner. They make their statements quickly, rather tensely, as if they are giving "answers" and meeting a standard, rather than being in touch with the other person or themselves. They remain tense instead of becoming more at ease as they go along. Then I tell them this as my imagining about them, for them to affirm or deny. Usually their response is vigorous nodding "Yes, that's what I'm doing." Then I ask them to slow down, not prepare their next response while the other person is talking. First, hear the other person, then say what is obvious *now*.

Becoming aware of the difference between observation and thinking is a good beginning for the body work. Learning to get in touch with your body is simply being aware of what is obvious inside your skin *without thinking about it.* Much as we often overlook what is happening outside, most of us are even more cut off from what is happening inside—and even more cut off from what wants to happen.

. . . Just then, I noticed that my eyes were tiring. I couldn't see very well. I have been editing this manuscript for several hours. I lay down on the floor, knees up, feet flat on the boards.

First: growls and groans. Then heavy sighing. Then inhalations followed by sighs. Then my cheek and jaw muscles began letting go. This was painful, but with an odd quality of knowing it was painful and not feeling pain.

Then my shoulders began letting go—as if dropping toward the floor. Nice hammock feeling with this.

More sighs, more dropping of my shoulders toward the floor.

Arms letting go. Then muscles in the palms—with the same strong pain/no pain feeling. Then muscles close to the groin letting go. I feel them do it. Thigh muscles . . . then calves . . . then in my feet.

My body (me—I'm strongly my body now through my not thinking, and so there is no "I") rolls over on the left side, left knee bent—right leg stretched out, toes almost hooked to the floor, increasing the stretching. Right leg bends, moving up, knee to waist — already I am feeling *good* . . . . I interrupt to write this down. Each time I had a thought to remember what was going on so I could write it, I let the thought go and simply *was* what was happening. In touch. And now this has written itself and I see it clearly accurate—no wondering if I've mixed things up, as happens when I'm not aware at the time of happening—like taking notes.

I got up after writing that and walked a little, feeling so much more free that I called it "free." But this is only relative freedom. My muscles still are letting go. I feel them do it . . .

When a person complains that he has a terrible headache and I say "Get in touch with it," often the response is "I am! Do I ever know I've got it! I can't think of anything else!" This "knowing" is different from awareness, or being in touch. I can walk down a street *knowing* there's pavement under my feet, buildings on both sides, people walking past—and not be in touch with anything. My head is full of fantasies or chatter and I'm not even aware of *that*. This is maya, the world of illusion. Nothing real. Nothing *present*. I'm not here.

When I walk down a street *aware* of the movement of my body, of my feet on the street or road, of people passing (their eyes, clothes, posture, whether they are awake or seem to be dreaming) the air, and so on, then my whole world is different. I cannot have this awareness by programming myself "Oh yes, I must pay attention to this, I must see that, I must be aware every moment." That's another should, another monkey on my back. I have to be rid of all the monkeys. This is where the trickiness comes in—arriving at something different, without giving myself another set of rules. With *any* rules, I'm still in the trap—the same trap.

I bought a small set of GO once and in it was a booklet which said that all the rules of GO were in it—about 57 as I recall—and that "Of course there are only a very few rules in GO. The rest are put in for the rule-minded westerner."

Gestalt is not rules. (Also the tao, zen, wu chi, and so on.) Whenever I notice that I'm going by a rule, I know where I'm not—even if my rule is to be aware. Going *against* rules, I'm in the same bag. Moving without rules is not difficult in itself: I simply move and do appropriately, within the circumstances at this time. *Conventions* require me to act in a certain way whether this is appropriate or not. Without rules, I sometimes move conventionally and sometimes not.

Any rule, however well-intentioned, gets me into trouble at some time because everything's always changing, and I can't foresee the future at the time I make the rule—for me or for anyone else. I had a rule of being honest with my young son. Then, when all my senses told me not to be honest at one time, and I followed this, I tortured myself because I had not been honest. This torture—self-administered—not only weakened me, but also often blocked me from awareness of what was going on at the moment.

It seems to me impossible to do a really good job of therapy with someone else without first having gone through it myself. Then, I recognize so much more of what is going on in the other person. I am in familiar territory, and can help to keep him away from the wrong side roads—while letting him explore down all the right side roads. By "wrong" I mean simply taking directions from his mind instead of from his body. In doing this, I am of course separating "mind" and "body" which is not possible. But it's a useful distinction that helps me come together and be free for a while of all splits, arguments, conflicts and so on.

When I de-control my body, which is what gestalt body releasing is, it acts unconventionally—for a while. I am my body. I act unconventionally for the time being. My body makes its own connections when I let my organism be. I tell people not to look for meaning, but I don't say that there is no meaning. When I *look* for meaning, I do this in my head, in my intellect, where the meaning cannot be found. I may get very frustrated looking for what I cannot find—and dismayed and confused. Or I may latch onto a meaning that satisfies my reason and is false. Sometimes meanings don't come and sometimes they do. Let be what is. I have freed myself or emptied myself of junk, my body has exercised itself, with its own knowing how to do it. I feel young and eager. When meanings come through on their own there is no looking for them, and they are simply accepted—like "Yes, that is true"—without confusion.

Let be what is. Don't try to make it into something else. That is manmade interference, not organismic, not me. When I let go of everything I *think* I am—"good" and "bad"—what's left is me. Any concept that I have of myself just gets in my way. Abe Maslow was unhappy with what happened with many people when they read what he wrote about "self-actualizing people." What they did with it was very strange. I have received a fair number of letters saying "I am a self-actualized person." Maslow said that he must have left something out. Fritz put it in. He saw that most people actualized a self-concept. This is not *self*-actualizing. My *self*-actualizing, when it happens, is full of surprises—surprises me. I am not actualizing a self-concept.

Knowing that I am a somewhat well-known writer, that some of my writing has been translated into other languages, does me no harm as long as I don't think about it. When I don't think about it, I have no image of myself as "a writer." If I had such an image (or any other image of myself) I would shape myself to the image, tailor myself to act and speak and respond according to my image. I would create an illusion and *think* that the illusion is me.

My body knows no such nonsense. It has no pretentions. *I* feel good when my body feels good to me—which it does when I'm good to my body. My body is *now,* and now is the only time that I can do anything. Try reading that sentence a moment ago—or a moment ahead.

By repeated doing, my body takes over more easily, more quickly. One of the fascinations in it for me is that I can arrive at a stillpoint, where I am neither pushing anything at all nor holding back. This is wu wei. No doing by me. This is a fine point to reach—like the razor's edge. As I observe more and more acutely, I discover how easy it is for me to *think* I'm doing nothing when in fact I am doing something—nudging a little to prolong something present, or holding back a little by notions from my head. This is particularly true when I feel the surge of life all through me that we usually call "sex." I want to nudge to increase it, like pressing for an orgasm, or hold it back a little so that I won't be disappointed by the lack of orgasm. When I drop all that and let this flowing surge of life be—just be—without expectations—I feel strong and alive and not needing anything more than this. No dissipation of this force or power or spirit, or whatever one wants to call it, into orgasm. Then I feel young—*very* young—before I was introduced to sex. My happiness is and I am whole, not needing anyone or anything to complete me. No need to touch or be touched to feel warm, easy and alive.

Voids, voids, voids — noddings!

Barry Stevens

When I went on a gestalt fantasy trip a year or so ago, at the end the instruction was to give something to the man in the store in exchange for what I had taken from him. I told him, in my fantasy, "There's only one thing I want to give you and I can't bear to give you that."

"What is it?" he asked, and I said,

"All the words and thoughts in my head."

"Oh," he said, "that's nothing! Give them all to me any time." His gestures said that I could pour them in whenever I liked. "They're nothing," he said again. I saw them then as all vapors that take no space and disperse rapidly, leaving nothing behind. What a relief! They had seemed so heavy and tangible in my head, but *really* they were nothing.

Words. What a strange life we live with words. All the words that have poured out of my mouth and from my fingers. All the words that I've heard, and all the words that I've read.

All the words in books and documents and records and orders and contracts and letters. All the words in files and vaults, in desks, on desks, in newspapers, billboards, subway and bus advertisements, magazines, journals, unpublished manuscripts, songs, movies, the Congressional Record, first-class mail, junk mail, pouring out of radios and TV . . .

And all the words that haven't appeared anywhere except in my head—sometimes seen, sometimes heard. How many words go on in my head in a day?

Words—spoken or unspoken—appealing, entertaining, agreeing, applauding, consoling, condoning, threatening, preaching, "teaching," manipulating, punishing, promising, reassuring, comforting, demanding, questioning, demeaning, confusing, praising, frightening, bluffing, condemning, answering, describing, forgiving, impressing, comparing, disagreeing, pleading, cajoling, persuading, seducing, labeling, resisting, approving, dismissing, placating, soothing, competing . . .

What a lot of activity in what the words are doing!

Where is my doing?

"What have you been most involved with all your life?"

How many of us would answer "Words"?

When I'm not aware how much of my life is spent with them, the fact remains.

"*Homo loquax,* the talking animal, naively delighted with his chief accomplishment," Aldous Huxley wrote. Krishnamurti said "Watch the thoughts behind the thoughts." I didn't know what he meant, but I looked for them and they were there. Pause now for a moment and look for them in yourself . . .

Fritz said of himself as therapist "I try as far as possible not to think." When I took the hot seat with him, for a while at least I had no thoughts. Then—and only then—I act and speak spontaneously—and what happens has never happened before.

At Cowichan, in the fifteen hours in the first week that we spent working on awareness, Fritz sometimes directed us to our thoughts—and to the thoughts behind the thoughts, or behind the words that we were saying. We were paired with someone else, talking in our usual way, when he asked us to do that. Behind what I was saying to the young man I was talking to, my thoughts were: (resentfully) "School! It's just like school!" When Fritz said "You are always talking to someone. Who are you talking to?" I recognized that I was talking to Fritz. I got up from the floor and went to him and told him. He nodded that he heard, and said nothing. I was a little unhappy that he gave no word of approval—and much more happy that he didn't. Approval is linked with disapproval. I can't have one without the other, and I live as though on a see-saw, high on approval, low on disapproval.

"Be aware of your thinking and the tone of voice . . ." Fritz said. I hadn't recognized before that the words in my head had tone, as voices always do. We had already worked on the spoken voice, saying "As my voice I am . . ." and describing our voice at the time as we heard it. Hearing the tone of the voice in my head was new to me.

Fritz had us get in touch with our voices in our chests, and let them come out like a song. When I did this, I had no thoughts—no words—only the sound.

Another way that Fritz used to get us out of our thinking was what he called "shuttling." He used the concept of two areas of awareness—everything outside my skin, and everything inside my skin. Interfering with this awareness was what he called "the middle zone." Sometimes he called it the DMZ. I call it my gabble zone, where all the chattering in my head goes on. Fritz had us practice shuttling between inside and outside awareness, which went something like this:

"Now I am aware of the smile on George's face. Now I am aware that his arms are crossed.

"Now I am aware of tension in my leg, and stiffness in my back.

"Now I am aware of the sunlight in the room, and the color of Ida's dress—it's red, the kind of red that has yellow in it. Now I am aware of the darker red in the shadows of the folds in the skirt.

"Now I am aware that I am breathing rapidly, and my arms are tingling."

And so on. When I do this fully, the chatter zone gets bypassed, and inside and outside awareness come together. I am whole—no thinking blocking me from what is. Saying "Now I am aware of—" often seems tedious, repetitious, and unnecessary at first, but this slows me down, and helps me to focus on something *now*. Without this, I tend to scan, moving rapidly from this to that. Even with the words "Now I am aware of—" some people did this quite a lot. Fritz called it the Supermarket Approach or grasshopper awareness—seeing this, that, and the other and not being really *aware* of any of it. I'm not in touch with anything. When I did this, once, I was trying to rack up a good score. That is not awareness. Just saying the words is not awareness. I am not doing what I say I am doing. My saying and

187

doing is not congruent. When I do it as I say it, then (in time) I am *here*—inside and outside coming together, vibrant, alive, with no interference from the chatter zone. To experience this even once is to want more. I arrive at it when I pay attention to what is going on outside and inside myself—no thoughts about. *Observation.* Observation simply observes, without judgment, without opinion. At such times I distinguish things like "green leaves" and "dead branches" without comparing them, without giving them different values. And, after all, what is the value of either one unless I am gathering brush for a fire or looking for a shady place to sit? These are *changing* values, changing in accord with my need at the time. When I have simply observed the green leaves and dead branches, I know where they are when I need them. My body knows the ease of this simple observation, not bound up in judgment or opinion.

In groups now, when I ask people to observe their thoughts, I sometimes ask "How does your body feel while you are doing this thinking?"

All the words going on in my gabble zone are fantasies. Even when there are mostly images rather than words, these images are tied to my thinking. What I *feel* then, in my body, is a reaction to what is going on in my head, disconnected from the world outside me. All of this is nothing but illusion. My body suffers, and sometimes develops what is called "organic" disease, but *I* am doing this to my body. It isn't simply happening of itself. When my fears are culturally acceptable—when people think that I "should" fear this—I get sympathy. This encourages me to go on doing it. I'm "rational" or "a sensitive person"—sometimes "courageous" or "noble." If what I fear is not culturally acceptable, then I am given a different set of labels—like neurotic or insane. In *either* case, what I am thinking is unreal and my body reacts to this thinking *as if* it were real.

When I think about all the work I have to do, my body feels tired—too tired to do even one of the jobs I have to do. When my thinking is angry, my body feels tight and bound and I am ready to explode. When I observe my thinking, I see how separated it is from reality. Sometimes my thinking starts writing letters in my mind— endlessly, going on and on, changing the words, the thoughts, revising the direction of what I'm saying. Cleverness is often bound up in this—trying to manipulate you into what would satisfy me. Not one of all these letters gets down on paper, but my body reacts to everything I'm saying in them—and if I am not pleased with these productions and keep trying, my body reacts to this frustration.

Observing my fears is easier when the fear isn't strong or long-lasting, so this is a good place to begin to see their absurdity. One afternoon I was working in my cabin, which is some distance from any other buildings. When I stopped working, I remembered that the other people here had gone on a somewhat hazardous drive that morning. I began to "worry" about them. Originally that word meant things like strangle, choke, twist—and that surely is what my worrying does to me. I watched my fantasies. The car was always going over a cliff, but the injured and the survivors kept changing. In each circumstance or combination, I fantasied what I would do, how I would rearrange my life. I became very interested, watching all these fantasies and what was involved in them, seeing their unreality. Then, when I went to Susan's house, I found that they had come back long before my fantasies began!

The more that I observe, the more that I see the process of thinking, the easier it is for me to let my fantasies go. When I am not observing them, they possess me, and my body reacts to my fears. How I do torture my body—*me*. How I suffer!

I don't mean that there's nothing to worry about. There are *always* lots and lots of things to worry about. It's just that there's no point or usefulness in worrying about them. My observation is that either what I worry about doesn't happen—or it happens anyway. All that my worrying has accomplished is to make me miserable. Usually I make some other people miserable too. When I am worrying, I am unaware of happenings around me which I otherwise would enjoy. And, in fact, when I am worrying I am unaware of something else going on which I could *do* something about. Maybe a child needs to talk to me, or my neighbor needs a ride to the store. I either don't notice or I'm too exhausted by my worrying to do anything.

By "not worrying" I don't mean ignoring what is happening if I can *do* something about it. If my income is going down, I can cut down on expenditures. If my husband is going off with someone else, or my grown-up child is going away, I can't do anything about *them*, but I can rearrange my own life to include this change, and let something new come into the space. Something always does, when I'm open to it.

If you read what I write and believe it or disbelieve it, both are nothing. Observe what goes on in yourself, accept the evidence. Then you are in touch with the facts of the process, not just dealing with words and building more illusions.

Last month I saw a Chilean whom I had known there two years ago, and he told me some of what had happened to him in between. He had been picked up by police and thrown into a prison where he saw people being tortured and killed. He was handcuffed and blindfolded and thrown on the floor of a bus. He was sure this was the end for him. He lost all hope—and knew the most beautiful peace. Bliss. He had never known anything like it before. From my own experience, I know that when I am truly hopeless all thinking stops and bliss is here. What we usually call "hopeless" is different. Then I am still hoping, *and* sure that my hopes won't come through. I am thinking all the time. This is a continuing "hopeless" that never completes itself: I don't let it become total. When I become totally hopeless, something changes.

Some other things that I say to people in groups who are exploring their thinking are:

What does this thinking do *for* you? . . .

Observe how your thinking is altogether tied to the past—and to the future . . .

Have you heard these words before? . . .

Do they have anything to do with the present, this moment . . . now? . . .

Is there any *new* thought in them? Or are they just old recordings? . . .

If you are judging or condemning your thoughts, then you are thinking about your thoughts. Make yourself an observer of what you're doing, simply seeing what goes on, like watching the changes in a sunset or a storm without opinion . . .

What is the theme, or themes, in your thinking? . . .

How often does "should" come in? . . .

These questions don't come in any kind of order. I ask them as I notice my own thoughts and what they are doing. Sometimes I ask "How can you be kinder to yourself than you are?" Many of us are so ruled by "be kind to others" that this is a mind-shaking question. Yet when I am kind to myself, kindness is, and I am kinder to others, too—in a very real, though often unconventional way.

Sometimes, after some of this experimenting, I ask people to keep their eyes closed and pay attention to their breathing. "Just pay attention to it, let it be, let it do its own doing." When I ask them to open their eyes, people often exclaim at how different people look to them—how much more vividly they see them.

The discovery that something is possible.

Sometimes I ask people to look into how grammar—the language that we've learned to speak—affects their thinking. Can you think without grammar—without the concepts you have learned? . . .

Suppose that in our language—as in some other languages—there were no concept of "could have" or "should have." Try dropping them out when they come into your thinking . . .

Try dropping out praise . . . No praise at all . . . How do you feel with that? . . . Now drop out blame . . .

Think of something that you did really well, that you felt good with the doing. Were you free just to feel good, and move on? The feeling of goodness needs no praise. In fact, praise wipes out the goodness. When I am praised, then I *think* "I did that well!" and the feeling that goes with the thinking is not the goodness that I have known from the simple accuracy of moving and doing without thought. With praise I become dependent on the approval of others, no longer moving with the good feeling of doing something on my own. Then, I do things *to* get approval. I have goals beyond the satisfaction in the doing. I become a slave, driven by others who approve me for doing what they want me to do.

Blame acts in the same way. I *intend* not to make the same mistake again. I'm so bound up with my intention that I am likely to make the same mistake again—and again—and again—and curse myself for being "no good." I'm thinking about it, and accuracy comes when I don't think—simply observe and act, free (for the moment) of all conditioning. I don't think "I can do it" or "I can't do it." I just do it, without thought. There is so much good feeling in people in emergencies when there is "no time to think."

Without words (or pictures, which are another form of words) I am accurate, I am right here and now with what is happening, and do what is appropriate in *this* situation *without thinking about it.* I am free of all conditioning and conventions at such times, simply moving on my own. At the same time, I am free and limited: free of conventions and conditioning, and limited in the sense that at this moment there are no choices. This does not in any way *feel* like a limitation: it's simply the only thing I want to do. I do it. An approximation of this in my daily life, although it is not the same as what I have described above, is asking "What do I want to do *now?*" and doing it. If I think I know what I want to do in the future, this is illusion. If I think I know what I don't want to do in the future, this also is illusion. Both limit me, and blind me to what is going on *now,* which is real. I lose touch with my life, which seems to slip away, lost between the phantoms of illusion. As one young woman said, "I feel as if life is going on out there—" waving her hand to outside the window.

When I have experienced *real* (experience is a bad word for it, but I don't have another) as the Chilean did, I don't make a production out of it afterward. That is impossible anyway because I have to use words and grammar that were invented to describe something else. But it's more than that, and I don't altogether know what the "more than that" is. I do know that when someone gushes, "Oh! I had the most wonderful experience!" I am very skeptical that it's real. Even if the experience *was* real, the memory of it is being used now to say "I'm such a wonderful/lucky, etc. person."

I do know that when I am out of maya, the world of illusion, all my past learning is available to me without my thinking about it. I use what is available to me in this moment. If I can't do anything, I do nothing, still without thinking about it. If I run from a rock that is falling from a cliff, I am not "saving my life." I simply run in accord with what is happening now, without intention or goals. It is simply the thing to do. Afterward, when I think, I may say "Whew! That was a close shave," and I may feel fear even though the real danger is past. But if I don't think about it afterward, it was nothing.

Try to feel fear without words . . .

When I focus on the feeling of fear, really get in touch with it, the fear disappears—and the same with anger.

The English language (and many others) makes it difficult for me to express what is real. The subject/object split becomes ridiculous when it says that "I save myself." Where is the "I" that saves "myself" and where is the "myself" who is saved by "I"? How can I be "a whole person" when *I* think about *myself* in this way? "I love myself." Absurd. I have split myself into I and myself, and without wholeness love is not. There is the illusion of love, along with the illusion of "I" and "myself." When I am whole, without words and thinking, love is. Love is not an idea. Love is when thought is not.

In the Hawaiian language there is not this split. When "I give you" something, you say "Mahalo" and I respond "Mahalo." Then it is like something going on between us, not a one-way street going from "me" to "you." When I truly give you something, that's the way it is: giving and receiving both going on at once, and both ways at once. "I give you" describes the outward action, what is visible. It can be seen going from my hands to yours. But what goes on between us—sensing, feeling, happiness—cannot be put into any of the words I know. Further corruption of what is real comes in when "*I* give *you*" and for this giving demand a giving back—whether in things or thank-yous. What kind of "giving" is that? It's more like barter. What kind of "giving" is it when I require that you keep what I give—or even that you accept it? No freedom. Clutch. In clutches is not freedom, is not love.

When I lived in the Islands, the Hawaiians were cooperative people. I don't mean "cooperative" in the sense of groups of people who come together and use competitive methods against another group. That's just disguised competition. I mean cooperation as a way of life. When I am not competing with you and you are not competing with me, there is no occasion for dishonesty. I don't "weigh my thoughts" or speech—I just say what is. Stop for a moment . . . take in what this means—feel the restfulness and ease of just saying what is. No one trying to get ahead of someone else . . . no comparing or trying to impress . . .

Each time I worked with Fritz, took the hot seat with him, something like this happened in me. I have seen the same thing happen with so many others. Just being here, present, disconnected from all the junk in my head. Fritz said that gestalt "leads to the discovery that something is possible." No matter how far away from it I may be later, still, I recall that it is possible.

In gestalt therapy, when someone breaks through to being real, anything he says is all right. What otherwise might be taken as criticism is simply factual and neutral. "Look around the group and tell each person how they look to you." The person goes easily from one to another, stating what he sees. The accuracy at such times is amazing to everyone in the group. He is not thinking, just observing and stating. An all-together knowing, involving (as it feels) every atom in the body. It has to be experienced to be known. Then, "forgiving" isn't just done in my head. I feel it all through me. There is no need to "forget." What I forgave is already gone. If I re-call it at any time, it's a dead memory, stirring up no agitation in me. Dead in the sense that it has no life, no feeling, no thoughts connected with it, no power over me. Just is. It no longer affects my body, my life or my doing.

Gestalt therapy, in its simpler levels, works to achieve this disillusion of the past that I have kept alive. This is a more one-by-one approach, like pulling scales from the eyes. The memories are all fantasies, and I get rid of them one at a time. Still, something happens in me in doing this. When I have let go of one memory that was binding me, I feel free. Then another appears. When I have got the habit of letting go of memories, I find more and more space in my head, and the ones that remain are softer-voiced, less clamorous. The pitfall at this stage is that it is easier for me to think they are not there. My awareness has to include softer and softer voices. Sometimes they feel like little sneaks coming in to trick me, to catch me unaware. If I don't pay attention to them, I mislead myself and think there's nothing there. As long as they are there, they influence me.

This is very different from setting them aside saying (thinking) that "I won't remember them," that "I won't let them bother me any more." When I set memories aside and say that I won't remember them, they're still actively inside me. They may not seem to bother me—perhaps for years—but any time that something triggers them, they break through with all their original vigor, and I have to work hard to shut them away again. Of course it is only "bad" memories that we do this with. One woman who did this a great deal, while remembering the "good" ones, said "I feel eroded." It's possible when "bad" memories arise to look them over, chew them up a little, and swallow them again. Doing this each time they come in can eventually clear them, but in my experience this takes several years or more, and during this time my energy is drained—energy that could be better, and more enjoyably, used for something else. When I let memories go, it's often difficult even to recall them, and when I do, they're nothing.

I am writing complete sentences. I have been taught to do this, as if it were always appropriate and meaningful. But when I say "I like you" this puts space between us which has nothing to do with "liking." When I like, liking is—and in this moment. "I used to like her" is said often enough to make clear that *liking* is not a permanent state. When I live with this fact—that sometimes liking is and sometimes liking isn't—just live with it like with clouds and sun and rain and clear sky and cold and hot and warm, life is much easier for me.

If I don't like someone or he doesn't like me, who is injured? Only ego, and as ego gets me into trouble in other ways too, I'm better off without it. Without ego, who would be in jail? Or in a mental hospital? What president would pay more attention to pomp and circumstance and keeping himself in office than to the people? In my own life, when would I be "hurt"? Who would think about "revenge"? When "he doesn't like me" is a simple fact, my life moves on without distortion. "Life is so complicated." Who makes it so?

And the point is, all of these complications are fictions. Thomas Szasz has remarked "There is no psychology. There is only biography and autobiography." Scraps and pieces of a total life put together in a way to make a *picture* of a man. What is your picture of you? Of me? "I am . . ." Say it fast, it isn't true any more. A moment ago, I was . . . Now, I am . . . When I am aware of the changes going on in me, I am in touch with the reality of me. With this awareness, I see how changing I am and everything else is. Then, "How are you?" is absurd, and any reply I make to the question is fantasy. It has nothing to do with the reality of me.

When I told Fritz of the 76th birthday party that was coming off for him in about half an hour, he was quiet for a while, then said "I don't like it, and I will go along with it." He did. What does how anyone *saw* Fritz at that party have to do with the reality of Fritz? At dinner, I said to him, "I don't give a damn about your birthday but I'm very glad you were born." He said, "Sometimes I have felt that way, not often." What light does that shed on the character of Fritz? I don't know. I don't know if what he said was largely true in his life, or seemed at that moment to be true. I don't know if he was playing the Old Sage, making a Memorable Remark. CBC had a twenty-minute television interview with Fritz, walking along a Vancouver beach. It was impressive. Many people told him so. Fritz said, "Yes, I played the Old Sage very well." I was fascinated, hearing him on TV. Only later did I realize that everything he said was fantasy, and that I had gone on fantasizing about his fantasies.

Many of us have latched onto some clues about change and about fantasies. You write me a letter. I "respond" to it. You write back as though I'm out of my mind, as if you hadn't written what you did. You wrote it and it went away. I read it and held onto it, thought about it, and wrote to you about it, thinking that I am in touch with you. But what bothered you went away, and I am writing to where you were, not where you are. My letter now is my fantasies about the fantasies you had at the time you wrote.

"You said—" "I did not!" There is no way of telling if you did say what I thought you did, or if I interpreted your words in my own context, which is different from yours, and changed your meaning to mine. Fortunately, it doesn't matter. Those words are all past, anyway, and we'll do much better if we state ourselves *now*. This was one of the delights to me in the Koolaupoko Improvement Club, which was devoted to keeping (most) improvements *out* of the Koolaupoko district in Hawaii. The Club kept no minutes. When someone said "That's not what we decided last time," it was just a statement. No one got into a discussion or argument about what was decided last time. Everyone simply looked into "What do we want now?" This was always arrived at without argument or debate. Anyone interested made a statement of how it looked to him. No one opposed him. A neutral statement of myself—not demanding—moving on to other such statements of other selves, and agreement was arrived at. Not compromise. No one "won" and no one "gave in." Everyone left the meeting with a feeling of happiness, of mutuality, and enjoyed the moonlight. There was no need of talk or touching to express what each/all of us was aware of. "Feeling" doesn't describe it. I don't know a word that does.

When I returned to the mainland, I stayed away from meetings, discussions, conferences and so on for years. Then I tried some encounter groups, which were supposed to get through this problem. So many words, so much mis-communication, so much pressure, and ego and one-upmanship. So much waste and war, even when it was expressed politely. People never really got together, even when they agreed on something. In fact, what was agreed on was satisfying to almost no one in the group. I discovered that as an observer I could see all these mix-ups. When I took part in what was going on, I got as mixed up as everyone else. As an observer, I wanted to throw everyone out of the window—not to harm them, just to wake them up out of that trance. I began to have some understanding of the violence in early Zen.

At Cowichan in the first two months I saw something really happening with people—not all of them, but many, enough to make a difference. Then, in August, Fritz brought in too many new people in relation to the nucleus that had begun to form, and the nucleus got fractured. It was like what happened when the military brought in 52,000 "defense workers" to the island of Oahu before Pearl Harbor. The life that I had loved there broke down very rapidly. In September, October and November, Fritz admitted even more people. He talked about cutting back to twenty, the original number, but kept bringing in more people. I asked him once how it happened that he talked one way and did something else. He said, "Well, Jerry is here because . . . and Lally is here because . . . and Dick is here because . . . and Marian is here because . . ." I told him, "I know all those reasons, but why do you do it?" He said, simply as a fact, "Because I am crazy." The two main factors in his craziness were being soft-hearted and ambitious. Both arise from thinking, which muddles me. I'm not very ambitious, but soft-heartedness has often got me into trouble, and wasn't good for the other people too. Hard-heartedness acts in the same way. Both these dualities take place in my thinking, my gabble zone, and influence my actions. I mix up facts and fantasies. When I have no thoughts about the situation, I simply do and my doing is right. Afterward, when I think about it, I wonder "Now why did I do that?" It is only recently that I know the answer, which can't be found in my head—where I was looking for it.

I am completely out of the world of illusion only at times, but I am much less in it than I used to be. I see the "drama" in my life as just that—some facts, mostly the illusion of what I thought about it and what other people thought about it that I took into myself and thought about too. Both the pleasure and the misery were in my thinking. This helps me now, any time I tend to be dramatic. I see the fantasy it springs from and let it go. What I learned at Cowichan from Fritz and from all of us there in the first two months is alive and growing. I don't have a gestalt community to live in, and don't know of one anywhere, and still I feel good with knowing that it is possible, and that sometimes I can live gestalt myself without it. Recently a man came here to see me. I didn't want to see anyone. I had received a letter the day before saying that this man was a bore. A lot of stuff went on in my head about "When you get well-known you have to expect this"—and also a lot of resentment that "I had to put up with it."

Then I really looked it over and saw what was going on, and out of that said "I must get rid of my slave mentality." I finished what I was doing, ate breakfast which I hadn't had yet at noon, and walked to the next building where he was—without thought, enjoying the air and the walking—and spent a half hour with him without thinking. What I got out of the half hour was the fact that I could do this. I was neither soft-hearted, as I tend to be, nor hard-hearted which sometimes comes in as a reaction, or as self-defense. I didn't need to defend, or to explain or apologize. I just was. The ease that I feel when I am just being is like never having had any burdens or dis-ease at all. The effort that goes into arriving at it—and sometimes this seems beyond what is possible—disappears. Nothing in my world has changed—only me.

One of the things that I have been aware of lately is that most of what I say is nothing, especially questions. When I am about to say something, I look it over. Often, I am just asking for attention, even with such questions as "Do you want this rock over here?" I know your answer. When I recognize the intention of the question, I let it go, and simply leave the rock where it is or move it somewhere else, aware of what I'm doing. I don't need your attention. I feel good in myself. I am aware of you, too, and feel close to you.

The command to "Think!" used to make sense to me. I often wished that people would, especially when they made so many mistakes that I wanted them to quit and let me do it myself. Now I know that their trouble *is* thinking, and that what they need to do is to pay attention to what they're doing, in the sense of being aware, exploring, observing. We fill our lives with an extraordinary lot of assumptions. A young man said to me today, "I like what Al Huang said in his book about talking with a student at Esalen, about being aware and flowing, and then, as he left her, tripping on the stairs." Al doesn't mention Esalen and it wasn't at Esalen. It doesn't matter at all that it was not at Esalen—or where it was that it happened. The extraordinary thing is that we fill in details that are sheer fantasy, and believe them to be real.

Another man watched an old Fritz film and said afterward, "At that time Fritz hadn't got on to using the pillow." I said, "I don't know whether he had or not." All that was obvious was that he didn't use a pillow in that short film. The man said "Oh!" clapped his hand to his forehead, and told me all the things that he had *imagined* while watching the film, and thought of them as fact. Fritz called gestalt "The philosophy of the obvious." That's like seeing a Christmas tree before I have hung it with decorations and embellishments of my own choosing. It is possible to see things as they are, as they are at this moment, before the decorating begins. Not easy, but possible. Then there is no sense of *I*. As Fritz wrote in the front of *Verbatim:*

> To suffer one's death
> and to be reborn
> is not easy.

It's only the fantasies I have about myself that die, and only because I have words and thoughts about them that I think they're real.

My Life Measured Out in Abandoned Words

Robert K. Hall

I have never been very interested in writing about gestalt. And yet, I have an understanding of what gestalt is. The understanding is intellectual in part, but mostly it manifests at a deep level—the level of my experience. The title of this book is very apt because, like my experience, gestalt just simply is. After the fact of what is, we can make up all kinds of things to say about it, but they'll always be things we made up to say *about* it. Experience is and gestalt is.

There are times in my life when I *know* that I'm living it. Not just thinking about it or planning it or worrying about living it, but really living it. When I'm aware, I know that I'm aware. I've noticed that when these awake-times come, I often have a desire to write something of my experience, and the words I put on paper come out looking vaguely like poems.

Recently, I noticed that there have been several distinct phases of my experience for about the past eight years. At times, during each of these phases, I climbed out of my internal dialogue long enough to experience the wonders of wakefulness. Often, I wrote a poem or two while I was awake. Looking back over the past eight years, those poems function rather like beacons. They reveal a great deal of what my existence was like during each phase. They are landmarks, signposts; they are descriptions of who I am. Because I am process, they reveal a process. Looked at in their created order, they are a string of illuminations that make a whole completed gestalt. Someone once said that poems are never completed, they are just abandoned. These poems are really abandoned words that are the wake of a process, the trail left by my awareness, wandering through time.

I have to begin somewhere, although there is really no signpost that says "beginning." I'll start with the period spent with Fritz in Big Sur: the learning period.

There was a small group of us in those days, four couples, who had made him our father-teacher. He responded to our devotion by having special group meetings for us. During these meetings, he terrorized us by tearing aside the masks we had assumed for protection against our personal demons.

In celebration of his 74th birthday, I wrote a poem for him. I remember that he came to the family dinner at my home all dressed up in his best clothes, including a tweed jacket and a beret. It was a candlelight dinner and we were all happy and full of love. Fritz was glowing. He was never very comfortable in social situations unless there was a gathering of loving friends or unless he could take the stage and perform. That birthday evening was a time when he did both. Each of us had brought a gift, something personal and made by hand. My wife had made him a beautiful shirt of green velvet. He wore it later at all the special occasions. After dinner and the opening of presents, as we were sitting around the table, Fritz read the poem aloud. While he was reading, he became very moved and wept. It was a great experience for all of us to have been able to please him so much. He had given us a priceless gift: the ability to see ourselves. Here is the poem he read that night:

Gestalt

Father, life is like a river,
each stone you drop into the clearness
becomes a new-pitched sound.
Each stick you throw will flow
down to the ocean
on a path alone its own.

Your only task while you are here
is learning to look around while gracefully
submitting
to the voyage down around.

Your teacher will be one who comes
to tell you where you are
so you don't drift away.
His words will sound a rushing stream
or wake you as a bell.

"Are you aware of your voice?
What are you feeling now?
What are your hands doing now?
Are you rehearsing something
or would you rather perform alive?"

There will be places where your aching chest
and pounding heart will tell you stay away.
But he will say to stay awhile,
for though the stream is cold,
only in its flow will you be free.

Your teacher's eyes will see you.
Will leave you on the shore to rest
another time
or tell you that he sees your pain
but knows the realness on the other side.

And every time you turn aside
the way it is right now,
his patient voice will ask you,
"What's so much better in the future?
Do you prefer stale thoughts
about a past
that's long ago upstream?"

And then you laugh.
You can't be now tomorrow.
You can't keep time in your watchpocket.
Your jeans are new.
A moth is following you.
There are daisies around here too,
and I wonder why the sky is blue.

You're really not awake, you know,
you're hiding in your head
and planning what to do.

Of course, the poem is about myself and my experience of his teachings. But it is also about the way all of us were: eager students, in awe of his wisdom, and afraid of plunging into the places where he was leading us. Those were very rich days.

That period, the learning period, began the first day I met Fritz. It was December, 1966. I was having lunch in the Esalen Institute dining room and Fritz was sitting at a table across the room. I knew who he was and I could feel the power of his gaze. I began feeling uplifted by the attention that this obviously great man was bestowing on me. He kept looking at me without shifting his eyes, and finally rose and moved to where I was sitting; he simply stood beside my chair and looked down at me. By this time, I had given up all pretense of eating my lunch and I knew that something momentous was happening. I had no time to think about what I was doing and I stood up. The energy passing between us attracted the attention of everyone in the dining room and they looked on in silence. I remember thinking then, "O.K., old man, if you are going to stare at me, I'll stare right back at you." As I looked intently into Fritz's legendary eyes, a shift occurred in my consciousness that I can't remember fully to this day. Something happened between our essences that is indelible. When I returned to my ordinary state of awareness, Fritz and I were embracing each other. Then he said to me, (the first words of the encounter), "I want you to come here and work with me." I said, without hesitation, "All right, I will."

How I managed to keep my agreement with him is another story.

At that time I was an officer in the Army but I told Fritz I would move to Big Sur, even though I knew full well that the military had refused to release me on other occasions. A general whom I knew in the Surgeon General's office was familiar with Fritz's work and he managed to get me a discharge; the following day I moved my family to Big Sur. Even then, before his fame, he was Fritz Perls.

From the moment I said "I will," a marriage was made that lifted me from the squeezing grip of establishment-orthodox psychiatry. I was tossed end over end (flailing and struggling to appear stable) into the intense world of gestalt workshops, where the madness of the mind and its emotions is made more and more explicit until the only appropriate response is one of laughter: loud, free, unrestrained, blessed laughter at the total absurdity of everybody's illusions.

I started laughing like that during one workshop in Fritz's round house on the cliff. He was training me to be his assistant by making me a participant in a world where everyone was encouraged to act out and freely reveal, through gestalt therapy, his own unique roomful of caged demons. Suddenly, I saw all of us sitting around being totally insane, and I realized that everyone in the world was doing the same thing! I started to laugh and couldn't stop: great loud bursts of laughter, bringing relief from all the tension I had been experiencing. I saw Fritz sitting there, toying with a long blade of grass, lost in his own dreams, while a neurotic, whining woman was complaining to her fantasy father about his withholding of love. As I was gasping for breath and rocking back and forth with laughter at this scene, Fritz looked up at me, recognized what I was experiencing, and, eyes shining with tears, he laughed with me. Everyone was amazed and indignant that we could be so irreverent before the great god, neurosis.

Here's another short poem that I wrote during that time. It's entitled *Aristotelian Schizophrenia.*

> I'm not sad anymore
> because I keep having
> this hallucination
> that makes me laugh
> when I'm sad.

So I keep laughing
all the time
and that makes other people
think I'm mad.

So they want to lock me up,
not knowing that I'm
laughing at *them*
for thinking I'm mad.

That's when my hallucination
(that I haven't told you about)
becomes them . . . .

That is, unless you can
laugh separately
at two things at the same time
without laughing twice.

I loved Fritz Perls with everything available to me. He was a hard teacher. He taught me to be a gestalt therapist secondarily, and a man first. He did this by assuming that I was already in possession of every skill I needed to function as a therapist, and he acted accordingly. He gave me no techniques for doing gestalt and gave me groups to lead without preparing me very much in any way. He simply let me watch him several times during five-day workshops and then said, "O.K., now you're ready. You do it." In doing this, he treated me with more respect than anyone in my life had done to that time.

When I first arrived to study with him, having moved my family to Big Sur with neither money nor prospects of being able to support them, Fritz put me in charge of a group of people who he said were to be trained to be gestalt therapists. They were all outrageous egotists, and each one of them knew much more about gestalt therapy than I did. That group was a disaster. But I had to work hard on myself and call on every shred of self-reliance available to my bumbling psyche. Every time Fritz visited the group to "observe" the progress of the training, I used the opportunity to work with him on my weaknesses and failings. He would never allow me more than a token support for those, however, and would respond to my protestations of ineptness by challenging me more. Once at a dream seminar, attended by 200 people, he announced that I would work with the next volunteer from the audience who had a dream. When he did that, without warning me in advance, I was seized with the most violent dread that no one would volunteer to work with me when Fritz was there available to them. I imagined myself sitting there, waiting, with a sea of hostile faces staring at me. But, they came. Many people were afraid of Fritz's refusal to compromise with dishonesty and his abrupt announcement, "You are lying, you are a phony." And they were eager to try the game with me. He once told me, "You won't have such a hard time as I've had, because you aren't such a prick."

Moving my middle-class nest to the intensity of Esalen, a community of "here and now" freaks, was an incredible experiment-in-living. The culture shock was as real as the one I experienced later upon my return to California from India. I moved my family to Esalen the day after my discharge from the army, where I had spent the previous *six years* as an army psychiatrist! The abrupt change from the world of military delusion to Esalen was experienced by my family like a move to Disneyland.

Here is another poem written during that period. It pretty much describes some of my experience during that confused and marvelous time:

> I'm visiting here
> and there must be
> a bed to lie
> next to someone
> in
> somewhere—
> whispers—an absurd
> number of voices—
>
> Each one straining
> to hear
> the other
> over the roar
> of its own sound.

        At times, one can
        hear them all.

Here's another one, rather in the same mood. My experiences with
Fritz were forcing me to confront my aloneness. Although the learning during that period was often exciting, and brought all the joy
that comes with finding out what I've known all along was true,
there was the inevitable sadness that comes with confronting what is.
Joy and sadness. They go together.

        I'm alone here
        but for everyone else
        whose minds
        are blinking
        on and off.

        So I'll slide along
        and keep warm
        by peering around
        corners
        before turning them.

        Then the distance
        from one to another
        will only seem
        like a small
        light
        wind.

When I arrived at Esalen, one of the first people I met was a
young lady, heavy with child, who announced to me that Fritz had
told her I would deliver her baby. Fritz was loved and trusted like an
ideal father by a small group of people there, and I soon discovered
that if Fritz said I would deliver the baby—that's exactly what
would happen. I hadn't seen a delivery in about six years, I had no
equipment for home deliveries, and I knew nothing of natural child-
birth. Several months later we delivered a healthy boy on the kitchen
table. This success was followed by a number of other natural de-

liveries among Fritz's circle. Each one became more ritualized than the preceding, until no birth occurred without flutes, guitars, chanting, incense, dogs, children, and me—standing rather redundantly in the vicinity, in awe of the innocence and love of these people who were real pioneers on the frontiers of consciousness.

While I was with Fritz, and at his suggestion, I had my first experience under the hands of Ida Rolf, in rolfing therapy, and later, as a student of Ida's. I had no idea that the body was anything other than the most immediately recognizable part of me or another person. My awareness of my physical self, prior to rolfing, was limited to sensations of sexual pleasures, eating, elimination, and the pain of tight shoulder muscles (that reflected an average amount of paranoid attitudes). The expansion of my consciousness to include the exquisite awareness of myself as a physical body was a process that stopped me from kidding myself about what the body is. I knew it was not permanent. That revelation was a huge step in my education on life and death. I saw everyone around me acting as if they were going to live forever. I became obsessed with the experience of my body-feelings and obsessed with thoughts of death. Almost all the people I worked with in gestalt groups were preoccupied with whether they were loved by others or not. Everybody was seeking after some childhood father's or mother's approval. I started doing Hatha yoga with fanaticism. I was so eager to feel the stretch of my own tendons because doing that made me feel alive! I became more and more in touch with the minutest tensions and vaguest sensations of my physical body. I began to identify myself with my body.

Here is a short poem from that time, which was the beginning of the black period. I call it the black period now, because it was a time of real despair. It came upon me as I realized that my mind wasn't going to be of any use in figuring it all out. I didn't know anything.

Metaphysical Circles

"What are you?"
is what I've been saying
for quite some time
now.

It seems to be
a question
asked of me
by some always flickering
center of me.

Which is not quite me
but part of something more
than me—
that includes me.

Now—
(by Aristolelian logic)
I must know already
that which I keep learning.

"Next question, please . . . ."

I saw myself clearly as a transitory being whose submission to illness, decay and physical death was inevitable. I became terrified at times that each heartbeat would be the last. I struggled to keep on breathing. Every moment became a hell of intense self-awareness. I knew a lot about myself, but I was crazy. I knew also, during this time, that what I was experiencing was being *avoided*, through mental trickery, by many of those around me. Real awareness of death is much too big a reality for an unprepared student to handle.

I read occult and quasi-mystical literature unendingly, searching for more meaning. I had an uneasy knowledge that I was going to enter a new country, and I was looking for road maps.

Then, one night during the peak intensity of this battle with my body, I spontaneously loosened my hold on "reality." Actually, my grip on the way I *thought* everything *should* be was gently, but abruptly, loosened for me. Probably I just got too tired to hang onto all the crap any longer. I sank deeply into a regression. I journeyed back into time until I saw myself as a baby lying on my back, kicking and protesting my delivery into this world. I think my body actually recreated those movements. Then I lost consciousness of my surroundings. I remember being very frightened and begging my wife to help me, and I remember her perfect response: "I can't help you." I had the most profoundly lucid understanding that I had no control over the beating of my own heart. It could stop without my permission at any time, so I might as well give up the struggle, submit to life/death and relax. I did.

I slipped into strange landscapes where beings I did not recognize appeared suddenly out of light and gazed at me, said nothing, then quickly disappeared. I do not know how long I travelled in that world, but it was nearly dawn when I came back into my body. For the first time, I felt that I was located in my legs, as well as in my upper torso. My body seemed to grow longer, like Alice in Wonderland when she drank out of the magic bottle. I had not opened my eyes yet, but I knew for certain that I had died, and I was reluctant to look around and see where I had come to. I remember keeping my eyes closed a long time before I found the courage to peep out.

When I opened them, I simultaneously experienced my own essence, myself, flowing through an opening in a dimension of consciousness, just as water flows through a drain. I instantly emerged, accompanied by a loud sound, like the sound of a vacuum breaking, into my old room. But the way I perceived myself was now astounding and filled me with the greatest ecstasy that I had experienced in all my life. I was golden light, and I filled that room with warmth and light. My dimensions extended far beyond the confines of my physical body, which I felt as weightless and fluid in motion, with more grace of movement than I had ever imagined possible. I remained in a joyous state of mind for days afterward. I knew that I was beginning on a long journey and that my life would never be the same. I could never again identify myself completely with my physical form. One more clinging hold had been loosened.

Much later, when I could look back on the black period with some perspective, I wrote this about it. It describes one aspect of that period:

"There's a center in my life now. It's the melody of the tao. I know about the tao, because I know when I'm *not* living in the tao." I feel the strain of living in opposition to the tao, and then I know that I have some adjustment to make somewhere. I feel the strain in my body.

A friend of mine says, "I know when I'm not loving." That's true. We all know when we're not loving.

When we moved back to Mill Valley from being with Fritz in Big Sur, we moved into a big comfortable house that had a swimming pool. It was the first home we had ever owned. There was plenty of work for me to do—actually too much, since I was working with four groups a week and six or seven people individually each day. My "practice" was quickly established, the house was a beautiful family home, the family was close and contented. My professional and personal star was on the ascendant. I, myself, was miserable. Too much success. I couldn't handle it.

I learned, indelibly written on my experience, that inner peace and contentment have nothing to do with what most of the world calls success. I learned that lesson firsthand in the school of the tao.

I made money, and I wanted more money. I had 150 patients (or clients or something—I never knew what to call them) and I wanted to accept more because I wanted everyone in the world to love me. I wanted power.

The results of my desires for more of everything were:

(1) I paid all my savings in income tax.
(2) I worked all the time, even weekends, because of weekend workshops that I held at the house.
(3) I became exhausted and depressed.
(4) I fought with my wife.
(5) I fought with my friends.
(6) I developed a martyr complex.
(7) I became terrified that I was going to die any minute of a heart attack.
(8) I learned a lot about myself.

When I had dug myself into a pit so deeply that I could no longer climb out to save myself, I was ready to listen to spiritual values. That is when they came, when I had defeated myself and was ready to accept that I was helpless. Fritz had been telling me that I was helpless all along. I'm a slow learner.

The next phase was what I call my devotion phase. I gave up expecting any answers from my intellect. I accepted a spiritual teacher, practiced his instructions, and I even travelled to India to study with him. The devotional period was a very intense and happy time. There was much to learn. Devotion to the teacher and regular meditation were the methods and I still use them.

My teacher taught me to meditate. Meditation became a really important part of my life, and sometimes I wrote about it. The teacher taught me to practice, in meditation, listening to an inner sound. He told me to concentrate on that inner sound and see what happens. At first I practiced meditation out of desperation. Then, later, the practice became really enjoyable. Now, it is my main way of enjoying myself, of playing. I've found that meditation and gestalt are very similar. Meditation is gestalt done inwardly and with oneself. Gestalt is meditation expressed. You need a teacher though, because learning meditation is the most difficult thing in the world to do.

Since I was experiencing devotion during this period, my poems were devotional poems. Sometimes they tended to be a bit extravagant. I've always tended to be dramatic about my feelings. Experiencing devotion made me more so. Here is one of the first poems I wrote during that period: (It is actually a love poem written in gratitude to my teacher).

I would sing a song to You
like the bird I hear who repeats
the same amorous caress over and over.

I would write a poem to You
like this man who empties these words
onto a page, and thinks them not enough.

The electric ineffable body of Your Love
is Here Now
and I would return the same to You
if I existed.

I remember how You descended
concrete steps to me and took my hand.
I looked into Your onyx eyes
but they did not gaze at me.

213

I would capture time with my mind,
for there is no other place
where I could drift and lie with You
and Your golden face will float
forever next to mine.

While I was in India, I had many experiences with my teacher that
affected me deeply. Somehow those experiences have become part of
the gestalt that is me, and have determined much of the flavor of the
way I work and live. Here is a description of one kind of experience
with my spiritual teacher. The intensity of the feelings I had for the
teacher are obvious:

"He is capitalized, because He is superconscious. He is obviously
different from the grayness of ordinary men, because there is something about the way He walks and something about the sound of His
voice that affects me. Sometimes He glances into my eyes, and a
shutter opens onto daisy-tossed filtered light-meadows where animal
spirits play, and just as quickly, the shutter closes. What was an
instant's tear in the fabric of dimensions is simultaneously closed
with the movement onward of His eyes. He just seems to be looking
around and turning His gaze to someone else.

"He sits in an awesome marble-floored room where occasionally a
swallow darts from the region of a balcony that rims the entire space.
There are windows and wooden doors that open onto the sunlight.
He rests in an oversized armchair that tilts backwards slightly, so that
He appears to be partially reclining. The marble floor is covered with
the bodies of 500 of His lovers. They squat on their haunches and
watch His every movement, as though there could be one quiver of a
finger that would bring them truth and must be seen to be known.
He sits facing them. No one speaks. There is an intensity in the air
that could be carved into a symphony, and He is the recurrent
theme. He gazes about this collection of persons and, although He
doesn't smile, there is some special kind of loving greeting in the
expression of His eyes. And then one lone voice from somewhere in
the crowd begins to chant a beautiful lilting song in praise of His
love. The sound is full, for the voice is strong. The echoes from the
lofty brick walls descend from all directions and cover us all like an

eiderdown made of gauze vibrations. Then the chant is taken up by 500 voices and repeats to the original singer. The great room is full of the joyous voices of this great inner circle.

"The singing stops, and there is a moment of silence when not even a breath is heard. The birds are not singing. He speaks, and His voice is the same as the sound of the 500, full and ripe and sonorous as bells. Then, one by one, His aides bring before Him the people who are seeking His gift. They are of all classes, these seekers. Some are simple farmers, some are finely dressed rich men. There are widows and young women, and some bear the look of merchants. But the expression of the face of each is the same—dazed, in wonder and awed. Some are unable to lift their eyes to meet His and stand meekly, watching the floor, as though waiting to disappear into the polished reflections of white marble. Others suddenly lift their eyes and stare like children into the face of the One who is Santa Claus, and Moses and Genghis Khan. Here is the loving conqueror, but His empire is not one of stone and earth, but of the Spirit, and they know that—it is written as plainly on their faces as the mark of recognition it is rumored that He reads on their foreheads. The mark of a returning soul, the brand of discipleship. One by one they are led shuffling forward. To each He asks a question and some respond by nodding their heads, while others whisper assent. Then the moment of reckoning arrives. He signals acceptance with His one hand or rejection with the other. Surely this is the Shepherd gathering His sheep, and He knows which are His, because He was present at their inception and not a breath has been drawn that He didn't witness and recognize. For some, the time is ripe, and their feet are planted on that narrow path as firmly as a loving father stands the firstborn son and teaches baby-legs to walk. For others, there is the slight movement of the hand, and they are led gently out of the hall, sometimes looking backwards over their shoulders as though to be sure that they had really seen that face. Many of them will be back another time to ask again, but only He knows when the waiting is finished.

"When all the seekers have made that short journey and have stood an eternity before the penetrating power of those eyes, instructions in the practice of an ancient science are begun. Very clearly, without any wasted explanation, that gentle voice describes what must be done and the method of doing it. They listen with every eye on that face, for what is being passed to them is the reward of lifetimes, the knowledge of a million schools and thousands of days of toiling the hard Earth in the broiling sun."

Looking back over things like that piece, written during the devotion period, is a bit embarrassing now. The feelings are so extravagant, the images are so rich. But the words reflect accurately the way I was. I was in love. A being had come into my life who was without the slightest trace of insecurity. I was very insecure, and I could see that everyone else that I knew was also.

I had come into contact with a man who moved through this world with complete grace and wisdom. Watching him go about his daily business of living was like watching a perfectly danced ballet. I recognized myself to be an awkward beginner compared to this Master. I watched him closely and carefully. In the unfolding of our drama together, I saw that his performance was flawless, but I wasn't yet willing to acknowledge that mine was too. I knew that he could teach me to experience my existence as perfection.

I fell in love with an example of what I knew I *could* be. His wisdom was so much more profound than anything I had ever experienced that I became at last willing to listen to what was being told to me.

He told me many things, but the essence of it all was, "Look within your body. Meditate." The more I looked, the more love I experienced and the more I watched my wisdom grow. He was teaching me true.

I travelled a lot during that devotion period. Here is a short poem written on a beach in Mexico. Everywhere I went, I was in love.

> The air is a fresh tangerine.
> Children laugh.
> The surf washes my ears and this page.
> Waiting for you to come
> is waiting.
> What can we do, Father, but think
> of you,
> if you allow it?

Will I always drift
between vertebrae
and sunburned flesh?
Is there such a thing
as not knowing?

My lungs fill and empty.
Is there still more to do?
I see the sea
but I can't see you.
I'm trapped by flesh and thought.
Pink, toothless and corruptible.

And again, here is a fragment taken from a journal I kept during
that time. The date is Dec. 30, 1972; the place, Zihuatanejo, Mexico.
"Another idyllic day of sun and salt water. If I could see you, I
would write words of love. My words now are a lament, a longing.
Yet I'm surrounded by life and beauty."

Gradually, meditation has become as much a part of my existence
as gestalt became back in the Big Sur days. Gestalt tends to infiltrate
one's being and alter one's whole perspective of life. Meditation does
the same. The two practices are very similar. In gestalt, we learn how
to watch ourselves unfold and become revealed to ourselves and
others. It is a way of making existence, and how we color it, more
and more explicit. Gestalt is meditation expressed. In meditation,
one sits quietly (without interfering) and watches the drama of mind
and body unfold from moment to moment. But we try to remain an
observer. The drama is watched closely, not acted out. The act of
watching is the only action involved. It is a very subtle work. And
then, very gradually and over much time, the distinction between the
observer and the drama being observed begins to blur. Finally, the
distinction is lost and there is just awareness process.

The poems that I have written about meditation have evolved
through phases, as the meditation has become more deep and meaningful. The first poems were devotional and were actually conversations with my teacher. Here is one:

Behind the moving mosaic
I feel you watching.

Random half-seen designs
grey blank spaces that burst open
like a ripe tomato
and one white seed in a moisture of red
takes my eye
and I am looking I don't know how long.

Again I search for your face
but an old friend calls me with happy memories
and I dance for another eternity
around imagined conversations,
old sexual movies, and future tactics
in a war of personal power.

I awaken suddenly, remember your names
and call you briefly
before the color of a lover's eyes sweeps me away
into a world of childish play
where I create towers of building blocks,
knock them down, and then begin to build again.

Somehow I sense your Grace again
and cry your names
but my sounds are lost in howling thoughts
that burn my eyes with dust
and shake my legs with desire.

FOOD! Perhaps a tangerine—
plays upon the screen and disappears
covered half over with plans
for some task to be completed later in the day.

What a dream this is!
I'm thankful that you've told me of the plot.
Behind the moving mosaic of my mind
I sense you watching.

But my popcorn is gone
The seats are half-empty (the cartoon is over)
I've seen the feature several times before
I'm afraid of the dark
And it's time to go home.

Later and more recently, the poems have tended to become a bit
more objective and less directed towards the teacher. This happens as
I get more familiar with the mind, more able to watch thoughts in
action. Here is another one about meditation and what meditation
teaches:

Those thoughts aren't necessary anymore.
There is just a habit of thinking
all the time all the time all the time,
there is no release there,
the path to liberation is camouflaged by all that thinking.

We get so fascinated by the moving mosaic
all the pretty colors of thinking
and thinking and thinking and thinking
and scheming and planning
and hoping that somehow we'll get satisfied.
But thinking is not moving onward, just moving around.

There's something else to do that's easier.
And I must hurry to write this down now
before I get lost in thinking
again.
Those thoughts aren't necessary anymore
they are revolving doors that keep us on the wheel.

Replace your thoughts with listening to the song of songs.
It is more real and brings more joy.
That song is sung in a clear voice just behind the
droning of your thought dreams
dreaming.

Listen to the unspoken Word and leave
your isolated prison.
There is the melody of love and liberation
being sung in raptured harmonies
so near to where you are
that one glance away from thought
will free your heart.

The most recent phase, the one following the devotional phase, and the one I'm in now, is what I call the period of digestion. At last I am opening to receive the message of both gestalt and meditation without confusing the message with the teachers. Things are getting simpler. I'm learning that everything is truly all right, that everything goes on just as it's supposed to and that I only have to enjoy. In short, everything is. That's all.

This digestion and absorption period seems to complete the gestalt begun with the learning phase. The understandings I've come to are simply the ones that were told to me in the learning phase. How simple. I passed through an entire process of growth in order to make them mine, in order to know what was told to me in the beginning.

Of course, the poems reflect this new phase, just as they have the other phases. The poems on meditation are starker, simpler, and less emotionally contrived:

Meditation
The mind drifts
while the spine hurts
and
the universe somehow fits
into this small body.

There is a triangle sitting here.
It is what I think is me
meditating.
At the top of the triangle
is a sound
ringing.

There are more poems about simply being now, also. They are merely descriptions of experience. Here is one about a moment in the sun of Guatemala:

> The vertebrae
> placed one on another
> like a child's building blocks
> have joined together with space
> and conspired to sit upright here.
>
> So this is the moment . . . . . .
> feet scuffling by on concrete,
> scraping, rasping sound
> out of the desire to move,
> and someone walks past this chair.
>
> Can it be true, there is no one
> who listens? Can it be true
> there is just the listening
> going on and on, related in some
> undramatic way to this pile
> of vertebrae and this
> chair and this sunlit
> dappled pattern?
>
> This body collects here toad-like,
> complacent and watchful,
> glittering eyes turning this way and that
> recording light and dark and color
> and movement.
> When the head moves, vertebrae turn.
> And gods change the world.

And here is one from the digestion phase that offers a clear statement on the mind and thinking:

The mind can't even know nothing.
because what it knows is thought,
and it can only know one thing at a time
and thought is some thing,
isn't it now?
So the mind can't know nothing
it can only know some thing
and some thing is not no-thing
I think.
Therefore I think I know something
when what I'm really looking for is
Nothing.

And here is one about reaching forty and finishing a gestalt and resting and being with what is:

I am growing older
I can tell, because I play with children lately
and I don't remember doing that before.
Yesterday, I knew what a grandfather is.
I just remembered that I knew.
And then later, I sat before the fire
like old men do.

And in between dreams
I thought a little about my heart.

Gestalt Therapy as a Meditative Practice

Stella Resnick

I like to think of gestalt therapy as an operational existentialism. This implies that gestalt therapy is not just a philosophy of being in the present but also a set of operations which, with practice, implement the skills of living in the present. We are so conditioned to live in our heads, to follow the dictates of conscience, habit, and expectation that by the time most people reach adulthood they have learned not to let their moment-to-moment experience interfere with their "lives." Gestalt therapy is a return to the present, not only philosophically but in practice as well. The practices most responsible for growth in therapy are along two intertwining tracks: one deals with expressing unfinished business, the other with self-awareness.

The old term for expression is catharsis; every major psychotherapy aims for the release of "pent-up emotions." We go through life experiencing our experiences in spite of ourselves, holding back our feelings because that's what we were taught to do. Everything goes in but not much comes out until, finally, we are so stuffed with unexpressed emotion that we either explode or withdraw from any further stimulation. We are like the zen master's overflowing cup; we get so filled with held-in past experience that there's no room for new data, new living. Gestalt therapy counters societal sanctions against expression by encouraging people to go after and get rid of their stockpiles of unexpressed feeling. People learn not only that expressing themselves is good and right but they learn *how* to express themselves. They reactivate unfamiliar release mechanisms, doing it safely by hitting a pillow or telling off an empty chair.

In this paper, I'm most interested in the second major psychotherapeutic track: insight, awareness and self-discovery. When most people first start out in therapy, they are unused to paying attention to their experience. When the therapist suggests that they close their eyes and report what they're aware of, they don't know where to look; it's dark in there. People frequently say that they don't know what they're feeling right now, although they can quite speedily respond with what they are thinking.

In order to learn to lead lives that are fulfilling, energetic and enjoyable, people have to be able to first discern what feels good or bad. Then people have to learn how to maximize the good feelings—the energetic flow of experience—and minimize the energy-stoppers—pain and lack of satisfaction as a way of life. Basically, what we need is information about ourselves. Who am I? What turns me on? How do I stop myself? How do I hurt myself? What do I want? What do I need? How do I satisfy myself?

In gestalt therapy, people pay attention to their inner mind-body process as a way of getting information for themselves about themselves. This doesn't come easy. Most of the time, we're so caught up in *what* we're doing that we don't notice *that* we are doing or feeling or wanting. We identify with the content of what we are saying rather than noticing the process. When people identify with the content of what they are saying and doing rather than simply noticing themselves saying and doing, they get stuck in the endless repetition of process: feeling sorry for themselves, blaming their parents, judging themselves, or whatever.

The difficulty is that much of our experience is so taken for granted that it recedes into the background of awareness. Marshall McLuhan said, "I don't know who discovered water but I'm sure it wasn't the fish." The fish is totally submerged within his medium; the only way he can discover water is if he gets out of it for a moment and gets back in. Then he might say, "Mmmmmmmmmm, I'm in something I wasn't in a moment ago." Another possibility is for him to stick his tail out of the water and notice that most of him is in something that a piece of him is out of. Somehow, we have to find ways of observing our process without being so immersed in it that we miss out on vital aspects of our living. To learn about ourselves, we need to not only be doing, but observing ourselves as well. Psychotherapy must be a practice of self-observation as well as self-expression.

Different therapists develop different styles of getting people to notice their process without being submerged in it. Fritz Perls was the great frustrator: he teased, chided, and sometimes condemned the process that the person was not aware of and not taking responsibility for. Other therapists align themselves with the person's healthy process and poke fun at the self-defeating process. In any case, the object of the therapist is simply to get the person to see the whole process clearly, without the blindness caused by taking parts of it for granted. For me, the best way to teach people to see their own process rather than to be submerged in it is to have them practice gestalt awareness as expressed meditation.

All the different forms of meditation, like Transcendental Meditation or Vipassana, have a common element of staying with the experience of the moment. Vipassana or insight meditation is very much like the gestalt process. In this Theravadin Buddhist practice, we start by anchoring our attention to the breath, making a mental note of the abdomen rising with the incoming breath and falling with the outgoing breath. We notice when the mind wanders from the breathing to a thought, sound, or daydream, and bring ourselves back to the breathing. Awareness of the moment-to-moment mind-body process in meditation is referred to as mindfulness. Noticing the process without identifying with the content, often spoken of as impartial witnessing, is a skill which, when practiced, leads one to a more complete and objective observing of one's inner experience.

This process of mindfulness in Vipassana meditation is very similar to the practice of expressing one's continuum of awareness out loud in gestalt therapy. In this exercise, the person pays attention to him- or herself and reports out loud what he or she is aware of: any thoughts, feelings, sensations and actions. "I'm gesturing now; I'm making a big circle with my right hand. Now my mouth is dry; I'm feeling scared." As in the Vipassana meditation, developing the ability to be an impartial witness to one's inner process is crucial to the gestalt awareness.

An impartial witness observes without judging. A witness who judges is not much of a witness, since bias generally restricts observation to confirming evidence. I instruct people to meditate out loud as though they were performing a soliloquy, a gestalt soliloquy where they are the audience as well as the actor. As audience, they are the impartial witness, watching the performance without judging it. As a result, the performance is not only cathartic but becomes informative as well, leading to insight and understanding. In gestalt therapy there are a number of practices that facilitate feeding information to the impartial witness as a way of maximizing objective self-observation.

Exaggeration—making a gesture, posture or vocalization larger—is one of the most effective ways of seeing oneself. If you simply do what you've been doing all along, the sensations and kinesthetic cues are very familiar and recede into the background. But if you exaggerate, doing deliberately what you ordinarily do unconsciously, you can see yourself more clearly. Exaggeration facilitates impartial witnessing. It keeps you from being totally submerged. Now you've got at least your tail out of the water.

The emphasis on precise language contributes to impartial witnessing by demanding that language accurately reflect experience. Changing it to I, turning questions into their underlying statements, turning fragments of thoughts into complete sentences, making the implicit explicit, are all ways to facilitate witnessing. In this way, people learn more by listening to themselves than by what they hear from others. Likewise, repetition of words, phrases, and gestures facilitates witnessing by repeating a spontaneously generated action for the purpose of observation.

By meditating out loud and using the variety of gestalt practices that facilitates witnessing, people learn to amplify the signals of their experience. It is as though certain signals which begin to rise as figure against the background of the constant internal noise are further developed to stand out clearly from the noise. Then people can do

226

on purpose what they originally did by default, in order to gain further awareness of the details of their patterns. But the clarity of self-observation is not the only effect of this gestalt meditation. An even more important effect is that watching oneself without judging encourages people to be more allowing with themselves, and this reinforces self-acceptance. When people first start out in therapy, one of the most frequently verbalized resistances is that they are afraid to see themselves because they think they won't like what they see. They are judging themselves, and this judging is experienced with pain. If people continue to judge what they see, the pain will keep them from really looking. They will get stuck in the judging and the pain of self-condemnation. On the other hand, if they learn to see without judging, the process becomes exciting and reinforces being allowing with oneself.

The impartial witness is an antidote to the topdog, the dictatorial inner voice that is endemic in our culture. Most people's unhappiness can be traced directly to the tone of voice in which they talk to themselves—often nagging, demanding and critical. But while we want to disempower, or even better, de-condition the topdog, we certainly don't want to strengthen the whining, resistant underdog.

The underdog makes the topdog. Without a victim to shove around, there would be no dictator. In fact, as the person takes responsibility for his or her experience, watching without identifying with either voice, a reconciliation of these opposites takes place. Duality and polarity give way to unity and integration. Another voice begins to emerge, a voice of caring and wisdom, which functions in a directing mode, taking account of the essential integrity of the organism.

The many internal voices are convenient ways of experiencing the multitude of different functions of the human organism. Each function is given a voice as a way of externalizing and witnessing that inner process. The topdog dictator is what happens when we are conditioned to invest too much power in the intellect. As the individual becomes more and more integrated, the power assigned to any voice begins to vary more according to need and circumstance than by intellectual fiat. The voice that rises out of the weakening topdog-underdog conflict functions as a democratic, compassionate, wise director rather than a dictator. People are always impressed and excited by their discovery of this part of them. Call it spirit guide, call it contacting one's divinity or simply call it a voice of integration and health, the experience is a high one and restores faith in self.

Giving up self-victimization as a way of enervating a dictatorial process, and achieving harmony and integration through realization, not condemnation, of the different parts has obvious implications for a healthy society as well as for the healthy person.

Simply noticing, then, inspires compassion and integration in gestalt meditation as it does in the more traditional meditative practices. Compassion toward oneself is the prototype of the compassion one has for others. Playing self-condemning and self-improvement games keeps people on the path of seeking but never finding. Witnessing without judging uncovers a directing function that assigns appropriate weights to all the different functions, reducing internal conflict and self-victimization. Decision, which is the usurpation of power by some functions over others, gives way to choice and preference: The human organism, instead of being an arena of internal strife, becomes a unit of different yet harmonious parts. Growth comes not through goals of unrealistic perfection, but out of a place of inner support and self love, through a continual process of realization of the parts. The effect is spiritual, an awareness of essence; something that many of us in gestalt therapy have ignored for too long.

Figure/Ground: Gestalt/Zen

Marc Joslyn

Years ago Fritz Perls discouraged a professional therapist in a group I was attending from calling himself a "gestalt therapist." Whatever Perls intended for that unique person, time and place, nowadays his remark reminds me of the statements of zen masters: "There is zen but no teachers of zen!" "Whenever you say 'Buddha' go wash your mouth out!" Perls used to disparage, during therapy sessions especially, all "talking about" or distancing oneself from one's immediate perceptions and feelings. But, like students of gestalt therapy, students of zen do on occasion "talk about," do "give lectures" and "write chapters." So let me start by affirming my arrogance in writing this. After I die I shall surely go to a hell for gestalt therapy students and zen students. Will you join me there?

A central theme in this paper is the figure/ground phenomenon. Prior to the gestalt psychologists, the main emphasis in academic psychology was on the gradual, quantitative or general aspects of experience. Research was directed mostly toward finding exchangeable "things" or "events" and reducing them to quantitative formulas. Change was seen mostly as a result of a gradual step-by-step process of quantitative accumulation. With the introduction of gestalt, attention was shifted to sudden, unprecedented changes; to the unique, spontaneous, qualitative, non-exchangeable and irreducible.

Still, with all the contributions made by the gestalt psychologists, they tended to limit themselves to the figural, visual, and spatial aspects of experience. They tended to ignore the field-like, non-formal, non-visual, temporal aspects. This was corrected somewhat by the work on visual figure/ground phenomena by Danish psychologist Rubin. Attention was then brought to the "holes" or nothingness aspect around and in the midst of forms or somethingness. Ground was quickly assimilated into the main body of gestalt theory and today "figure/ground" or "figure/field" is almost synonymous with gestalt.

Work on "reversible figures" by Rubin and others showed that a figure could be alternately figure or ground. Work on "field theory" by Lewin and others showed that fields can take on figural attributes and vice versa, but somehow the interpenetration of figure and field did not become an important feature in gestalt theory. Even the imaginative work done by Metzger on the "ganzfeld" or "total field" did not go much beyond the visual implications.

Koffka devoted five long chapters to "the environmental field," one of which is entitled "visual organization" and another "figure and ground." But though Koffka in the same book made an extensive attempt to develop figure/ground and other gestalt laws to incorporate memory, will, action, and though he referred to the "silent organization" in human experience, figure remained limited essentially to inside-the-form visual phenomena, and ground to outside-the-form phenomena. The gestalt psychologists were so occupied with creating a "scientific psychology" and refuting traditional metaphysics that they perhaps could not afford to take a more complete phenomenological approach.

Koffka may have come closest to realizing the problem when he referred in passing to a "supersensory ground," a ground from which all sensory figures arise and to which all figures return. When this approach is followed through radically, there is no such thing as "*a* field." There is only "field," just as there is only "eternity." It is meaningless to talk of imposing any condition or limitation whatsoever outside or inside eternity. Likewise, as soon as any condition like "visual" or "auditory," "personal" or "environmental" is appended to "field" it is no longer field but a figure of sorts, loosely defined though it may be.

But how does field become figure? And how is it that a figure after appearing from field and developing what the gestalt psychologists called "good form," "pragnanz" and "physiognomic character," tends to disappear into field once again?

It took the "organismic" research of Goldstein and others to show how the figure/ground and related principles could be applied to the total motivation and action process of human beings, and that physical and mental pathologies could be more economically viewed in terms of these principles.

But it was Perls, together with his wife Laura, who most insightfully and thoroughly applied the gestalt discoveries, especially figure/ground, to psychotherapy. I have looked in vain for some discussion in one of Perls' books which would link figure/ground on the one hand and hunger, desire, willing, caring on the other hand. I have searched in vain through my memories of conversations with him for other signs of a theoretical link. There are various precedents in the form of hints and speculations such as Koffka's discussion of the "demand character" of figures or Wertheimer's remark that "a transformation takes place from 'what I want' to 'what the situation requires,'" or Goldstein's statement that "the foreground-background relation is . . . the basic form of the functioning of the nervous system." But somehow Perls was the first to assume (modestly or arrogantly, and in his very first book *Ego, Hunger and Aggression*) the identity of figure/ground on the one hand, and the birth, fulfillment, and disappearance of hunger and interest on the other hand. All Perls' subsequent discussions are elaborations of this initial assumption, not explanations or proof of how he arrived at it.

In his therapy sessions there was the ever-present working hypothesis that our most current need or interest tends to come naturally to the foreground of attention while all else tends to recede into the background. Or, to put it in another way, if I am attending properly, I will discover that what is in the foreground of attention is indeed the most important thing here-and-now, whether it is an itch that needs scratching, an idea that needs clarification or a tree that needs planting in a particular garden location. I recall how I once interrupted the flow of awareness in a session. Perls asked me where my attention was during the interruption. When I told him, he chided me: "What's the matter? Being just an ass-scratcher is not enough for you?"

Perhaps Perls' discovery went past all his preceding experience with psychoanalysis and gestalt to an everyday etymological identity between perception and emotion and motivation. Are not our very words "lack," "want," "longing," "need," synonymous with "separation," "limitation," "interest," "direction"? When figure is born of ground, is not hunger or interest of one sort or another born simultaneously? Assuming proper attention, when the figure returns to ground, doesn't hunger die also? And this is true no matter how we conceptually allocate the source of hunger, whether as the hunger of an idea or the hunger of a garden.

Can you realize your whole life as a changing reversible figure, or as a moving kaleidoscope with all the differentiation which experience provides and yet with no loss or gain, no coming or going? When or how does a child realize that he is separate from his mother? Where was this paragraph before you read it?

Gestalt therapy as it is practiced nowadays has come to include a great variety of techniques, some original, some borrowed. Most of these techniques have the purpose of evoking awareness or increasing sensitivity. At times, it is difficult to see what connection with gestalt a particular technique might have in the mind of the therapist who is practicing it, other than it seems to work with his therapees. The very creativity and freedom of Perls' therapy and training style tended also to foster a kind of theoretical looseness in Perls' followers.

As I understand it, one of the fundamental things that makes gestalt therapy more than just a collection of sensitivity methods with little or no relation to the discoveries of the gestalt psychologists is this: the theory that human problems are interruptions or fixations at various stages of the naturally unfolding figure/ground process. And in this area, one of Perls' most brilliant theoretical achievements was the recasting of psychoanalytic ideas about ego functions and ego defenses into the here-and-now terms of gestalt psychology.

Most of the Freudian topological terms can be used more economically and experienced more directly as types of inappropriate figure/ ground differentiation or figure/ground integration. The "unconscious" can be viewed as those aspects which are frequently or always allocated to the ground of experience. "Introjection" can be viewed as inappropriate allocation of non-ego to ego; "projection" as inappropriate allocation of ego to non-ego. "Egotism" can be viewed as maintaining an inappropriate unity in the figure, "confluence" (Perls' word) as maintaining an inappropriate unity in the ground.

When viewed as part of the figure/ground process, each term allows a variety of interpretations, each one of which is economical in itself. "Confluence" can be interpreted as a superfluity of sameness or as a lack of differentiation: as an interruption of differentiation or as a premature arrival at sameness. And each term of the figure/ground process has diagnostic meaning as well as therapeutic meaning, unlike most traditional psychiatric terms. "Confluence" describes not only what is "wrong" but also suggests "what can be done" about it, such as (prescribing the symptom) telling the therapee to be deliberately confluent by ignoring the distinction of himself and his environment, by putting on a phony euphoria, by holding his breath, by playing dead, etc. until some differentiation occurs spontaneously.

Other schools of therapy could criticize gestalt therapy for being only "suggestive" in many areas, for lacking a more worked-out, systematic theory. As Perls grew older, he seemed less inclined to bother with systematic theory. Perhaps in the future, another genius of Perls' calibre will make a fresh attempt to systematize all the developments of Perls' late years as well as all the innovations since Perls' death. It would be a thankless task because gestalt therapy, like zen, like your life, is open-ended, never completely finished: any systematic presentation, no matter how good, must of necessity fail.

When human problems are viewed as fixations or interruptions, as misallocations in the figure/ground process, there is just one criterion of "mental health:" the just-so response, the spontaneously appropriate, the completely free yet fittingly determined action or word. If you ask a zen master why he does something in particular, maybe he will "repeat" his previous action or words, maybe he will remain silent, maybe he will strike you, maybe he will offer you a cup of tea, maybe ... It all depends here-and-now on what is peculiarly appropriate. Whenever a dispute about opinion or taste arises between people and someone says finally "Well, who's to say?" the commonplace mystery of appropriateness is being evoked. Yes indeed, who is to say? And who is to systematize this profound sense of fittingness? But now and again someone like Perls tries.

Another good example of Perls' insightfulness was his recasting of Freud's "repetition compulsion" into the gestalt principle of "unfinished business." In the Freudian system this is one of many *ad hoc* principles; in gestalt it is part and parcel of the whole system. Years before, in a series of experiments with children, Zeigarnik discovered that incompleted activities tend to be remembered with more clarity and urgency than completed activities. Lewin, Koffka and others realized later that this modest discovery could have been deduced from the general principle that a figure tends toward closure or toward completing itself. Perls realized that most human problems could be regarded as incompleted figures or interrupted needs from the past intruding into the present over and over again in an attempt to be solved or completed. And Perls saw this as a much more economical way of viewing self-obstructive and self-destructive behavior in human beings than Freudian theories such as the "death wish."

There is a future dimension to this principle as well. I recall how Perls frustrated me into an insight about a fixation I had on "decision making." Eventually, I came to see that whenever I was faced with a conflictful decision, an either/or choice, it was often either the outcome of *post*maturely having to attend to something I could have attended to in the past more appropriately, or the outcome of *pre*maturely speculating about something I could leave more appropriately to the future. True maturity is now, neither premature nor postmature. Most effortful self-willed actions are somewhat false. With proper attending, there is a more or less immediate and effortless process where what is of here-and-now importance engages my full attention until it is taken care of. It is not that we should avoid musing about the past or rehearsing for the future, it is just that it is unwise to mistake these activities for complete reality.

A person can have unfinished business in not letting a figure be born from ground, as in confluence; or in not letting a figure come to its full development, as in retroflection. That much relates rather clearly to gestalt principles of closure and good form. But Perls went beyond this in his therapeutic use of unfinished business. In his description of "egoism" he completed the figure/ground circle by pointing out the phenomenon of not letting a figure die, not letting it become ground again. With this he moved gestalt therapy closer to zen and bypassed the dispute between the older "drive" theorists (Freudians, Behaviorists) who maintain that basic motivation is to satisfy or wipe out needs (return figure to ground) and the newer "novelty" theorists who maintain that motivation is to awaken curiosity, needs, sensation (to return ground to figure). To what does this return, figure or ground?: as I wait for the next thought, pine trees and boulders are playing with the wind.

One of Freud's contributions was his delineation of the human ability to negate via postponement, substitution, and symbolization. A child, for example, can deny a need for his absent mother by substituting various aspects of his relation with her such as sucking his thumb, warming himself and rubbing his face with a blanket, rocking himself to and fro, singing to himself, repeating a verse centered on the word "mama," imagining her face or voice, etc. By the time the child gets into therapy as an adult, his problem is not the unfulfilled childhood needs and the attendant pains, but rather his defenses against those needs and pains, defenses which are now out-of-place and out-of-date. Meanwhile (and this is more gestalt than Freudian) the child develops an "ego" in the gap between "what is" and "what should be" (or "what could be"), and he develops emotional states which resemble shock in that they entail a less involved, less feelingful attitude—as if he were a spectator of his own life, rather than the liver of it. He distances himself from his problem with substitutions and symbolizations which eventually become obstacles in his here-and-now existence, leaving a lot of unfinished business.

But a necessary part of growing up as a human being is learning how to put off, distance, objectify and symbolize, so how can we distinguish the "neurotic" and the "normal"? This seems to be what Suzuki referred to when he said that the trouble with the human mind is that it has a gift of creating concepts in order to articulate and handle reality but that it tends to fool itself and regard its self-created concepts as "real things" or as "externally imposed upon reality" and that as a consequence, the mind altogether misses the inner workings of life.

This conceptual rigidity hinders the natural unfolding of the figure/ground process. Psychotherapy can take care of the "neurotic" aspects of this rigidity, but only an intense and long-term training such as zen (and potentially gestalt therapy) can take care of the "normal" aspects. Aside from the personal interruptions of fixations of the figure/ground process which constitute neurosis, there is the more general human problem: we tend to conceive of ground as other than our self, as unknown, unattainable, alien, inanimate, meaningless or dead. Unless we can make ground into a loose or vague figure, we do not recognize it as such. To perceive the figure/ground process from the dualistic point of view of figure is the usual human way. To perceive the figure/ground process from the unitary point of view of ground is the zen way.

My zen master once said that everything in the world exists, forming self (figure) by limiting a part of absolute being (ground). To be enlightened means to realize absolute being again (we never really left it) and then to realize the coming and going (ground to figure and back again) as the natural working of absolute nature. On another occasion he said that God, Buddha or true self has no eyes, ears or nose. When you have no eyes, ears, or nose, you will be able to perceive your true self. When you are separated from parts of the world then you must "have" those parts. When you are completely at one with this world, you no longer need to have it or any of its parts. When you can use your eyes, ears and nose, freely unifying this world, then you will thoroughly understand that your true self has no eyes, ears and nose.

In gestalt therapy, awareness of ground is often realized through Perls' "empty chair" technique. The therapist asks the therapee to occupy one of two chairs and to talk to someone or something "in" the empty chair, then to develop a dialogue between two distinct roles by alternately sitting in and speaking from each chair. Perls gave due credit to Moreno, Berne and others for originating such methods, but Perls took dialoguing further. Talking to others and talking to ourselves are of equal importance. I cannot talk to others without "projecting" internal roles, or talk to myself without "introjecting" external roles. But although we spend most of the time talking to ourselves, we are most ignorant of this internal process, perhaps because it is closer to ground or the subjective. (Note that "subject" derives from the Latin "to throw down or under," like ground, out of sight and awareness.) So, with internal dialoguing we need more awareness, and it is there that Perls focused much of his therapeutic attention.

All our daydreams and speculations are forms of internal dialoguing "On the one hand; on the other hand," back and forth. While we take the by-products of internal dialoguing as ultimate realities, we are largely unaware of the ways of this process, and how tied up we are in the time and energy that is expended on it. We do not see that we incessantly allocate our living experience into two or more roles which are in conflict because one at least is fixed by some ideal of what "should" happen. We do not see that in trying to escape the painful consequences of this division, in trying to put things together again, all we succeed in doing is to create a false unity: We identify with one role and take it for granted with deadly seriousness, and allocate the complementary role elsewhere as though we were not responsible for it. Most of what zen calls "relative mind" or "small mind" and what western psychology calls "ego" stems from the false conceptual unity of this incompleted dialogue.

So how do we get free of "ego"? By realizing that there is no freedom from ego; by realizing that the attempt to escape from that which we have ourselves created is the source of the problem; by realizing both roles of a dialogue as complementary rather than antagonistic; by realizing that ego is not a self-contained, independent entity; by realizing in brief what ego truly "is," simply a figure rising out of ground. Perls once quoted to me a passage from a German poet, saying in effect that we are always playing (a role) (a music instrument) (a game) and that it is the heart of wisdom to realize this. Another therapist with whom I once worked commented that the sneakiest, dirtiest, most destructive games are played by people who are convinced that they are beyond playing games. But this is true of most of us at least some of the time. Our favorite roles, our most serious roles, are precisely our "deadly virtues," the phony roles of "no roles," the false games of "no games." From a zen point of view, when I am playing a role completely, *then* I am free of it.

The empty chair procedure with "topdog" and "underdog" dialoguing is a formalization of play and humor as well as work and seriousness. By using separate chairs, Perls facilitated the process of distinguishing "inner roles," of taking "this" *and* "that" role seriously and thereby freeing oneself to take any role. By leaving one chair empty, Perls facilitated putting any role there, whether it is absent or present in the "outer" world, whether it is animal, vegetable or mineral. The empty chair is like the blank wall or blank floor facing the meditator in a zendo, the beginning of realizing the complete ground of all dialogue, roles and games.

True meditation, in the zen sense, results when there is no object of attention, no concern for form, meaning, or intention: when attention itself is the object of attention and when all things perceived, including oneself, are experienced as manifestations of attention. Such attention could be likened to someone who waits alertly and patiently for he-knows-not-what, yet waits with the conviction that he-will-know (   ) when (   ) occurs. One zen metaphor for such attention is the mirror which reflects all, is manifested in all it reflects, and yet is free of all it reflects. How do you realize such a mirror?

People now often seem to think of zen in terms of bio-feedback. That is, they seem to conceive of zen as a means of producing more alpha waves or slowing the pulse rate, a means of tranquilizing and gaining control of the body and mind. But zen is not tranquilizing or controlling, nor is it a means to an end. Zen is most simply and intimately you, the reader, when you have no ends or means left; when you have nothing more to control or tranquilize, when you are thoroughly realizing your self.

Dialogue is essential in zen practice also. Most zen mondos and koans are short, intense dialogues where one or both participants are enlightened, freely realizing self, or where one of the participants comes to a deep realization during or after the dialogue. These dialogues are both "external" and "internal." A zen master was overheard talking to himself: "True self! Yes. Wake up, wake up! Yes,

yes. Don't let yourself be made a fool of! No, I won't." Elsewhere, it is recorded that Buddha, after his enlightenment, stated that he finally had succeeded in catching the masked man or builder of the tabernacle; he finally saw in action the self which is beyond all dialoguing yet which creates all dialogues and is present in all roles.

Gestalt therapy and zen can both be regarded as radical empiricism or radical existentialism. No final faith in any dogma or teacher "out there" is needed. The doubt or problem is all important, and the authority of the gestalt therapist and the master stems from their returning us to our living experience, affirmative and negative, for the solution to our doubts. Unless I believe in something, I cannot doubt. Unless I take something for granted, I cannot ask a question. Ultimately, then, my life cannot be totally affirmed until I get to the root of my negation or self-limitation. Any problem is already a negation of some kind, but most of us, most of the time, also negate our negation: We treat the problem as if it were alien to us, something to escape from.

Perls used what he called "therapeutic frustration" to block this habitual escape and avoidance. Paradoxically, although it is affirmation of the therapee's problem, doubt or resistance, it is negation of his usual way of negating or avoiding the problem.

For example, someone with whom Perls was working said that he could not recall his dreams. Such a statement could easily seduce a therapist into taking up an oppositional role of being "helpful," thus unwittingly aiding the therapee to continue with a false dialogue. The therapist might be drawn into giving the person advice about remembering dreams, or into telling the person that he is resisting. Perls just bypassed this seduction by telling the person to put his dreams or his dreaming self into the empty chair and to start a dialogue with it. Perls removed himself as figure (rewarder, chastizer, advice-giver) leaving the person an empty ground in which he could generate his own figure, or leaving the person free to discover that he was "projecting" his own oppositional role onto the therapist. On other occasions, Perls had the therapee put his notion of the therapist into the empty chair and have a dialogue with him instead of arguing with Perls. On still other occasions, Perls suggested that a therapee pretend or deliberately "put on" a problem which he was otherwise trying to get rid of, such as feeling nervous or helpless or getting a headache. In effect, Perls killed himself as a therapist, thus frustrating the therapee into becoming his problem, becoming his here-and-now self, by reversing the habitual figure/ground relation.

This practice has been named in various ways by other contemporary therapists: "paradoxical intent," "therapeutic double bind," "prescribing the symptom." Some therapists seem unaware that it is known, in one form or another, to other therapists and that it is actually an ancient practice. In gestalt it can be viewed as a natural outcome of the figure/ground process. In zen, it is manifested in every exchange between master and student. Again and again a zen master will affirm in one sense, negate in another, until the student has nothing left to do but become his koan. This is also one meaning of the zen sayings: "Put no head above your own" and "If you meet a zen master, kill him!" Someone once said that men have a tendency to create their own gods and then to kill them. What do you do if your god kills or negates himself before you have a chance to do so?

Where are we after therapy? Are we not faced with the same question of self, albeit better prepared, that we had before therapy? Is not this question just simply the fundamental negation involved in being human? Looked at this way, neurosis may be regarded as negation of negation; gestalt and zen as affirmation of negation, in the trust that it will lead to complete affirmation or solution to the problem of self. If you, the reader, are in doubt at this point about the basic negative aspect of human awareness, try nurturing that doubt by pondering something like the following:

Try imagining a completely free or completely happy state of existence and notice how negative aspects, whether they be called "despairing" or "challenging," "exciting" or "frightening," creep in, apparently uninvited. Who creates these?

In the relative world of time and space, we must negate to affirm and affirm to negate. We must say "no" to a multitude of other stimuli (make them ground) in order to say "yes" to one (make a figure). And we must assume something (make it figure) in order to say "no" or pose a question about it (make a ground in the figure).

Again and again it is stressed in zen literature that the enlightenment experience is sudden and abrupt. It would seem therefore that there are no steps or precedents leading up to the experience. This is not altogether true. Suppose we try to describe it in figure/ground terms. The first problem is how we experience ground. In gestalt therapy this is appropriately evoked with silence and waiting. Until I became a zen student, I had never encountered anything so intense as the feeling in Perls' group at the beginning of each session. Perls sat quietly and waited while each group member struggled with a silence that grew louder as the minutes ticked by. We knew that the first person who spoke up had to be "genuine" in his problem presentation or else suffer disinterest and maybe even censure from the rest of the group and Perls. So we each had a personal struggle; balancing our need for attention to ourselves and what we thought was our "problem" vs. our need to remain as safe spectators in the group. The very emphasis on silence and waiting created a "purer" ground against which anyone's problem became a more clearly defined gestalt, once that person got the courage, or felt the desire strongly enough to speak out.

The same principle of emphasizing ground or holding back gestalt-formation until it reaches a certain level of intensity and clarity can be seen in many other forms of therapy and religious training. I have heard that drug addicts, turning to Synanon for help, used to be put in a circle of ex-addicts and bombarded over and over again with questions like "What did you come here for?" until they dropped their rationalizations (weak gestalts) and burst forth with a "Help me please!" And there are various forms of therapy which grew from the research on sensory deprivation following the effects of the "brain-washing" methods used by the Chinese in the Korean war. Some of the spectacular results claimed by abreactive therapists such as primal therapists may be due to adjunctive deprivation techniques which simplify the ground of personal experience, thereby intensifying the subsequent gestalt-needs and facilitating the therapy.

In zen, figure-withholding and deprivation are not special techniques but are a natural part of the whole process. Primarily, there is the simple fact that true zen masters have always been few and far between, even in the heyday of zen one thousand years ago in China. What is valuable because it is hard to find or hard to reach is likely to evoke longing and concentrated attention (without any special effort to remove peripheral distractions) leading finally to a clear gestalt. Though zen students no longer have to walk many miles to interview some master on a mountain top, during the modern sesshin (seven-day meditation period) they must do zazen for hours before seeing a master for a minute or two.

Taking this principle further, we could say that the reason a child's actions are so spontaneous is that his experience of ground is less cluttered with concepts, fixed hopes and fears, etc. As we grow older we tend to accumulate more fixed memories and to impose more fixed expectations on our immediate experiencing, gradually crowding out the awe, wonder, newness, freshness, and surprise which accompany intense gestalts. In terms of communication theory it is as though increased background static makes it difficult for clear messages to come forth.

When we say that some action is "spontaneous" or "original," are we not saying that it seems to have no precedent in time or that it seems to arise beyond the causation of its spatial context? Are we not saying that it seems to come from nothing: from an uncluttered ground? Zen training is often referred to as "unlearning" rather than "learning." If we unlearn our cluttered ground, will we not experience the here-and-now as having no beginning and end, or as beginning and ending with every gestalt we experience?

So far so good. But what about the ego? What about the needs and problems of the adult human world? If you attempt to stay in the perfectly homogeneous and empty ground, how can you live in the world of causation, plans, successes and disappointments. If you face a zen master in the state of samadhi (intense meditation) as though you were perfectly calm and have no ego left, he might strike you suddenly and then inquire "Who is it that feels this pain now?" or "How is it that your non-ego feels anger now?" Maybe you will realize something if this happens to you.

Gestalt therapy leads to clear, strong gestalts, to warmth, aliveness and so on. But it does not seem to lead to what is expressed in one of the Buddhist sutras: "Form is emptiness, emptiness is form," which can be rephrased as figure is ground and ground is figure or the two are separate but interpenetrating. Though Rubin discovered reversible figures where visual figure and ground are interpenetrating, though Koffka proposed a supersensory (not just visual) ground which might be interpenetrable with all empirical figures, though gestalt therapists developed these and other related discoveries as far as possible, figure and ground still tend to be treated as separate though no longer antagonistic.

When a zen master raises his staff and declares that it is the whole universe, he is not indulging in a figure of speech or a rhetorical gesture. He is saying exactly what he experiences. He does not experience a gestalt as an object separate from himself, surrounded by a lot of empty ground. He sees exactly what everyone else sees but with the difference that all ground or self is manifested in this staff, no more, no less. In any gestalt he can realize all of eternity and infinity as a reversible figure or as completely interpenetrating figure/ground. He has no longer any need to search for the universal, god, or such things as I am absurdly talking about here, like zen and gestalt therapy. He needs only to raise his teacup to his lips to realize all of this quite simply.

I sometimes think that some of the human problem originates in vision, that marvelous sense which is so highly developed in human beings and which seems to be so closely linked to our intellectual processes. All logic is based on what could be called "visual metaphors": A is A and C is C and the two cannot occupy the same space at the same time; the relationship of A, B and C cannot be understood unless they are all contained in a larger space or higher level of abstraction; and so on. I cannot see two dense objects in the same place at the same time. If one dense object is standing in front of another object, I cannot see the back object unless I walk around the front object. If I want to see the relationship between two objects, I must back up far enough to allow enough space to see both of them at the same time.

Now, if I told you that I can perceive things in a finely articulated way but without any of the foregoing conditions, you might tell me that I am crazy, that I have been taking a drug or that I have had a mystic experience. But I assure you that you too perceive things in this manner except that you probably do not notice it because it is not visual but auditory. You can hear two, or two dozen, musical tones in the same space at the same time. You can hear a tone around or through another tone. You can hear any tone as contained in or as containing all other tones. None of the usual visual space allocations are necessary to the wonderfully complex discriminations we can make in music or speech. It is probably not an accident that more people are said to have come to a zen realization via hearing than by any other sense.

One of the main differences between zen and gestalt therapy is that zen training is both more spiritual and more mundane and it goes on for years. Though a zen student is exhorted to realize infinity and eternity and answer the deepest spiritual questions, at the zendo he has no place and no time to answer them but in the midst of his everyday activities. When you have been sitting for long periods of time, just to stand or to walk is a miracle. When you have been doing zazen, walking and working for twenty hours at a time, to sleep four hours is a miracle. Everything is a miracle when you give it your full attention and yet everything is still quite ordinary. So, when you hanker after "the supernatural" you are admitting that you are taking "the natural" for granted. When there is nothing more of the natural to take for granted, where is there any place for the supernatural to exist? And when you are squatting on a mat in a little bare room facing a zen master, how else can you answer him but with your natural everyday actions and words?

To compare zen and gestalt therapy is to limit both to systems of therapy. Since *you* are much more than a therapeutic system, so is zen, and gestalt. The zen notion is to return after training to everyday society, indistinguishable from other people except ... two people interacting with no mention of zen, yet with each word or action full of zen: that is the final realization. Even in the zendo, the master teaches you the zen of being free of zen—like when you approach him during an off-moment with a zen question and he replies, "I am just a sock-darner now!" What is the final gestalt ideal? Hopefully, it is not just to turn out more therapists or ex-patients playing the "psychiatry talk" parlor game.

When we learn somewhat to attend, we discover that we are spending a good bit of our life in the past or the future, in some "elsewhere" outside or inside of what we conceive ourselves to be: in plans, reveries, hopes and daydreams. We learn that we are not really as here-and-now as we previously thought. Potentially at least, all human beings could come to a zen enlightenment or a gestalt fulfillment by simply attending uninterruptedly during their everyday affairs. But the simplest of all things turns out to be the most difficult of all things. Though we humans long for a true identity, for a fundamental experience that will put to rest all the doubts and struggles about the meaning of our lives, we are lazy. Furthermore, we are enamored with the byproducts of our analyzing and fantasizing.

Perls once told me that when I had some experience as a therapist, I would discover that though people complain of a problem, if I tried to relieve them of the problem I would be surprised to see how hard they would try to hold on to it. As a human being, I can adapt and learn to make the uneasy easy, the abnormal normal, the unnatural natural, but if someone tries to relieve me of even part of this elaborate ego and all the work that is entailed in maintaining it, I am afraid, I hesitate, I resist. What guarantee do I have that an easy, natural mode of being will be as exciting and interesting as my present neurotic state? Indeed, how do I even know for sure that I will continue to exist if I give up some favorite, habitual, but phony role?

In his later years, a pet phrase of Perls' was "Lose your mind and come to your senses." As I understand it, Perls meant "Give up your pretending and speculating about the world and yourself and come to your immediate experience of the here-and-now." But how few of us listen!

A zen master was asked by a newly arrived monk if he would give some instruction about how to realize Buddha nature. The master asked the monk if he had eaten his rice yet. When the monk answered "Yes," the master told him to go wash his rice bowl, and the monk came to enlightenment. This paying attention as you go or one-thing-at-a-time process is integral to the here-and-now. The open-ended-ness or transitoriness of existence is not ignored or denied. On the contrary, it is most immediately affirmed by the master; in effect, whether you live only forty minutes more or forty years, whether you are happy or miserable, whether you understand or not, whether whatever, give over to the next event: "Go wash your rice bowl!"

Everything has its will. Giving over to wherever or whenever you next find yourself is a way of realizing the will of everything. As we grow up, we learn to restrict the notion of "will" to higher animals, humans and god. But how do you realize the will of a mountain, a tree, a river? There is a self-regulating process in human beings, in all sentient creatures, indeed in all things of the universe. In the self-regulating process there is a time and place for everything, for all experience.

The gestalt therapist doesn't "cure" a person, he doesn't add or subtract anything, such as giving a patient medicine or removing a diseased organ as would be dictated by a medical model. When the here-and-now is truly seen and attended to—that is, when being and becoming sees itself, attends to itself—there is no superfluity, no lack. The gestalt therapist attempts to put a person into contact with the self-regulating process; to realize himself and the world as that self-regulating process, to cease interfering with that process, to stop obstructing the perfectly clear "is" with notions of what "should be." Ultimately, the gestalt therapist, like the zen master, has nothing to teach other than that there is nothing to teach. And all gestalt and zen "techniques" are merely for evoking the realization of oneself and the world as the here-and-now process.

All is with you now; what are you clinging to that keeps you from realizing it? Is there anything really wrong with your present existence? If you ask what you conceive to be an outside power, what can you receive but an outside answer? If you ask in a half-spirited manner, what can you expect but a half-spirited answer? Who or what put you in that bondage? Who or what is going to release you from bondage? The purpose of zen and gestalt therapy is that there is no purpose: that is, no purpose aside from your every act, your every experience. The "therapy" is "successful" when you realize the self that all along has no need for therapy.

Hypnosis, Intention, and Wake-fullness

John O. Stevens

One way of looking at the human condition is that we are all hypnotized. By hypnosis, I mean any time you accept words as a substitute for your own experiencing. When the hypnotist tells his subject, "It's getting cold, soon you'll start to shiver," the subject pays attention to the words of the hypnotist and ignores his own senses, his own experiencing of his world.

There is the hypnosis of parents, society, authorities, friends, spouses, etc. telling you how you should be. All the beliefs and injunctions saying "You must be this; you can't do that," etc. There is also your own self-hypnosis telling yourself that you must be a certain way or you won't be loved, won't be successful, etc. For each of us our hypnosis has a somewhat different content, a different message. But always there is the involvement with the words as a substitute for reality, which is judged to be not adequate in some way.

Much of gestalt work can be seen as revealing the hypnosis and uncovering the reality beneath the words. When I notice that I say "I'm angry" in a dead, expressionless voice, or that I say "I'm calm" while gritting my teeth, I can realize that the words are lies. We have all been hypnotized throughout our lives, and much of the work we have to do is *de*hypnosis or *un*hypnosis, waking up out of the trance. We have to discover the words that we take for granted, the words that distort, disguise or deny our experiencing.

There are essentially two ways you can falsify yourself. One is by denying something that exists, and the other is by artificially creating something that doesn't exist. You want to be strong, so you put on the appearance of strength. Or you *don't* want to feel angry, so you put on the appearance of calm. Actually, of course, there is always complementarity, a polarity of opposites. If you want to be strong, you don't want to feel some weakness; if you don't want to be angry, you want to be calm. Self-discovery is seeing both: those parts of yourself that are pretense, and those parts of yourself that are denied.

Self-falsification is the illness, and the means is words and images. But beneath this is a deeper and more basic illness: the unwillingness to be what you are, and the frantic efforts to be something that you are not.

These efforts are revealed in all sorts of *intention:* trying, struggling, wanting, wishing, hoping—all the activities directed toward the *not* now, the *not* here, the *not* real. All these efforts take you farther away from yourself and they also result in a fragmenting of your existence. As soon as I have a hope, then immediately I have a fear: If I hope to impress you, the other side of the hope is the fear that I won't, that you'll think me stupid. Fantasies always come in opposite pairs. Instead of being centered here in my own experience right now, I become spread out between the hopes and the fears; I become scattered and *dis*integrated. As soon as I have intention of *any* kind, then I start to become split between these two poles of hope and fear, *both of which are unreal!* They are both possibilities, things that are not now. Rather than being settled and collected into what I am experiencing right now, I become scattered and bounce back and forth between hopes and fears. The person who is truly hope*less* is blessed. If I have no hopes, I have no fears. What we usually speak of as hopelessness is being suspended between hope and fear—still hanging on to hope *and* being certain that the hope will not be fulfilled.

Hoping for something is essentially a statement of dissatisfaction, or non-acceptance, of my present situation. If I am truly acceptant of my situation, I have no need to hope for something better or different. By noticing my hopes and examining them, I can discover what it is that I am not accepting. Realizing what I am not accepting is already a step toward making friends with the denied aspects of my life. No matter how scattered I am, or what kind of mind trips I am involved in, it's possible to settle back down into what's happening right this instant. Scattering happens automatically with involvement in fantasy, and centering happens automatically with involvement in the present. True centering is not something that comes through effort and will: It comes by itself when intention ceases and I become willing to allow myself to return home.

All the foregoing has equal relevance for my relationships with others. If I am centered in my own experiencing and I express this to you, simply and directly, then I am giving you something of myself. A real gift is something that is given with no expectation of being given to in return. Expression is a gift that doesn't require an answering response. If you give me something in return, that's very nice, and perhaps we can be together for a while. If not, that's O.K. too.

As soon as intention enters, and the focus shifts from the present to the future, then expression becomes manipulation. Now I speak not out of my experiencing, but out of my hopes and fears. And now what I say is not a gift, but a loan, a bribe, or a threat, requiring that you answer.

Any act can be either manipulation or expression (or both). I may smile out of joy, or to please you or placate you. I may cry out of grief, or to make you feel bad. Expression is a welling up, an outpouring that needs no response, while manipulation requires a response. Expression is a fountain; manipulation is a whirlpool. With expression I feel moved, filled; with manipulation I feel sucked, drained.

Often we are so hypnotized by the content of people's words that we lose touch with the process, the way the words are being said. Often the essential interaction lies in the process, *how* the words are being said. I can say "I'm angry at what you did" forcefully, directly, with anger, a clear expression of how I feel. Even anger can be a valuable gift. Or I can say the same words quietly, coldly, without looking at you, making an implicit announcement that you'd better do something to make me feel better—or if you get angry with my manipulation, then that gives me an excuse for unleashing my anger while blaming you, etc.

Since expression requires no response, while manipulation does, one way of making manipulation stand out more clearly is to not give a response to it. Often what follows is disappointment, anger, or a clearer overt demand for something.

The result of manipulations is that life becomes a wrestling match, a struggle with other people. I'm continually trying to get from you what I want and you're trying to get from me what you want, falsifying us both in the process. We try to make an unsatisfactory relationship satisfactory by manipulation.

Another possibility is that I give to you whatever I have to give, and you give to me whatever you have to give. Sometimes that's nice and sometimes it isn't. With luck we may find a situation in which we can be with someone in a satisfying way. Our interaction will be more like a dance, much nicer than wrestling.

Hypnosis plays a large part in manipulative struggles. Underlying every manipulation is a set of implicit hypnotic messages something like this: "I need (x). If I present myself as I am, you will not provide (x). I must do (y) so that you will provide (x)." Usually (x) is something pleasant, a convenience, which I have *misidentified* as something terribly important. I am unaccepting and distrustful of my being, *believing* that you will not respond to me as I am. So I *think* I have to falsify myself, and thereby also falsify our relationship.

Perhaps the one place that hypnosis might be valuable is in a kind of *counter*-hypnosis. If a guy says "I can't do anything. I'm a total failure" and you hypnotize him and you say "You are not a failure. You're a success" then maybe he will try something because now he thinks he can do it. Maybe he will find out he *can* do it. Then that experience will be healthy and the hypnosis is a means to that. But it's still hypnosis. To tell a person that he's a total success or that he *can* do something, is just like telling him that he *can't*. It's not the zero point of just trying it out and seeing if he can.

A lot of therapies are simply another dose of hypnosis. Now we have the "human potential topdog" saying "You should be open, you should be warm, you should love everyone." That might be a little better than some other forms of hypnosis, but it's still hypnosis. It still isn't paying attention to your own process, paying attention to your own needs and desires.

Even an apparently healthy intention such as "I want to make good contact" is destructive. Good contact comes from being what you are, not trying for anything. Perhaps at this moment I want to be far away from you. If I tell you this, that's contact, that's something real. You make contact by being honestly however you are. If you are trying to manipulate someone else, and you tell them that, that's contact, too—you are revealing yourself as you are at that moment.

Some of the more traditional therapies still do a great deal of "interpretation." This is translating the experience of the patient into the belief system of the therapist.

In transactional analysis, there is script analysis, which is to see clearly the hypnotic injunctions and predictions that have constricted a person's life. Fine, but what is to replace this? *Rescripting*, another hypnosis—perhaps less destructive, but still hypnosis. As they call out while selling programs at the Rose Bowl Parade, "You can't see the parade without a program!"

If the therapist has any intention, any goal beyond simply being what he is clearly, then falsification enters the "therapeutic" relationship in the same ways as discussed earlier. Any attempt to change someone else is a statement of non-acceptance of him as he is now. In gestalt, the only goal is to make the present stand out clearly, so that it can be seen clearly. (And if the present is confusion and obscurity, to make *that* stand out clearly.)

Most other therapies and therapists have goals for their patients: to get them to feel better, to adjust their "parent/adult/child profile," etc. The therapist is at least partly occupied with a fantasy of how the person *could* be rather than how he *is*. There is no essential difference between this and the manipulation discussed earlier, no matter how humanitarian the intent. (The road to hell is paved with good intentions.) Even "comfort" can be destructive, because it often violates the experience of the person who is in difficulty. If you can be with a person and acknowledge and receive what they're experiencing, without any need to cover it up or erase it or change it in any way, that's fine. That's deep human contact. But often people try to make someone else feel "better" (different from how they *are* feeling now) by saying "It's all right. You'll feel better soon," etc. That's really a non-acceptance of the person as he is now, a violation of his experiencing.

Any effort by a therapist to change his patients is a statement of his own symptoms, his own unhealthy process. Let's take the most common symptom of therapists as an example, the goal of "helping" the patient. When I attempt to help someone else, I immediately structure the situation as one in which I am a capable helper and the patient is incapable and helpless. (See what a help I have been already!) Most "help" is an attempt to mold the patient in a particular way (guided by the hypnotic beliefs of the therapist), rather than to let the person develop out of himself. But even if the "help" is open-ended, there is still the implicit statement that the patient needs the therapist's help, making him seem weaker than he is. Many people are already good at the helpless role, and quickly accept it and pursue it with a strength that belies their apparent weakness.

Meanwhile, what is happening to the therapist? He has put himself in the role of capable helper. This must do something for him—perhaps allaying his own feelings of helplessness, perhaps making him feel useful or important. But he is caught by his own intention in a paradoxical trap. If the patient dutifully follows the helpless role, then he frustrates the therapist's need for the patient to improve. If the therapist truly helps the patient, then the patient won't need him any more. This is exactly the sort of "double-bind" situation that has been delineated in families of schizophrenics and other disturbed relationships, and it has the same consequences.

In contrast, the only goal in gestalt is awareness. And the working *assumption* is that if you become aware of yourself as you are, wherever you are, whatever your situation is, that out of that awareness change will occur spontaneously—not out of effort, not out of will or intention but simply out of awareness. Here's a simple example. Be aware of how you are sitting right now. Do you feel some discomfort? If you feel some significant discomfort in the way you are sitting, then out of that awareness you'll do something about it. If you *really* become aware of your situation, you don't need outside instruction or outside guidance to tell you how you should be or what you should do. Gestalt puts into *practice* the idea of organismic self-regulation: that the organism can be trusted to find its way if it is not separated from its organismic information by hypnosis.

This makes the gestalt therapist's job very simple. All you have to do is listen and watch and comment on the parade of events you see. You don't have to think about anything or figure anything out. You don't have to decide what is a "therapeutic intervention," or what is healthy and what isn't, what to reinforce and what not to. If your head is stuffed with all that theory and speculation, then you can't see the person. That's like looking at the program instead of at the parade. You leave behind all concern with *in*tention, and that leaves all your energy free for *at*tention, for seeing what is. It's as if you are watching a play and commenting and reporting about it for someone who can't see it.

It's so hard to get across that all that is necessary is to see things clearly. Really being aware is seeing all the detail and differentiation of events, but without judging and comparing. As soon as I judge, I am accepting some aspects and rejecting others. My awareness diminishes as some aspects get pushed aside or swept under the rug. With full awareness the world is deliciously complex, yet simple and unconfusing: Everything is O.K. as it is, including the fact that sometimes some things seem to be not O.K.

But most people are convinced that they need willpower, a magic pill, a new therapy or something else to change them. So in addition to all the other manipulative games, we now have a lot of self-improvement and therapy games. Even gestalt therapy often degenerates into a "struggle to be real," a "breakthrough contest" or a "nower than thou" game. What makes games so destructive and entangling is the fact that the essence of the game is hidden, unclear. As soon as the game is explicit, then it becomes an enjoyable pastime. For example, let's say I am playing a helpless game in order to manipulate you into doing things for me, and I have hypnotized myself into believing that I really am helpless. And let's say also that you are only aware that you are feeling dragged down by all the work you are doing for me and resenting this. When you want to do less for me, I begin to feel abandoned and try to get you to do more, etc. The more we get bogged down in this struggle, the more serious it seems to be.

The moment we both see things clearly, the game becomes ridiculous: As soon as I see that I'm not helpless, I see how silly I am to spend all that effort to get you to do something for me. And as soon as you see that I'm not helpless, any pressure to do things for me vanishes. Just the fact of seeing the game clearly takes away all its power. Now you are no longer lost in the tangles and confusion. If someone is caught up in "trying to stop" a game he is in, that is a clear message that he doesn't yet see the game clearly, or that "trying to stop" is the game.

When we both see what is happening clearly, when we both know the rules, then the same game becomes fun. We can play the ridiculous game simply for enjoyment, as we would a game of chess, or we can easily stop when some other game, or something else, becomes more appealing. The difficulty with games is that we get lost in them by giving them an importance beyond the enjoyment of the game itself. Even though a game like chess is explicitly a game, many people get so involved and invest so much importance in it that it is no longer a game, and no longer enjoyable. The chess game becomes a pawn in another game: it becomes a contest, a test of intellect or masculinity, sometimes a life-and-death matter. It becomes an obsession instead of just something that you do for enjoyment, and only when you feel like it.

There is a very special, very beautiful movie called *The King of Hearts,* which is all about playing games, sanity and insanity. The context is world war I, and the Germans and English are fighting over a French town. The Germans plant a time bomb and leave the town, and the French learn about the bomb and leave town. All the people in the insane asylum come out and take over the empty town, and have a wonderful time. They all put on different clothes and enjoy themselves thoroughly. Everyone takes on some role in the town:

General, duke, lady, madam, bishop, etc. One guy becomes a barber, and he pays customers because he enjoys being a barber and he gets more customers that way. They are all living these roles, living in the moment and enjoying it completely.

A British soldier is sent to the town to disable the bomb. He gets frustrated and starts ranting and raving, shouting "We're all going to die!" So everyone brings lawn chairs to watch him perform, and they clap and cheer. The next day both the Germans and British march back into town, and all the crazy people treat it as a parade. Then the soldiers see each other and shoot and kill each other. The duke, up in a balcony, looks down at all the bodies disdainfully and says, "They're overacting." A young woman looks down sadly and says with puzzlement, "Funny people." It's a beautiful movie about the difference between playing games for fun and getting lost in them.

I have only used psychedelics about three times, and in general I don't recommend them. But one of the things they can do is to drop you into that space where everything just happens and you are participant/observer, seeing people doing their roles and doing everything just right. "Ah, there's Will doing his grim old man act. Ah, there's Chris doing her wide-eyed young girl act." Everyone is perfectly cast and acting perfectly. You see all this drama happening, both your own and others, without being caught up in it, without giving it any importance beyond the fact of its happening. Psychedelics can give you a glimpse of that kind of being.

This is close to what Castaneda's Don Juan calls "controlled folly." You know the world is a ridiculous drama. You see that what you are doing won't make any difference, and doesn't matter anyway. But you go ahead with whatever interests you, simply because it's the most interesting and enjoyable thing for you to do. It's controlled folly because you don't make the mistake of thinking that your folly is serious, very important.

One of Don Juan's instructions is to lose self-importance. Self-importance is the greatest folly, since it keeps us from seeing our folly. It's easy to see self-importance. Just notice when you say something not because anyone asked or wanted to hear it, but because you wanted to appear intelligent or expert. Notice when you do something not because you wanted to do the thing itself, but in order to impress someone.

A useful frame of mind for losing self-importance is to imagine that we are all small children playing in kindergarten. There are no adults; but some children are playing at being adults, some seriously and some with enjoyment. We are all kids and we are playing together. Right now I am playing at being a writer/philosopher/seer. What role are you playing as you read this? Diligent student, awed disciple, haughty critic, proofreader? I am enjoying my role; are you enjoying yours? If not, perhaps you can find one that you enjoy, or stop reading this and do something else.

Another of Don Juan's instructions is to erase your personal history. Your personal history is mostly a way of maintaining your identity, your self-importance. Examine your own personal history and ask for each item: "How does remembering this maintain my importance?" Another experiment you can try is to rewrite your personal history so that it is more satisfying and makes you even more self-important. Actually, most of our personal history has already been rewritten many times, just as the histories of nations are rewritten to justify the beliefs of those in power.

Another experiment you can try is to go into a new situation where you don't know anyone and refuse to reveal your personal history. Just stay with the now, in present events. If someone asks a historical question, just answer "I don't want to discuss the past. I am enjoying being with you"—or whatever your now experience is. You will find that others will keep trying to push you back into the categories of your personal history. They prefer dealing with your past history (as you reveal it) rather than respond to your present being. And you participate in this by keeping your personal history alive, by anchoring yourself in your history.

You can also go into a new situation where you don't know anyone and invent a whole new history for yourself to draw upon in a conversation, and notice how this history establishes your identity and self-importance.

When I am trying to impress someone with my self-importance, this is a signal that I don't accept myself, that I think I'm not very important as I am. So we are back again to the hypnosis of my thinking, which judges and rejects part of me, and the intention that shows the self-falsifying struggle to be something other than I am.

In all the foregoing I can see much substantiation for the essence of many eastern teachings, particularly zen: Much of our world is maya, hypnosis, illusion. We sleep and drowse in this realm of maya, unaware of the real world of wakefulness. The problem is our desires, our attempt to be other than we are, and our attachment to our fantasies, beliefs, and illusions. Our desire to escape or break out only strengthens the walls of our self-created prisons. Liberation is not a matter of breaking out but of letting go, and can only come through settling into your existence with acceptance, by willingly submitting to what is. Fulfillment comes when you stop emptying yourself by trying to fill yourself, and simply allow the world to fill you.

It's really strange to realize that we are all hypnotized, that we are all in the process of waking up, seeing and hearing perhaps ten percent of what goes on. I have times when I wake up *again*, and I realize that I've been asleep for a week, just sort of going through the motions of living. So I use whatever helps me to wake up or to realize when I'm asleep.

I don't consider myself religious, yet when I'm somewhat awake, I feel an involvement with my living that often brings tears to my eyes. If I *really* wake up, who knows what I may discover. I prefer to leave that an open question. The Pima Indians in southern Arizona have a prayer:

The creator has made the world. Come and see it.

Engagement and Attachment

John O. Stevens

Healthy behavior is relational; it always relates to something, always engages the world. I feel hungry, I want a ham sandwich, I go to the refrigerator, I take it out and eat it. My sequence of actions is a loop that arises out of my interests, reaches out to engage the world and returns to myself. I want to meet someone, I go to meet him, and maybe then I don't want to be with him any more, so then I come back. My actions involve both myself and the world. I want to dig a hole. So I go get a shovel and I shovel the world for a while and then I stop when I'm done.

All mind activity—thinking, planning, imagining, fantasying, guessing, worrying, etc. is autistic, relating to the self and no longer relating to the world. It is a short circuit when compared to behavior that engages the world actively. Now, instead of actually digging a hole, I can dig it in fantasy. The advantage of this, of course, is that I can dig the hole in my mind in different ways, review the advantages and disadvantages of these ways, foresee difficulties, etc. without lifting a finger. Then, at the conclusion of my mind activity, I can re-engage the world and actually dig the hole, probably saving myself a lot of effort by having rehearsed it in my imagination—provided that my thinking is a fairly accurate representation of the real world. My thinking will only be an accurate representation of the world if it is tentative, and continually checked against real events. If I have never dug a hole, my thinking about it probably won't be much help. This thinking is useless to me unless it is periodically actualized into some kind of behavior that engages the world. The hole isn't going to get dug by my mind: at some point I have to actually dig the hole.

If you *do* something with your fantasy, then it works for you and becomes a valuable part of your living. When children fantasy, it is part of their playing and doing and feeling. The creative artist doesn't just sit and think beautiful thoughts. He has to write them on paper, paint them on canvas, or build a house. As you bring fantasy into the world, you find that it develops and changes through this contact. If I have designed a house in my mind, when I start to actualize it into wood and nails I find that certain ideas don't work, that I left out details that have to be worked out, that the material is a little different from "what I had in mind," etc. Perhaps I find that it is impossible to actualize my design with the materials available, or perhaps I discover qualities in the materials that make a much more satisfying design possible. Whatever the outcome, the products of my mind are continually interacting with real materials and events. My conceptualizations are simply ways of working with the real world.

This is how a scientist treats his conceptualizations: not as truths, but as useful tools. A physicist knows that electrons aren't little balls of something. He knows they aren't rays. He says "I don't know what they are, but these are ways of describing them that are useful, and if you use these equations, you'll get results that can be useful." If you can keep that kind of tentativeness in your thinking, then you don't get hypnotized by your own conceptualizations.

The difficulty with mind is that the short circuit frequently remains disengaged from the world and becomes a substitute for it, instead of only a tool for dealing with it. If you pay a little attention to the activity in your mind, you quickly realize that most of it is totally disengaged from the real events of your living. It is mostly totally useless chatter and clutter: endless internal dialogues, repeating reruns of past events, worrying about the future, all sorts of "talking about" that is totally isolated from any kind of doing. The more I am preoccupied with these mind productions, the less I can be involved with the world. The extreme of this is the back ward schizophrenic who is almost totally involved with his mind and almost totally oblivious of his surroundings.

Thinking blocks your exchange with the world in two ways: It can block your senses, your taking in, and it can block your responses, your going out. The extreme of this is hysterical blindness or paralysis, but most of us have deadened ourselves in lesser ways. Every assumption makes me less likely to take in information that is in conflict with it; and every thought makes my responses more planned and less spontaneous.

Let's take an example of a simple unfinished situation like mowing the lawn. The lawn needs mowing, and I have put it off. I keep thinking "I've got to mow the lawn," day after day. Perhaps I avoid sitting in the shade because I will be reminded of the lawn. Every time my attention goes to the unmowed lawn, it goes away from something else. This preoccupation clutters and impoverishes my living until I *do* something about it—mow the lawn, or move to an apartment with no lawn, etc. Then I can forget about it. With a little less clutter in my mind, I have a little more room for something new, something that's happening now. Some people live in mental houses that are so cluttered there's no room for anybody to live there. It's so full of old boxes, broken refrigerators, faded photographs, pieces of string and all sorts of stuff that there's no way anything can come in or go out.

If I could clear my mind of all that clutter, then I would have more room to let the world in and be really open to people and events, without blinding prejudices and preconceptions. This is close to the zen idea of no-mind. With no mind there is no interference with your experiencing. Think of the mind as a flute. The flute is totally empty except for the air that resonates inside it. It has a hole that air goes into, and several holes that air can come out of. If you block either end, or if you put stuff inside it, the music dies. The music is created in the resonating space as it exchanges air with its surroundings. This is the useful, fruitful emptiness that is spoken of so often in the *Tao te Ching*, and in other Eastern teachings.

There are a number of ways to clear out the clutter of the busy, chattering mind. One way is to simply give the mind a mantra, or something else to chatter with. While my mind is busy with the mantra there is no space for the usual chatter. The mantra is simply a sound, displacing, at least for a while, the usual chatter of words, meanings, and images that I get attached to and lost in. My favorite mantra is "Blah, blah, blah."

Another way to clean house is to meditatively focus attention on the chattering itself, examining it without attachment until I see its workings and wanderings clearly. When I see the chattering clearly it is so absurd that it's easy to let go of it as my attention shifts to the more interesting events of the real world.

Another way to clear the mind is to simply shift my attention to real events whenever I find myself occupied with mind chatter. I can direct attention toward the world around me, and become receptive to sounds, colors, things, etc. or I can look inward and notice bodily sensations and feelings. In either case I am simultaneously withdrawing my attention from the chattering and lessening my involvement with it and my attachment to it.

Often, my attachment to my mind chatter is so strong that these ways of clearing the mind don't work: I need a better broom. Since the only difficulty with mind-chatter is its isolation from real events, another way to clean house is to focus on the chatter and explicitly reengage the world with it. By directing my autistic, short-circuited mind activity toward the world I can make it relational again. As my useless chatter reengages the world, it turns into useful messages that can become part of my living again.

One means for doing this is the "two chair" technique in gestalt. If I have an unexpressed resentment chattering in my head, I can express it to an empty chair or pillow. Sending this message involves my voice, body movements, gestures, etc. Now at least I actively engage the world in fantasy. Later I may send the same message to someone real in the group. Eventually I may be able to express it to the person who originally provoked it. Through dialogue with the empty chair I may go beyond this and come to a realization of the basis for my attachment to this old resentment. When I see this clearly it is easy to let it go, and I then have no more need to express it to anyone.

In the two-chair dialogue, I am always working with my own mind chatter: with my memories, images, impressions, etc. Some of this may be labeled "father," "mother," "ex-wife," etc., but I am forced to realize that all these are parts of myself. After all, no one else is here: I produce *both* sides of the dialogue. Usually when I have a problem I feel as if I am the victim of circumstances, and I blame others for my troubles. As I switch roles, I have to temporarily give up my attachment to my victim role, and play the other role. By doing this, I can realize what I am doing to myself, how I do it, and also feel my power in this doing. When I see this clearly I am free to continue it if I enjoy it, or drop it if I don't. Whatever I do, I am no longer a victim.

In many conflict dialogues, one side is something organic or organismic: anger, love, resentment, grief, tears, some kind of concrete experience that a person has. The other side is usually some words, images or injunctions: "Men don't cry," "It's not right to get angry," "Loving is too dangerous," etc. In this case the work involves discovering the reality of my experience and the unreality of the hypnotizing words that I'm attached to and take for real.

Sometimes both sides of the dialogue are unreal images, and if the dialogue is continued long enough I may realize that they are both phantoms. For instance, many people still feel like a small child in relation to powerful parents (often long dead). Both these images are phantoms, except that the person *acts out* both those phantoms in his behavior. He plays the small child when someone else is in a position of power, and then becomes a tyrant with his own children. Through the dialogue, he can realize the power in playing powerless, and the weakness of the tyrant's apparent power. He can even come to realize that personal power is neither power over others nor power under others, but simply being himself as he is.

The reason for the dialogue is to reengage the world, and it will only be useful if the two speakers really do talk to each other and contact each other. At the beginning of the dialogue, my words may be vague generalizations, heavily qualified, and broadcast to the ceiling without feeling: "Well, I think maybe I might possibly sometimes get a little bit annoyed at someone who did something like what happened just now." The dialogue is a laboratory for the discovery of all the ways that I avoid sending and receiving clear messages. Much of the work is clarifying the messages so that they come through simply, directly, and are delivered with the impact of feeling. And, of course, a good message also has to be received, taken in, for it to really engage. When the dialogue develops into direct feelingful communication and listening on both sides, it usually moves rapidly toward resolution.

If the dialogue is to be fruitful, I must be willing to pay attention to my awareness in the moment of my experiencing: the awareness of where my attention goes—the integration of attention and awareness. I have to be willing to focus my attention on my awareness, so that it has a chance to grow and change and develop on its own. I must be willing to do this even when this involves unpleasant experiences and feelings of discomfort; I have to be willing to suffer myself as I am. For me, this is the only context in which the idea of "will" or intention has any use. It often takes effort to focus my attention and settle into my experiencing. Once I really immerse myself, then I become a follower and student of my developing awareness, discovering and learning from a source much wiser than my usual thinking and knowing.

In principle, all I need is this willingness to pay attention, and the willingness to accept whatever I discover. This process may sometimes be slow, tedious, and meandering but it will not lead me astray. In principle, then, I don't need a therapist, or anyone or anything outside to show me how to live or how to be.

In practice, however, a therapist or guide can be very useful, as a facilitator or a midwife, assisting the natural process. He can express his awareness of his own functioning, showing by example what is meant by paying attention to awareness. He can be particularly useful by pointing out when my attention and awareness are divided—moments when I avoid full contact with my experiencing or full identification with my actions. Then I am faced with the choice of either refocusing my attention to discover more about what I'm avoiding, or realizing and taking responsibility for my present *un*willingness to stay with my existence. My awareness of avoidance and unwillingness is itself a factor that draws me back toward willingness to contact whatever I am avoiding.

The therapist may also be useful by suggesting an experiment which serves as a context for discovery. If the suggestion is a poor one, the experiment falls flat and can be dropped. If the suggestion is a good one, it may lead me into a discovery of a new experience or way of being, or rediscovery of something I have forgotten or ignored. A good experiment is a short-cut that can save a lot of time and cut through a lot of confused meandering.

Some of the simpler gestalt experiments involve alternate ways of communicating—talking in the present, saying "I" instead of "it," etc. By trying these experiments, I can experience for myself how speaking like this differs from my usual way. Unfortunately, some people think of these experiments as rules to be followed, laying on another set of "shoulds" to clutter living.

If the therapist hears my voice whining, he can ask me to deliberately whine, letting me discover that when I whine deliberately, my voice sounds the same as it usually does. My whining, which was previously in the unnoticed background of my living, can become aware foreground through this experiment. Many other experiments such as shuttling between fantasy and reality, reversing my usual view of things, and the two-chair dialogue focus on the figure/ground aspect of awareness. In the dialogue, I have to reverse my usual view of a difficulty by playing the role of the antagonist periodically, bringing into the foreground what is usually in the taken-for-granted background.

One common experiment in dialogue is the shift from feeling "guilty" to expressing resentment. Rather than dwell on the experience of guilt, the person is asked to shift to an experiment in expressing resentments, which nearly always produces good results. This short-cut is so widely used and accepted that it tends to be unquestioned, and I think also poorly understood.

What is the situation of a person who feels guilty? As I see it, the essence is that I have done something that someone else doesn't like, and I identify strongly with that person's views. The situation is actually one of conflicting demands. The other person demands that I "should" be a certain way; my acting contrary to this demand is itself a demand to be allowed to be different.

The conflict of demands does not necessarily lead to guilt. What does lead to guilt is my identification with the other person and his demands, an identification that is usually unquestioned, taken for granted. I experience guilt when my identification with the demands of the other person exceed my identification with my own demands, and my actions are in conflict with the other's demands. The extremely guilty person identifies so strongly with the demands of others, or their belief systems, that he even condemns and punishes himself for forbidden thoughts. He may physically punish himself, and may even kill himself to destroy the "evil" that he *thinks* himself to be. He takes for granted that his introjected ideas about himself are correct, and that his wants and needs are bad and must be stopped or eliminated. He has lost touch with his own awareness and the sensing of his own wants and needs.

Besides the negation of self and identification with the other, there is a sense of defeat, worthlessness, unhappiness, a sort of agitated stagnation. Although a person can "feel" guilty, there is no localization of this feeling in any specific parts of the body (as there is in anger, for instance) and no possibility of mobilizing the feeling of guilt directly into any sort of movement or action. Guilt is such a muddled state I don't quite know how to describe it. Some guilt, particularly when expressed to the other person, is part of an underdog plea for forgiveness: "See how bad I feel; I'll try not to do it again, etc." How do you describe a tangled ball of yarn—and where do you start to unravel it?

With developing awareness, a guilty person can become more accepting of his own needs and more questioning of the demands of others. This awareness could be developed by simply paying attention to the details of feeling guilty. Rather than doing this, we can ask the guilty person to try a dialogue experiment: Find someone in his life who would be most upset by his guilty act, and express his resentments and demands that lie buried beneath the guilt, here and now. This short-cut plunges the person back into the unsettled conflict, and it asks him to try a different approach: to take a stand by expressing his resentments and demands, directly engaging the other person. Out of this direct engagement can come awareness, clarification, understanding, and even resolution of the conflict. By taking this short-cut, we can avoid a lot of muddling around in the confusing experience called guilt, and go directly to a useful point for working and clarification.

I use essentially the same orientation for working with what is usually called "hurt" and "pain." I first ask how the person experiences the hurt or pain, and whether they are speaking about a physical feeling they can localize in some part of their body. When the hurt or pain is actually localized in some part(s) of the body, and the pain is not clearly the result of unrelated recent injury or disease process, then the person must be causing his pain himself by tensing his own muscles. Chronic muscular tension is the result of an action that is not allowed to complete itself, an action that is retroflected, held in, held back, blocked from expression, by opposing muscular activity. The pain is both a signal for a retroflected action, and a useful point of focus for remobilizing the interrupted action and allowing it to complete itself.

A useful shortcut in this context is to ask the person to continue to focus on the pain, and at the same time inflict the same kind of pain upon someone else. If a person has a headache, I first ask him to get acquainted with the details of the headache, and then continue to do this and at the same time give *me* the same sort of headache. When the retroflected action completes itself in the world, the chronic tension is relieved, and the self-caused pain disappears. Usually, then, other material emerges that can be worked with further.

When the hurt or pain is not localized in the body, then the situation is even closer to what exists in guilt. Often when a person says, "I feel hurt by what you said" or "I feel such pain" he doesn't actually feel any physical hurt or pain. By saying this, he is trying to manipulate someone else into changing their behavior. As with guilt, there is a situation of conflicting demands, and one party in the conflict feels "hurt." Let's examine an extreme example, the person who plays the role of the martyr. Here it is obvious that the "hurt" is a vindictive gimmick to control others' behavior by inducing guilt in them. Hurt is the counterpart to guilt. The martyr suffers publicly, and by doing this, makes those "responsible" feel bad so they will change their ways.

The therapeutic short-cut is to mobilize the anger and resentment that lies hidden beneath the "hurt" by asking the person to confront the person who "hurt" him, and ask him to hurt in return, to express himself by lashing back in some way. Again the conflict of demands can be joined directly without the smokescreen of manipulation and confusion, and it is possible to work toward some kind of resolution.

The process of resolution through dialogue is the process of discovering my attachment to ideas and my non-acceptance of things as they are, and the gradual letting-go of this attachment and interference. If I have some unexpressed anger at you, it means that I didn't accept something that you did; it also means that I didn't accept my own resentment enough to express it. I still don't accept either, or I would let go of the memory and no longer be attached to the idea that things could have been different. Perhaps what you did challenged my image of myself that I am attached to. Perhaps I am attached to the memory because it justifies something nasty that I did to you. Perhaps you told me you were leaving and I was attached to the idea that we would continue to be together. The possibilities for attachment are endless, and include attachment to the idea of being unattached. Attachment is always a signal of non-acceptance, an unwillingness for things to be as they are.

Acceptance is a matter of discovering my attachments, and then letting go of my interference, my avoiding, my fighting, my holding on, etc.

The gestalt dialogue is an operational means for discovering attachments and non-acceptance, and also a means toward acceptance. In the dialogue I can move toward accepting myself as I am, and become willing to send my messages clearly. I can move toward accepting you as you are, and accepting your messages without distortion. Together, we move toward mutual understanding and acceptance, as I discover and become us both in the dialogue. As I see the situation from your standpoint, I can realize that at that moment that was the only thing you could do—and that my resenting and not expressing was the only thing I could do. Time moves on, and I can't go back to change anything. Go back five minutes in time in imagination: Is there anything that you could have done differently *then*? At this moment, is there anything you can do other than what you're doing? You may have a sense of choosing but that choosing is also part of your being at this moment and arises out of your life, background, desires, etc. Acceptance is saying "Yes" to what is, including the "isness" of my dislike of some of it. Acceptance comes when non-acceptance yields to the nature of things and events. It is not something that I *do*: it is something that I *allow*.

Support and Balance

John O. Stevens

There are two ways I can find support for my existence. I can be centered in the reality of my physical existence in the present: my sensing of my body, my feelings, and my sensory experience of my surroundings. Or I can find support in the fantasy world of memory, roles, self-concept, hopes, plans, expectations, etc. All this thinking about living provides a very different kind of support than that provided by my own experiencing.

My own experiencing unquestionably *is*, even when it is fuzzy, unpleasant, dull, or partial, etc. Even when I feel dull, and my body is tight, these are solid, real facts, no matter how much I or someone else may wish otherwise. My own experiencing gives me a solid base in reality that is not dependent on the opinions and views of others. In contrast, fantasy support is always questionable, and usually heavily dependent upon the view of others. If my self-concept involves being important, than I must repeatedly look to other people and events for confirmation. If my role involves being a good father, then my children must be outstanding to support my belief. Since my plans and expectations usually involve others, they must behave properly or this support will be threatened. Instead of being centered in the unquestionable facts of my experiencing, I scatter myself in dependence upon the opinions of others for confirmation of my fantasies.

When I find my support in fantasy it is always uncertain—even memory is suspect, subject to attrition, distortion and falsification.

Involvement in fantasy support attaches me to other people and events, as I become involved in manipulating them so that they will continue to support (or at least not threaten) me in my fantasies, thinking, planning, etc. The actions of others become not merely pleasant or unpleasant events, but essential for the support of my existence. When my manipulations are not successful, my existence is threatened and I become more frantic in grasping for confirmation. And when my manipulations are successful, the resulting support is contaminated by doubt: "Would he have supported me if I had done nothing?"

Whenever I leave the solid base of the present, I become unbalanced as I lean into the unsolid future. Since the future is always doubtful and multiple with possibility, I also become scattered among my many questioning hopes and fears, lost in the endless alternatives of "What if . . . . ?"

My attention has limited capacity. When my attention is focused on fantasy, I lose touch with the real events of my experiencing, and vice versa. To the extent that I am involved with fantasy support, I lose touch with my real support, my real functioning. For example, here's an experiment you can try for yourself. Notice when you make a physical goof: when you stumble, when you drop something, spill something, bite your tongue, etc. When that happens, take one little step back in memory and notice what was going on in you at that time. Usually you were thinking about something or your attention was focused on something far away. Often you were hoping to impress someone, or trying to do something very well, etc. It's a nice way of seeing how your thinking and intention interferes with your functioning. When your attention is right here with real events, you function fine.

When I find my support in the solid facts of my experiencing, my fantasies are mostly fleeting messages, reminding me to my current interests and needs. I think of a glass of juice, reminding me of my thirst or signaling that I'm not much interested in the current conversation. As long as I pay attention to these messages and act on them, they are a useful part of my ever-changing existence, returning me to my experiencing. Fantasy is the servant of reality.

When I find my support in thinking and fantasy, then I try to make reality the servant, adjusting reality to confirm my ideas about it. One of my fantasy supports used to be playing the righteous "good boy" who is always hard-working, always nice and kind, who gets angry only when provoked or in the defense of good causes, etc. There is no room in this "good boy" role for just being angry, or for the simple selfishness of doing something I want to do even though it conflicts with the wishes of others, etc. Any such self-concept is never fully human and requires that certain actions in conflict with it be inhibited or denied. As I interfere with my functioning, I further lose touch with the solid support of my own existence and reach for more fantasy support and confirmation of this from others.

Many people think that giving support to someone else is helpful or beneficial. But all this does is perpetuate looking outside himself for the basis of his existence. I cannot give real support to someone else, any more than I can eat food for him. I can be myself and show by example what self-support is, and I can refuse to participate in his attempts to find support outside himself. I can point out when he is involved in fantasy or reality. I may even be able to suggest some self-discovery experiments. But each person has to find his own support. Real support for your life is your experience as you find it, and is not necessarily "good" "nice" or "helpful." You may find that much of your support is in anger, despair, quivering, grief, etc. Support comes from contact with your present, ongoing experiencing, whatever that is. Even if it is unpleasant, it is nourishing.

Most of us tend to abandon our experiencing whenever it becomes unpleasant or comes in conflict with others. We are aided in this by the socialization process that encourages us to adopt some belief system in place of experiencing. Much of this social hypnosis is in the form of statements and injunctions that erode self-support by making the individual doubt and distrust his own experiencing—and thereby have more need to accept the rest of the social belief system.

Much of the work of returning to our self-support is discovering the thinking and beliefs that make us distrust ourselves. Notice the critical words in your head that say "Gosh, that was dumb," "That's ridiculous," "You should have thought of that," and so on—all the words that prevent you from simply accepting yourself as you are. Many of these "put-down" words are borrowed from parents, friends, spouse, etc., while others are self-created. Whatever the origin, it is unreal thinking: judging and comparing that rejects, and takes you away from yourself.

Often the words seem to be instruction and encouragement, such as "You can do better," "Think of something intelligent to say," etc. Beneath these words is the implicit message "You didn't do very well," "What you're saying isn't very smart." And if I'm trying to impress you, that is a signal to me that I don't think I'm impressive enough as I am. When I have this kind of talking in my head, no amount of success will make me feel good for long. That's like pouring water into a bucket with holes in it. When I can realize the unreality of the put-down words, then I can move toward an acceptance of myself in which there is no need to be special, better, impressive, etc., no need for effort.

I can also look for the words behind my words. I may be talking to you, saying "Ah, look at the beautiful sky." What's behind those words? Perhaps it's "I'd like you to notice me," or "See how perceptive I am," or whatever. This is a way of seeing into my process —seeing how I *think* myself inadequate in some way, and how I try to compensate for this imagined lack.

Another thing I can do is *not* talk, and notice what I *would* say and what I would be doing for myself if I said it. Recently I heard someone say something that I knew was wrong. I wanted to say "Oh no, it's really *this* way." Then I saw both that I wanted to show how smart I am and that I must not think myself so smart if I have to prove it. So let it go, it's all unreal. I'm neither smart nor dumb; I just am, and there's no need to prove anything.

In the present moment is the firm support, the balance, the center of my ongoing, changing experiencing. And now I am here, writing words, with tears of gratitude in my eyes, remembering Fritz Perls, and the last words in *Garbage Pail:* "Will I ever learn to trust myself completely?"